P9-CPY-219

The Least You Should Know About English

FORM A
Third Edition

The Least You Should Know About English

Basic Writing Skills

TERESA FERSTER GLAZIER
Western Illinois University

HOLT, RINEHART AND WINSTON
New York Chicago San Francisco Philadelphia
Montreal Toronto London Sydney
Tokyo Mexico City Rio de Janeiro Madrid

This text is available in Form A, Form B, and Form C so that a different form may be used in various semesters. The three forms are essentially the same except that they have different exercises, writing assignments, and essays.

Library of Congress Cataloging in Publication Data

Glazier, Teresa Ferster.
The least you should know about English.

Includes index.
1. English language—Rhetoric. 2. English language—Grammar—1950- . I. Title.
PE1408.G5589 1985 808'.042 84-9077

ISBN 0-03-069779-4

Address correspondence to:
383 Madison Avenue
New York, NY 10017

Printed in the United States of America
Published simultaneously in Canada
5 6 7 8 090 9 8 7 6 5 4 3 2

CBS COLLEGE PUBLISHING
Holt, Rinehart and Winston
The Dryden Press
Saunders College Publishing

To the Instructor

This book is for students who need to review the rules of English composition and who may profit from a simplified approach. The main features of the book are these:

1. It's truly basic. Only the indisputable essentials of spelling, grammar, sentence structure, and punctuation are included because research has shown that putting too much emphasis on mechanics is not the way to help students learn to write.
2. It stresses writing. A new writing section, EIGHT STEPS TO BETTER WRITING (pp. 196–229), provides writing assignments to be used along with the exercises. The section has been kept brief because students learn to write by *writing* rather than by reading pages and pages *about* writing.
3. It uses little linguistic terminology. A conjunction is a connecting word; gerunds and present participles are *ing* words; a parenthetical constituent is an interrupter. Students work with words they know instead of learning a vocabulary they'll never use again.
4. It has abundant practice sentences and paragraphs—enough so that students learn to use the rules automatically and thus carry their new skills over into their writing.
5. It includes groups of thematically related, informative sentences on such subjects as pigeon racing, state birds, Epcot, grizzly bears in Yellowstone, Henry Ford's first auto, the history of clocks, harvesting wild rice, making maple syrup . . . thus making the task of doing the exercises more interesting.
6. It includes five essays to read and summarize. The students improve their reading by learning to spot main ideas and their writing by learning to write concise summaries.
7. It can be used as a self-tutoring text. Simple explanations, abundance of exercises, and answers at the back of the book provide students with a writing lab in their own rooms.
8. It's an effective text for the "one-to-one conference" method of teaching because its simple, clear organization makes it easy for students to use on their own, thus keeping the conference hour free for discussing individual writing problems.

The instructor is provided with an enlarged packet of ditto master tests covering all parts of the text (four for each section). These tests are free upon adoption of the text and may be obtained through the local Holt representative or by writing to the English Editor, Holt, Rinehart and Winston, 383 Madison Avenue, New York, NY 10017.

Students who have heretofore been overwhelmed by the complexities of English should, through mastering simple rules and through writing and rewriting simple papers, gain enough competence to succeed in further composition courses.

TFG

Macomb, Illinois

Contents

3. PUNCTUATION AND CAPITAL LETTERS

4. WRITING

The Least You Should Know About English

What Is the Least You Should Know?

What Is the Least You Should Know?

Most English textbooks try to teach you as much as they can. This one will teach you the least it can—and still help you learn to write acceptably. You won't have to bother with predicate nouns and subordinating conjunctions and participial phrases and demonstrative pronouns and all those terms you've been hearing about for years. You can get along without them if you'll learn thoroughly a few basic rules. You *do* have to know how to spell common words; you *do* have to recognize subjects and verbs to avoid writing fragments and run-together sentences; you *do* have to know a few rules of punctuation—but rules will be kept to a minimum.

Unless you know these few rules, though, you'll have difficulty communicating in writing. Take this sentence for example:

> Let's eat Mike before we start the game.

We assume the writer isn't a cannibal but merely failed to put commas around the name of a person spoken to. If the sentence had read

> Let's eat, Mike, before we start the game.

then no one would misunderstand. Or take this sentence:

> Max said the police officer was driving without a license.

Do police officers usually drive without a license? Perhaps the writer meant

> "Max," said the police officer, "was driving without a license."

Punctuation makes all the difference. What you'll learn from this text is simply to make your writing so clear that no one will misunderstand it.

The English you'll learn to write is called standard English, and it may differ slightly from the English spoken in your community. All over the country, various dialects of English are spoken. In northern New England, for example, people leave the *r* off certain words and put an *r* on others. President Kennedy said *dollah* for *dollar*, *idear* for *idea*, and *Cubar* for *Cuba.* In black communities many people leave the *s* off some verbs and put an *s* on others, saying *he walk* and *they walks* instead of *he walks* and *they walk.*

But no matter what English dialect people *speak*, they all must *write* the same dialect—standard English. You can say, "Whacha doin? Cmon," and everybody will understand, but you can't write that way. If you want your readers to understand what you write, you'll have to write the way English-speaking people all over the world write—in standard English. Being able to write standard English is essential in college, and it probably will be an asset in your career.

It's important that you master every rule as you come to it because many rules depend on the ones before. For example, unless you learn to pick out subjects and verbs, you'll have trouble with run-together sentences, with fragments, with subject-verb agreement, and with punctuation. The rules are brief and clear, and it won't be difficult to master all of them . . . *if you want to.* But you do have to want to!

Here's the way to master **the least you should know:**

1. Study the explanation of each rule carefully.
2. Do the first exercise (ten sentences). Then tear out the perforated answer sheet at the back of the book and correct your answers. If you miss even one answer, study the explanatory page again to find out why.
3. Do the second exercise and correct it. If you miss a single answer, go back once more and study the explanatory page. You must have missed something. Be tough on yourself. Don't just think, "Maybe I'll hit it right next time." Go back and master the rules, and *then* try the next exercise. It's important to correct each group of ten sentences before going on so that you'll discover your mistakes while you still have sentences to practice on.
4. You may be tempted to quit when you get several exercises perfect. Don't! Make yourself finish every exercise. It's not enough to *understand* a rule. You have to practice it. Just as understanding the strokes in swimming won't help unless you actually get into the pool and swim, so understanding a rule about writing isn't going to help unless you practice using it.

   If you're positive, however, after doing five exercises, that you've mastered the rules, take Exercise 6 as a test. If you miss even one answer, you must do all the rest of the exercises. But if you get

Exercise 6 perfect, then spend your time helping one of your friends. Teaching is one of the best ways of learning.

5. But rules and exercises are not the most important part of this book. The most important part begins on page 196—when you begin to write. The writing assignments, grouped together for convenience, are to be used along with the exercises.

Mastering these essentials will take time. Generally, college students are expected to spend two hours outside of class for each hour in class. You may need more. Undoubtedly, the more time you spend, the more your writing will improve.

1 Spelling

1 Spelling

Anyone can learn to spell. You can get rid of most of your spelling errors by the time you finish this book if you want to. It's just a matter of deciding you're going to do it. If you really intend to learn to spell, master the first seven parts of this section. They are

YOUR OWN LIST OF MISSPELLED WORDS
WORDS OFTEN CONFUSED
CONTRACTIONS
POSSESSIVES
WORDS THAT CAN BE BROKEN INTO PARTS
RULE FOR DOUBLING A FINAL CONSONANT
A LIST OF FREQUENTLY MISSPELLED WORDS

Master these seven parts, and you'll be a good speller.

YOUR OWN LIST OF MISSPELLED WORDS

On the inside back cover of this book write correctly all the misspelled words in the papers handed back to you. Review them until you're sure of them. That will take care of most of your errors.

WORDS OFTEN CONFUSED

By mastering the spelling of these often-confused words, you will take care of many of your spelling problems. Study the words carefully, with their examples, before you try the exercises on page 10.

a, an

Use *an* before a word that begins with a vowel sound (*a*, *e*, *i*, and *o*, plus *u* when it is sounded like *uh*).

an apple, an essay, an icicle, an heir (silent *h*), an honest man (silent *h*), an umbrella, an umpire, an ulcer (all the *u*'s sound like *uh*).

Use *a* before a word that begins with a consonant sound (all the sounds except the vowels, plus *u* or *eu* when sounded like *you*).

a pencil, a hotel, a history book, a university, a uniform, a union, a unit (all the *u*'s sound like *you*), a European trip (*Eu* sounds like *you*).

accept, except

Accept is a verb and means "to receive willingly." (See p. 55 for an explanation of verbs.)

I *accept* your gift. (receive it willingly)

Except means "excluding" or "but."

Everyone came *except* him. (but him)

advice, advise

Advise is a verb (pronounce the *s* like *z*).

I *advise* you to go.

Use *advice* when it's not a verb.

I don't need any *advice*.

affect, effect

Affect is a verb and means "to influence."

The lack of rain *affected* the crops.

Effect means "result." If *a*, *an*, or *the* is in front of the word, then you'll know it isn't a verb and will use *effect*.

The lack of rain had a bad *effect* on the crops.

all ready, already If you can leave out the *all* and the sentence still makes sense, then *all ready* is the form to use. (In that form, *all* is a separate word and could be left out.)

I'm *all ready* to go. (*I'm ready to go* makes sense.)

Dinner is *all ready.* (*Dinner is ready* makes sense.)

But if you can't leave out the *all* and still have the sentence make sense, then use *already* (the form in which the *al* has to stay in the word).

I'm *already* late. (*I'm ready late* doesn't make sense.)

are, or, our

Are is a verb.

We *are* studying English.

Or is used between two possibilities, as "tea *or* coffee."

Take it *or* leave it.

Our shows we possess something.

Our class meets at eight.

brake, break

Brake means "to slow or stop motion." It's also the name of the device that slows or stops motion.

You *brake* to avoid an accident.

You slam on your *brakes.*

Break means "to shatter" or "to split." It's also the name of an interruption, as "a coffee break."

You *break* a dish or an engagement or a record.

You enjoy your Thanksgiving *break.*

choose, chose

I will *choose* a partner right now.

I *chose* a partner yesterday.

clothes, cloths

Her *clothes* were attractive.

We used soft *cloths* to polish the car.

coarse, course

Coarse describes texture, as *coarse* cloth.

Her suit was made of *coarse* material.

Course is used for all other meanings.

Of *course* I enjoyed that *course.*

complement, compliment

The one spelled with an *e* completes something or brings it to perfection.

A 30° angle is the *complement* of a 60° angle.

His blue tie *complements* his gray suit.

The one spelled with an *i* has to do with praise. Remember "*I* like compliments," and you'll remember to use the *i* spelling when you mean praise.

She gave him a *compliment.*

He *complimented* her on her well-written paper.

conscience, conscious

Conscious means "aware."

I was not *conscious* that it was raining.

The extra *n* in *conscience* should remind you of NO, which is what your conscience often says to you.

My *conscience* told me not to cut class.

desert, dessert

Dessert is the sweet one, the one you like two helpings of. So give it two helpings of *s*.

We had apple pie for *dessert*.

The other one, *desert*, is used for all other meanings.

Don't *desert* me.

The camel moved slowly across the *desert*.

do, due

You *do* something.

I *do* the best I can.

But a payment or an assignment is *due*; it is scheduled for a certain time.

My paper is *due* tomorrow.

does, dose

Does is a verb.

He *does* his work well. She *doesn't* care about cars.

A *dose* is an amount of medicine.

That was a bitter *dose* of medicine.

feel, fill

Feel describes your feelings.

I *feel* ill.

I *feel* happy about that *A*.

Fill is what you do to a cup.

Will you *fill* my cup again?

forth, fourth

The number *fourth* has four in it, but note that *forty* does not. Remember the word *forty-fourth*.

This is our *fourth* game.

That was our *forty-fourth* point.

If you don't mean a number, use *forth*.

She walked back and *forth*.

have, of

Have is a verb. When you say *could have*, the *have* may sound like *of*, but it must not be written that way. Always write *could have, would have, should have, might have*.

I should *have* finished my work sooner.

Then I could *have* gone home.

Use *of* only in a prepositional phrase (see p. 60).

I often think *of* him.

hear, here

The last three letters of *hear* spell "ear." You *hear* with your ear.

I can't *hear* you.

The other spelling *here* tells "where." Note that the three words indicating a place or pointing out something all have *here* in them: *here, there, where.*

Where are you? I'm right *here.*

it's, its

It's is a contraction and always means "it is" or "it has."

It's too late now. (It is too late now.)

It's been a long time. (It has been a long time.)

Its is a possessive pronoun. (Possessive pronouns such as *its, yours, hers, ours, theirs, whose* are already possessive and never take an apostrophe. See p. 31.)

The committee gave *its* report.

knew, new

Knew has to do with knowing (both start with *k*). *New* means "not old."

I *knew* I wanted a *new* job.

know, no

Know has to do with knowing (both start with *k*). *No* means "not any."

I *know* she has *no* money left.

EXERCISES

Underline the correct word. Don't guess! If you aren't sure, turn back to the explanatory pages. When you've finished ten sentences, tear out the perforated answer sheet at the back of the book and correct your answers. Correct each group of ten sentences before continuing so that you'll catch your mistakes while you still have sentences left to practice on.

□EXERCISE 1

1. Of (coarse course) I should (have of) learned to spell these words long ago.
2. I (all ready already) (know no) some of them, but I (do due) misspell others.
3. Learning them won't be (a an) enormous task, and it will have a good (affect effect) on my writing.
4. I'll (accept except) my instructor's (advice advise) and strive for mastery.
5. (It's Its) going to take time, but I (knew new) when I registered for this (coarse course) that it would take time.

6. I'm (conscience conscious) that if I want mastery, I must allow myself (know no) errors.
7. If I (choose chose) to learn these words perfectly, I'll be starting a (knew new) way of studying.
8. I'll (know no) longer (do due) things halfway.
9. I (hear here) that mastery in one field helps one achieve mastery in others.
10. I'm (all ready already) to learn (a an) useful (knew new) way to study.

□EXERCISE 2

1. I took some soft (clothes cloths) to polish my car and some (coarse course) ones to clean the wheels.
2. I did all of the car (accept except) the inside, and I (knew new) I should (have of) done that too.
3. My (conscience conscious) told me that I wasn't doing (a an) uniform job.
4. But I was (all ready already) (do due) at work and couldn't (do due) any more polishing.
5. Finally I was (all ready already) to go (accept except) for putting the polishing (clothes cloths) away.
6. Then just as I drove out of (are our) driveway, I had to slam on my (brakes breaks).
7. Someone was (braking breaking) the speed limit and almost ran into me.
8. That driver deserves a (does dose) of his own medicine.
9. My car is (knew new), and I don't want any scratches on it.
10. I'm (conscience conscious), of (coarse course), that it won't keep (it's its) fine finish forever.

□EXERCISE 3

1. We're looking for a (knew new) house and (all ready already) have seen several we like.
2. The house (doesn't dosen't) have to be large so long as (it's its) in a good location.
3. I (know no) the location of a house can (affect effect) (it's its) price.
4. We told the realtor we trust her (advice advise), and she liked the (complement compliment).
5. We're not looking anywhere (accept except) in this area, for we like it (hear here).
6. We intend to (choose chose) a house not far from where we (are our) living now.

7. Of (coarse course) we (know no) there may be problems.
8. We're (conscience conscious) that (are our) old house may not sell quickly.
9. That might (affect effect) our ability to raise (a an) adequate down payment.
10. Perhaps we should (have of) sold the old house first (are or) at least tried to.

□EXERCISE 4

1. I'm writing (a an) ecology paper that's (do due) Monday.
2. I (choose chose) a subject that I (know no) something about.
3. (It's Its) the (affect effect) of lumbering on animal populations.
4. I (know no) I should (have of) finished the paper yesterday.
5. But at least (it's its) (all ready already) to type now.
6. And of (coarse course) I have (a an) entire weekend to type it.
7. Our instructor (does dose) not (accept except) late papers.
8. I think (it's its) going to have a good (affect effect) on my grade.
9. (Are Our) grades (are our) based on the paper and the final exam.
10. I (hear here) the final (doesn't dosen't) count as much as the paper.

□EXERCISE 5

1. I've just read (a an) article about the birth of some baby condors at the San Diego Zoo.
2. I never (knew new) before what a condor is, but now I (know no) that (it's its) (are our) largest land bird, with a wingspan of more than nine feet.
3. (It's Its) feathers are black, and (it's its) head is orange with beady red eyes.
4. These chicks will have a good (affect effect) on the total condor population because only about 20 adult condors exist in the wild.
5. I wasn't (conscience conscious) that the condors had been brought so close to extinction.
6. In the wild, condors produce only a single offspring every two years, and even then the chick may die from a fall from the nest (are or) from (a an) attack by predators.
7. So scientists from the National Audubon Society (choose chose) to snatch some eggs from nests and transfer them to (a an) incubator at the zoo.
8. After each chick chipped (it's its) way out of (it's its) shell, it was given a meal of chopped-up mice.
9. Meals are given with the help of a puppeteer's glove designed to look like the head of (a an) adult condor.

7. (It's Its) the tallest freestanding structure ever built.
8. I rode in a glass-faced elevator to the world's highest observation deck. The views (are our) breathtaking.
9. Of (coarse course) I had lunch in the revolving restaurant and could look out a hundred miles as I ate my (desert dessert).
10. I'm (conscience conscious) that it was my best vacation ever, but I (do due) wish I could (have of) been there when the Toronto Maple Leafs were playing.

JOURNAL WRITING

The surest way to learn these words is to use them immediately in your own writing. Therefore begin to keep a journal, writing each day at least three sentences that make use of some words or rules you have learned that day. If you write about things that interest you, then you'll be inclined to reread your journal occasionally and thus review what you've learned. You might write about your changing ideas, your relationship to a friend, your opinion about something that has happened, your goals . . . .

WRITING ASSIGNMENT

The writing assignments, grouped together for convenience at the back of the book, are to be used along with the exercises. Turn to page 196 for your first writing assignment.

WORDS OFTEN CONFUSED (continued)

Here are more words often confused. Study them carefully, with their examples, before attempting the exercises. When you've mastered all 40 of the word groups in these two sections, you'll have taken care of many of your spelling problems.

lead, led

The past form of the verb is *led.*

She *led* the parade yesterday.

If you don't mean past time, use *lead,* which rhymes with *bead.* (Don't confuse it with the metal *lead,* which rhymes with *dead.*)

She will *lead* the parade today.

loose, lose

Loose means "not tight." Note how *l o o s e* that word is. It has plenty of room for two *o*'s.

My shoestring is *loose.*

The other one, *lose,* has room for only one *o.*

They are going to *lose* that game.

moral, morale

Moral has to do with right and wrong.

It was a *moral* question.

Morale means "the spirit of a group or an individual." Pronounce these two words correctly, and you won't confuse them—*móral, morále.*

The *morale* of the team was excellent.

passed, past

Passed is a verb.

He *passed* the house.

Use *past* when it's not a verb.

He walked *past* the house. (It's the same as *He walked by the house,* so you know it isn't a verb.)

He's living in the *past.*

He's coasting on his *past* reputation.

peace, piece

Remember "piece of pie." The one meaning "a *piece* of something" always begins with *pie.*

I gave him a *piece* of my mind.

The other one, *peace,* is the opposite of war.

They signed the *peace* treaty.

personal, personnel

Pronounce these two correctly, and you won't confuse them—*pérsonal, personnél.*

He had a *personal* interest in the election.

Personnel means "a group of workers."

She was in charge of *personnel* at the factory.

principal, principle

Principal means "main." Both words have *a* in them:

princip*a*l
m*a*in

The *principal* of the school spoke. (main teacher)
The *principal* difficulty is time. (main difficulty)
He lost both *principal* and interest. (main amount of money)

A *principle* is a "rule." Both words end in *le*:

princip*le*
ru*le*

He lived by his *principles*. (rules)
I object to the *principle* of the thing. (rule)

quiet, quite

Pronounce these two correctly, and you won't misspell them. *Quiet* rhymes with *diet*.

Be *quiet*.

Quite rhymes with *bite*.

The book is *quite* interesting.

right, write

Right means "correct" or "proper."

I got ten answers *right*.

Write is what you do with a pen.

I'm going to *write* my paper now.

than, then

Than compares two things.

I'd rather have this *than* that.
The movie was better *than* I had expected.

Then tells when (*then* and *when* rhyme, and both have *e* in them).

Then he started home.

their, there, they're

Their is a possessive pronoun (see p. 31).

Their house is painted pink.

There points out something. (Remember the three words indicating a place or pointing out something all have *here* in them: *here, there, where.*)

There is where I left it.
There were clouds in the sky.

They're is a contraction and always means "they are."

They're happy now. (They are happy now.)

threw, through

Threw means "to throw something" in past time.

He *threw* the ball. I *threw* away my chance.

If you don't mean "to throw something," use *through*.

I walked *through* the door.
She's *through* with her work.

to, too, two

Two is a number.

I have *two* brothers.

Too means "more than enough" or "also."

The lesson was *too* difficult and *too* long. (more than enough)

I found it boring *too.* (also)

Use *to* for all other meanings.

He likes *to* snorkel. He's going *to* the beach.

weather, whether

Weather refers to atmospheric conditions.

This *weather* is too hot for me.

Whether means "if."

I don't know *whether* I'll go.

Whether I'll go depends on the *weather*.

were, where

Were is a verb.

We *were* miles from home.

Where refers to a place. (Remember the three words indicating a place or pointing out something all have *here* in them: *here, there, where.*)

Where is he? There he is.

Where are you? Here I am.

who's, whose

Who's is a contraction and always means "who is" or "who has."

Who's there? (Who is there?)

Who's been eating my pizza? (Who has been . . . .)

Whose is a possessive pronoun. (Possessive pronouns such as *whose*, *its*, *yours*, *hers*, *ours*, *theirs* are already possessive and never take an apostrophe. See p. 31.)

Whose book is this?

woman, women

Remember that the word is just *man* or *men* with *wo* in front of it.

wo man . . . woman . . . one woman
wo men . . . women . . . two women

you're, your

You're is a contraction and always means "you are."

You're very welcome. (You are very welcome.)

Your is a possessive pronoun.

Your toast is ready.

EXERCISES

Underline the correct word. When you've finished ten sentences, tear out the answer sheet at the back of the book and correct your answers. WATCH OUT! Don't do more than ten sentences at a time, or you won't be teaching yourself while you still have sentences to practice on.

☐EXERCISE 1

1. That (peace piece) of pie is (quiet quite) small.
2. I should (have of) ordered more (than then) that.
3. (You're Your) not ready for (desert dessert), are you?
4. (Hear Here) is the menu for you to (choose chose) from.
5. I (know no) you don't need my (advice advise).
6. Of (coarse course) it (doesn't dosen't) matter what you order.
7. (It's Its) bound to have (to too) many calories.
8. I hope you won't (brake break) (you're your) diet rules.
9. (Who's Whose) that (woman women) at the next table?
10. I think I (knew new) her sometime in the (passed past).

☐EXERCISE 2

1. (Were Where) are those notes I (threw through) away?
2. I'm at (loose lose) ends and about ready to (loose lose) my mind.
3. (It's Its) (all ready already) past midnight.
4. I (knew new) I shouldn't have waited (quiet quite) so late to finish my paper.
5. I (know no) I've got to (right write) my final draft before morning.
6. It will be my (forth fourth) draft, and (it's its) got to be good.
7. (It's Its) true that rewriting (does dose) improve a paper.
8. My (principal principle) worry is that I'll have (to too) many misspelled words.
9. I should (have of) worked harder on spelling in the (passed past).
10. This (coarse course) is having a good (affect effect) on my writing.

☐EXERCISE 3

1. I've been reading (a an) article about pigeon racing.
2. (It's Its) not a (knew new) sport; pigeons were raced in Palestine in the second century.
3. And (there, they're) was a pigeon postal service in Baghdad in A.D. 1150.
4. Pigeons (are our) raced over mapped (coarses courses) all over the United States.

5. One of the longest races is from East Moline, Illinois, to Pawtucket, Rhode Island. (It's Its) 1,000 miles.
6. Of (coarse course) (their there) is no explanation of how the pigeons find (their there) way.
7. But they fly home faster (than then) their owners can drive in a car.
8. If pigeons are let (loose lose) 700 miles from home, they'll be home in about 12 hours, depending on the (weather whether) and (weather whether) they have a tail wind.
9. The exciting part of pigeon racing is seeing the pigeons come out of the sky at last to (their there) own loft.
10. Thirty-two pigeons got medals in World War II, including one American bird, G.I.Joe, who flew (threw through) the lines with a message that saved the lives of hundreds of soldiers.

☐EXERCISE 4

1. On my way to the game, a (peace piece) of (loose lose) gravel hit my windshield.
2. I slammed on my (brakes breaks), but (than then) I realized (their there they're) was (know no) emergency.
3. The gravel merely made a little crack (right write) on the driver's side of the windshield.
4. (It's Its) (quiet quite) inconspicuous really.
5. Finally I got to the stadium (were where) the game was to be played.
6. They expected a larger crowd (than then) last year, but not (to too two) many came.
7. As usual, the captain (lead led) the team to (it's its) victory.
8. Next week he will (lead led) them in (their there they're) second game.
9. The (moral morale) of the team is higher (than then) (it's its) ever been before.
10. The coach thinks (their there they're) ready for the championship.

☐EXERCISE 5

1. The rhinoceros is threatened by extinction unless the (advice advise) of the ecologists is followed.
2. Poachers kill the rhino just to get (it's its) horn, which sells for more (than then) silver.
3. The Yemen Arab Republic has recently (passed past) a law forbidding the import of rhino horns.
4. (It's Its) the world's biggest market for the horns, which are carved into handles for the daggers worn by 80 percent of the adult males.
5. I (hear here) that the daggers sell for up to $1,000.

6. If such a law could be (passed past) in all countries, (their there) still might be a chance to save the rhino.
7. We heard a lecture on the subject that was (quiet quite) informative.
8. It was presented to a (woman's women's) conservation society.
9. Of (coarse course) the (woman women) are working to get laws (passed past).
10. (It's Its) (to too) early to say (weather whether) (their they're) efforts will be successful.

□EXERCISE 6

1. By January 2, I usually (brake break) my New Year's resolution.
2. Probably most people (do due) the same.
3. I had resolved to (do due) (a an) hour of homework before dinner each evening.
4. But (their there) I sat reading a magazine.
5. Finally I (threw through) the magazine down and started to (right write) my psychology paper.
6. But I couldn't decide (were where) to begin, and I didn't (know no) (weather whether) to include personal examples (are or) not.
7. Of (coarse course) my problem was that I hadn't worked out (a an) adequate thesis statement.
8. Finally I decided to (right write) a thesis statement, and (than then) I was on the (right write) track.
9. The supporting points of my thesis (lead led) me to organize my paper (quiet quite) well.
10. Before (to too) long, I had a rough draft that included all my (principal principle) ideas.

□EXERCISE 7

1. The (moral morale) of the (personal personnel) (were where) I work is excellent.
2. The employees all take a (personal personnel) interest in (their there) jobs.
3. (Their There They're) all happy in (their there they're) work.
4. No matter (who's whose) job it is, we all try to help each other.
5. (Are Our) supervisor is (quiet quite) a sympathetic (woman women) and helps us (threw through) difficulties.
6. She has high (principals principles) and strict (moral morale) standards.
7. The (personal personnel) are encouraged to invest (their there) savings in the firm.
8. We feel (quiet quite) sure that we'll never (loose lose) either (are our) (principal principle) or interest.

9. I don't (know no) (were where) I could work that would be as pleasant.
10. (Their There) is no question that my job is the (right write) job for me.

□EXERCISE 8

1. My little son is never (quiet quite) (accept except) when he's asleep.
2. Only when the little guy's asleep do I get any (peace piece).
3. I can't decide now (weather whether) to rest or to make some (desert dessert) for dinner.
4. I guess I'd better (do due) the latter because (there they're) isn't much time left.
5. In this kind of (weather whether), I'm sure a cold (desert dessert) will be best.
6. Perhaps I'll offer (too two) choices because my children (are our) big eaters.
7. They go (threw through) a meal and (than then) ask for more.
8. I'm going to make (to two) entrees tonight and see (weather whether) I can fill everybody up.
9. If (your you're) not busy, why don't you stay for dinner?
10. (Than Then) you'll understand (were where) my time goes.

□EXERCISE 9

1. I don't (know no) (weather whether) I'm going to remember all these words.
2. My (principal principle) difficulty in this (coarse course) (does dose) seem to be spelling.
3. But (its it's) no wonder we all have problems with spelling because (are our) English language is so difficult to (right write).
4. Over 80 percent of (are our) words aren't spelled phonetically.
5. For example, the *ow* in *crow* sounds (quiet quite) different from the *ow* in *cow*.
6. A sound may be spelled in four (are or) five different ways.
7. But since taking this (coarse course), I spell better (than then) before.
8. I now (know no) most of these often-confused words.
9. And if I forget them, I (know no) (were where) to look them up.
10. I'm (quiet quite) sure I'm making progress, and I'll learn more before I'm (threw through).

□EXERCISE 10

1. I wonder (weather whether) the (weather whether) will (affect effect) the attendance at the game.
2. I'm (all ready already) to go if you are.

3. (Were Where) did you find that (peace piece) of cake?
4. I was (quiet quite) sure (their there they're) was none left.
5. Do you like the (coarse course) texture of the cake, or do you prefer a finer texture?
6. (You're Your) (right write) that (it's its) time we were going.
7. Let's walk (passed past) the park and (than then) down (Forth Fourth) Avenue.
8. It (doesn't dosen't) matter (weather whether) we're on time.
9. Since we have (are our) tickets, we're sure of seats.
10. Do you (know no) that (woman women) (who's whose) waving to us?

JOURNAL WRITING

In your journal write several sentences using words you may formerly have had trouble with.

WRITING ASSIGNMENT

From now on you will be expected to continue the writing assignments (which begin on p. 196) along with doing the exercises.

Proofreading Exercise

See if you can correct all six errors in this paragraph before checking with the answers at the back of the book.

THE ALARM CLOCK

When I was a freshman in high school, I took apart a old wind-up alarm clock that wouldn't run. I new I could fix it. Their sure are a lot of wheels and levers and gears and things in an alarm clock, but they all fit together beautifully. I could see how they all worked, but when I started to put the parts back were they logically belonged, I couldn't remember the exact pattern. When I was all threw, I had two gears left over. And of coarse the clock didn't work. However, the day was worthwhile because I learned a lot about wind-up alarm clocks. I learned not to take one apart unless I'm positive I can put it back together!

CONTRACTIONS

Two words condensed into one are called a contraction.

is not	isn't
you have	you've

The letter or letters that are left out are replaced with an apostrophe. For example, if the two words *do not* are condensed into one, an apostrophe is put where the *o* is left out.

do not	don't

Note how the apostrophe goes in the exact place where the letter or letters are left out in these contractions:

I am	I'm
I have	I've
I shall, I will	I'll
I would	I'd
you are	you're
you have	you've
you will	you'll
she is, she has	she's
he is, he has	he's
it is, it has	it's
we are	we're
we have	we've
we will, we shall	we'll
they are	they're
they have	they've
are not	aren't
cannot	can't
do not	don't
does not	doesn't
have not	haven't
let us	let's
who is, who has	who's
where is	where's

One contraction does not follow this rule:

will not	won't

In all other contractions that you're likely to use, the apostrophe goes exactly where the letter or letters are left out. Note especially *it's, they're, who's,* and *you're.* Use them when you mean two words. (See p. 31 for the possessive forms—*its, their, whose,* and *your*—which don't take an apostrophe.)

EXERCISES

Put an apostrophe in each contraction where a letter or letters have been left out. When you finish ten sentences, tear out the perforated answer sheet at the back of the book and correct your answers. Be sure to correct each group of ten sentences before going on so you'll catch your mistakes while you still have sentences to practice on.

☐EXERCISE 1

1. Im not sure why I didnt learn these rules earlier.
2. If Id learned them in grade school, Id be better off now.
3. Im sorry I didnt learn them at least in high school.
4. I wish Id mastered them when I didnt have so much else to do.
5. But since I didnt, Ive got a big job ahead of me.
6. Its a demanding task, but its not impossible.
7. Its important to learn standard English now, or Ill have trouble later.
8. Anyone who cant write acceptably isnt going to make it in college.
9. One cant expect professors to correct sentence errors, for theyve more to do than that.
10. But if I spend enough time, Im sure Ill make up for what Ive missed.

☐EXERCISE 2

1. Im probably going to lose the part-time job Ive had for a month.
2. If a firm isnt getting business, naturally its going to lay off workers.
3. In the firm where Ive been working, theres a threat of layoffs.
4. The management hasnt made any statement, but weve heard rumors.
5. Of course anyone whos been hired recently cant expect to stay.
6. Its only fair that someone whos been with the firm a long time should stay.
7. Since Im one whos been hired recently, Ill be one of the first to go.
8. Im already looking for another job, but theyre hard to find.
9. In fact Ive decided theres not much use in continuing to look.
10. Ive been thinking that spending all my time on my studies wouldnt be a bad idea.

☐EXERCISE 3

1. Ive been reading that scientists are studying noise levels.
2. Theyre looking for ways to reduce noise levels near airports and other places where noise cant be eliminated.
3. Theyve found one way to muffle sound is to plant small forests.

4. The forest floor with its heavy layer of decaying leaves absorbs sound like a sponge.
5. Also its been found that tree trunks deflect sound to the forest floor.
6. But forests not only muffle sound; theyre also useful as visual screens.
7. If people cant see where sound comes from, they arent so disturbed by it.
8. Thus city planners find its worthwhile to plant small urban forests.
9. But the forests arent only sound barriers.
10. Theyre pleasant recreation spots as well.

☐EXERCISE 4

1. Ive discovered its not difficult to paint a room.
2. Id always thought Id have a painter do our living room.
3. But after learning the price, I decided Id do it myself.
4. Even if youve never painted before, its not hard.
5. First its important to buy a good grade of paint.
6. Then youll need to fill in nail holes and sand uneven places.
7. Then youre ready to paint a six-inch border around the woodwork so youll be able to do the rest of the walls with a roller.
8. Next youre ready for the fastest part—rolling the paint on the walls.
9. Its almost always necessary to add a second coat, and youre lucky if you dont need a third.
10. Soon youll be in a paint store again choosing colors for the next room.

☐EXERCISE 5

1. Ive been reading about the data *Voyager I* sent back to Earth in 1980.
2. Scientists didnt know much about Saturn before, but theyve learned a lot.
3. For example, theyd always thought Saturn had six rings, and now theyve learned there are about 1,000.
4. Theyd never before been able to get a good look at Saturn.
5. Isnt it amazing that a spacecraft no bigger than a compact car could discover so much that scientists didnt know?
6. One scientist said, "Weve learned more about the Saturn system in the past week than in the entire span of recorded history."
7. Its impossible to imagine *Voyager I*'s speed of 91,000 km an hour, isnt it?
8. Whats amazing is that the spacecraft completed all its maneuvers flawlessly in its two-day close encounter.
9. Scientists havent begun to analyze all the information thats been sent back.
10. Itll take years before theyve interpreted all the findings.

☐EXERCISE 6

1. Havent you noticed how many people are riding bicycles these days?
2. Ive just read that in 1972 bicycles outsold cars for the first time.
3. Today bicycles arent merely for diversion; theyre an important means of transportation.
4. And they arent only energy savers; theyre health builders as well.
5. Theres nothing better for the cardiovascular system than a bicycle ride to work.
6. If youve had a bicycle ride in the morning, youll feel better all day.
7. A few cities are aware of the trend; theyre putting in bicycle lanes.
8. Its a problem, however, to make room for bicycle lanes in busy city streets.
9. Its going to take time to solve the conflict between bicycles and cars.
10. But its certainly true that bicycles save fuel, provide healthful exercise, and leave the air clean; theyre not to be taken lightly.

☐EXERCISE 7

1. Ive just come back from Epcot, and I cant begin to describe all thats to be seen there.
2. Theres so much that I didnt begin to see it all.
3. Ill never forget my amazement at the exhibits of nine countries in the World Showcase.
4. Its exciting to "ride a buckboard" at the Calgary Stampede and to walk in a real Indian village.
5. Id never before seen a Japanese house or a Mexican hacienda.
6. Its fascinating to go to the end of the Great Wall in China and to a pub in England.
7. Then theres Future World, in which I flew aboard a space vehicle.
8. Youll learn a lot if you visit Epcot, and youll want to stay awhile.
9. Its an education to go there, and Im planning to go back.
10. Also Im now planning to see the originals of some of those places.

☐EXERCISE 8

1. Im doing more reading now, and I find that its helping my writing.
2. Id never before realized that its important to read widely.
3. Ive begun to notice good sentences and how theyre put together.
4. And just by reading Ive improved my vocabulary.
5. Im beginning to look up words I dont know.
6. Its amazing how many new words Ive already learned.
7. Ive found that reading has helped my spelling too.

8. Im getting used to seeing words spelled correctly, and Im automatically spelling better.
9. And its good to know whats in the books I hear people talking about.
10. Ive found that reading can do a lot for me that TV cant.

□EXERCISE 9

1. Ive been reading about some famous people who didnt do well in school.
2. Its made me feel better.
3. Woody Allen says he didnt get any awards in school, and his grades "varied from below average to way below average."
4. I hadnt known before that Einstein failed his entrance exams to the Zurich Polytechnical Institute.
5. Louis Pasteur didnt fail but had the word *Mediocre* written after *Chemistry* on his diploma.
6. Winston Churchill didnt do well in school and says he stayed in the lowest grades three times longer than anyone else.
7. Charles Schulz, the cartoonist who created Charlie Brown, not only wasnt good in school but didnt even succeed at first with his cartoons.
8. Its a fact that his high school yearbook rejected them.
9. Perhaps grades arent the most important thing.
10. Hey, with my grades, maybe Ill become famous!

□EXERCISE 10

1. Ive just learned that bats are mammals and that theyre the only mammals that fly.
2. A bat cant walk or run.
3. Its legs and feet arent strong enough to do anything but hold onto a perch when its time to sleep.
4. A bat can chase insects through a dark forest and wont ever strike a twig or branch.
5. Its not its eyes but its ears that guide it.
6. It gives a continuous cry thats so high-pitched that people cant hear it.
7. The sound waves of the cry are reflected by obstacles back to the bat's sensitive ears, and thus it doesnt hit any obstacles.
8. There are 2,000 kinds of bats; the only place they dont live is in the coldest climates.
9. The female doesnt have a nest but gives birth to a single pink, blind baby.
10. When shes ready to go out, she simply hangs the baby up by its feet.

POSSESSIVES

The trick in writing possessives is to ask yourself the question, "Who does it belong to?" (Modern usage has made *who* acceptable when it comes first in a sentence, but some people still say "*Whom* does it belong to?" or even "*To whom* does it belong?") If the answer to your question ends in *s*, simply add an apostrophe after the *s*. If it doesn't end in *s*, then add an apostrophe and *s*.

one boys bike	Who does it belong to?	boy	Add *'s*	boy's bike
two boys bikes	Who do they belong to?	boys	Add *'*	boys' bikes
the mans hat	Who does it belong to?	man	Add *'s*	man's hat
the mens hats	Who do they belong to?	men	Add *'s*	men's hats
childrens game	Who does it belong to?	children	Add *'s*	children's game
one girls coat	Who does it belong to?	girl	Add *'s*	girl's coat
two girls coats	Who do they belong to?	girls	Add *'*	girls' coats

This trick will always work, but you must ask the question every time. And remember that the key word is *belong*. Who does it *belong* to? If you ask the question another way, you may get an answer that won't help you. Also, if you just look at a word without asking the question, you may think the name of the owner ends in an *s* when it really doesn't.

TO MAKE A POSSESSIVE

Ask "Who (or what) does it belong to?"
If the answer ends in *s*, add an apostrophe.
If it doesn't end in *s*, add an apostrophe and *s*.

Cover the right-hand column and see if you can write the following possessives correctly. Ask the question each time.

the womans dress ______	woman's
the womens ideas ______	women's
Stephens apartment ______	Stephen's
James apartment ______	James'
the Whites house ______	the Whites'
Mr. Whites house ______	Mr. White's

(Sometimes you may see a variation of this rule. *James' book* may be written *James's book.* That is correct too, but the best way is to stick to the simple rule. You can't be wrong if you follow it.)

In such expressions as *a day's work* or *Saturday's game*, you may ask how the work can belong to the day or the game can belong to Saturday. Those are simply possessive forms that have been in our language for a long time. And when you think about it, the work really does belong to the day (not the night), and the game does belong to Saturday (not Friday).

A word of warning! Don't assume that because a word ends in *s* it is necessarily a possessive. Make sure the word actually possesses something before you put in an apostrophe.

A few words, called possessive pronouns, are already possessive and don't need an apostrophe added to them. Memorize this list:

my, mine	its
your, yours	our, ours
his	their, theirs
her, hers	whose

Note particularly *its, their, whose*, and *your*. They are already possessive and don't take an apostrophe. (They sound just like the contractions *it's, they're, who's*, and *you're*, which stand for two words and of course have to have an apostrophe.)

As a practice exercise, cover the right-hand column below with a sheet of paper, and on it write the correct form (contraction or possessive). If you miss any, go back and review the explanations.

(It) raining. ________________	It's
(You) car needs washing. ________________	Your
(Who) to blame? ________________	Who's
(They) planning to come. ________________	They're
The cat drank (it) milk. ________________	its
(Who) been sitting here? ________________	Who's
The wind lost (it) force. ________________	its
(Who) going with me? ________________	Who's
My book has lost (it) cover. ________________	its
(It) all I can do. ________________	It's
(You) right. ________________	You're
(They) garden has many trees. ________________	Their
(It) sunny today. ________________	It's
(Who) car shall we take? ________________	Whose
The club lost (it) leader. ________________	its

Here's one more practice exercise. Cover the right-hand column with a sheet of paper, and on it write the possessives.

1. My cousins love their Aunt Anns house.	Ann's (You didn't add an apostrophe to *cousins*, did you? The cousins don't possess anything.)
2. Students grades depend on their study habits.	Students' (Who do the grades belong to?)
3. I invited Charles to my parents house.	parents' (Charles doesn't possess anything in this sentence.)
4. My parents went to Charles house.	Charles' (The parents don't possess anything in this sentence.)
5. Robins job is similar to yours.	Robin's (*Yours* is a possessive pronoun and doesn't take an apostrophe.)
6. Last years crop was the best yet.	year's (The crop belonged to last year.)
7. The Fowlers cottage is near the lake.	Fowlers' (Who does the cottage belong to?)
8. The Fowlers went to their cottage.	(No apostrophe in this sentence. *Their* is the possessive pronoun telling who the cottage belongs to. The sentence merely tells what the Fowlers did.)
9. Our computer is newer than theirs.	(No apostrophe in this sentence because the possessive pronouns *our* and *theirs* don't take an apostrophe.)
10. The womens team played the girls team.	women's, girls' (Did you ask who each team belongs to?)
11. The girls were proud of their team.	(No apostrophe. *Their* is the possessive pronoun telling who the team belongs to, and the girls don't possess anything in this sentence.)
12. The jurors verdict was fair.	jurors' (Who did the verdict belong to?)
13. The jurors gave their verdict.	(No apostrophe. The sentence merely tells what the jurors did.)
14. The gardens need rain.	(No apostrophe. The gardens don't possess anything.)

EXERCISES

Put the apostrophe in each possessive. WATCH OUT! **First,** make sure the word really possesses something; not every word that ends in *s* is a possessive. **Second,** remember that possessive pronouns don't take an apostrophe. **Third,** don't be confused because the word seems to end in *s*. You can't tell where the apostrophe goes until you ask the question, "Who (or what) does it belong to?" In the first sentence, for example, "Who does the watch belong to?" "Man." Therefore you will write *man's.*

□EXERCISE 1

1. Here's a mans watch on the table.
2. And whose book is this on the floor?
3. It may be either Kimberleys or Sarahs.
4. Have you seen Alfredos guitar?
5. Perhaps he left it in its case at the Student Union.
6. Everyones possessions seem to be lost today.
7. That colleges chief claim to fame is its football team.
8. The team was tired, however, after Saturdays game.
9. And yet yesterdays game was the best of the season.
10. Now the team is going to the governors reception.

□EXERCISE 2

1. Yesterday the professor read everybodys paper in class.
2. The professors comments were interesting.
3. Someones paper had excellent specific details.
4. Another persons paper was amusing.
5. Two students papers were exceptionally well organized.
6. All the students comments were helpful too.
7. Jims grades show his determination to get ahead.
8. And most of Michaels time seems to be spent studying.
9. But Mikes main interest these days is track.
10. The track teams trophy is displayed in the entrance to the Union.

□EXERCISE 3

1. Chauffeuring is a big part of a days program for me.
2. My first trips are to Tonys grade school and to Sues morning kindergarten.
3. In the afternoon it'll probably be to Sues ballet or violin lesson.
4. After school I pick up Tony and take him somewhere—perhaps to his Cub Scouts meeting or to the orthodontists office.

5. One or two more trips in the evening will finish the days driving.
6. It's all part of a mothers day.
7. I've been listening to todays weather report.
8. Chicagos temperature is higher than Miamis.
9. I need to know about tomorrows weather.
10. Then I can plan the childrens activities.

□EXERCISE 4

1. We went to the Womens Club yesterday.
2. We wanted to hear the senators speech.
3. The presidents introduction was excellent.
4. And the women all enjoyed the chairpersons jokes.
5. Then we were all impressed with the senators presentation.
6. The audiences applause was tremendous.
7. But who will win the primary is anybodys guess.
8. After the speech the women planned for the librarys annual book sale.
9. Jennifers mother chairs the library committee.
10. The Library Board appreciates the womens help with the book sale.

□EXERCISE 5

1. A visitors first impression of the Science Museum of Minnesota in St. Paul will be surprise.
2. Here are exhibits that people can touch, try out, and experiment with.
3. The museums unusual exhibits attract more than 10,000 visitors a week.
4. Childrens voices are heard asking questions, and people are interacting with the exhibits.
5. The museums 400 volunteer interpreters answer the visitors questions.
6. Visitors can help set up and take down an Ojibwa Indian wigwam and touch the Ojibwa Indians pots and bows and arrows.
7. In the weaving section a visitor is allowed to sit at the seven-foot-high loom and weave a strand of wool in and out of the looms warp.
8. The museums second floor boasts the most advanced space theater and planetarium in the United States.
9. The theaters semicircular dome and rounded walls seem to wrap around the visitor.
10. And in a film on the Great Barrier Reef, a visitor gets the impression of swimming right among the fish and sharks and marine plant life.

□EXERCISE 6

1. Sallys chief interest these days is butterflies, and she's been telling me about them.

2. Butterflies and moths look much alike, but a butterflys antennae or feelers have little knobs at the end of them.
3. Also a butterflys feeding time is during the day whereas a moths feeding time is at night.
4. I was amazed to learn that a moths size may vary from one-fifth of an inch to ten inches.
5. These insects bodies are divided into three sections with three pair of legs and, in the middle section, two pair of wings.
6. A butterflys mouth is a long slender feeding tube that is coiled up like a watch spring when not in use.
7. Birds are these insects main enemies.
8. But the monarch butterflys foul taste and odor make birds avoid it.
9. Sallys term paper is going to be about the contribution of butterflies to conservation.
10. One way they contribute is that as they feed they rub against the stamens and pistils of flowers and thus aid the flowers pollination.

☐EXERCISE 7

1. Lincolns gaunt frame was a comforting sight to the North during the Civil War.
2. And the settlers hard work and courage helped them through the long winters.
3. Beethovens Fifth Symphony is a masterful elaboration of the "fate motif."
4. This motif was one of the French peoples secret symbols during World War II.
5. Childrens symphonies are now being organized in many cities.
6. The Girls Athletic team has its meeting tomorrow.
7. Pablos motor scooter is faster than Leroys.
8. Everyone is pleased about Cheryls new job.
9. Since she has no car, she borrows Heathers bicycle to get to work.
10. Each days work gives her a sense of satisfaction.

☐EXERCISE 8

1. Our visitors were impressed with Dads garden.
2. My fathers hobby has always been gardening.
3. And my mothers hobby is flower arrangement.
4. The chief asset of Mr. and Mrs. Jones property next door is its fine lawn.
5. Mr. Jones lawn is always in beautiful condition.
6. Mr. Jones keeps the lawn that way in all seasons.
7. The car in front of our house isn't ours.
8. It's the Johnsons car.

9. Have you seen Erics new Fiero and Dennis new Corvette?
10. Charles car is a really old model.

☐EXERCISE 9

1. I've decided to buy some gifts at Saturdays sale.
2. Then I'll have them ready for everybodys birthday.
3. I'm going to look at mens ties and womens scarves.
4. That store sells only boys and mens clothing.
5. Of course I'll look at childrens toys for my nephews.
6. And perhaps I can find a book for my nieces gift.
7. Jewelry is always a safe choice for my sisters gift.
8. And my parents gift will probably be records.
9. It looks as if I'll have a mornings work buying all these things.
10. But I enjoy choosing gifts for peoples birthdays.

☐EXERCISE 10

1. Matthews mind isn't exactly on his studies these days.
2. And Victors motto seems to be to study hard—the night before exams.
3. Jeffreys ability in dramatics may carry him far.
4. Hurrying out of the room, he grabbed someone elses books instead of his own.
5. Have you read Haleys account of finding his relatives in Africa?
6. It was hard to accept that judges decision.
7. I'm not asking for anyones advice.
8. I'm going to stay at my brother-in-laws camp.
9. We spent Thanksgiving at Aunt Rebeccas cottage.
10. He wasn't listening to his wifes explanation.

JOURNAL WRITING

In your journal write five sentences using the possessive forms of the names of your family or the names of your friends.

WRITING ASSIGNMENT

Turn to the section beginning on page 196 for your writing assignment.

Review of Contractions and Possessives

Put in the necessary apostrophes. Try to get these exercises perfect. Don't excuse an error by saying, "Oh, that was just a careless mistake." A mistake is a mistake. Be tough on yourself.

☐EXERCISE 1

1. Ive been reading about how bananas grow.
2. Id always thought they grew on trees, but they dont.
3. The banana plant doesnt have a trunk like a tree; its trunk is made of overlapping leaves like a celery stalk.
4. When the stalk is full grown, its from 8 to 16 inches thick but so soft it can be cut with a knife.
5. A banana plants leaves may be 12 feet long and more than 2 feet wide.
6. In some countries the leaves are torn into strips to make mats, and the fibers are used to make twine.
7. When a banana plants blossoms fall off, a cluster of tiny bananas pointing to the ground can be seen.
8. Thats the way Id always thought bananas grew, but they dont.
9. As they grow, they begin to point upward until when theyre fully grown, theyre all pointing to the sky.
10. Then theyre harvested and may travel as much as 4,000 miles to our grocery stores.

☐EXERCISE 2

1. Id been traveling with Doug for a week, and wed never thought of stopping for any sightseeing.
2. Dougs goal was to get to his home in Nevada as soon as possible.
3. Then as we approached the Colorado-Utah border, we saw signs advertising the Dinosaur National Monument.
4. We decided wed stop, and weve always been glad we did.
5. Wed never seen anything like it before; its one of our countrys most amazing sights.
6. It contains the worlds largest known deposits of petrified skeletons of dinosaurs, some as small as a chicken and others as long as 60 feet.
7. Its impressive to see them embedded there just as theyve been for millions of years.
8. And at the visitors center we saw how the excavators work.
9. We learned a lot wed never known before about dinosaurs.
10. It was like reading a chapter of the Earths history.

☐EXERCISE 3

1. One of my friends cant bear to throw anything away.
2. Now shes found a use for the familys old Christmas tree.
3. Shes decorated it with strings of raisins, apple bits, and popcorn and stuck it in a snowdrift with its trunk firmly on the ground.
4. Shes also added ears of dried corn and pinecones stuffed with suet.
5. Already the birds and squirrels have found the feast, and most of its been eaten.
6. Some people say everythings good for something.
7. Ive just learned that even poisonous snake venom is good for something.
8. Doctors are now separating its enzymes to make various medicines.
9. Theyve made medicines that stop bleeding, that dissolve blood clots, and that kill pain.
10. So a poisonous snakes bad reputation is getting a second thought.

☐EXERCISE 4

Its going to be a summer of traveling for my brothers. Theyre going to the West Coast in Marks car. They had thought of taking Miles van, but its a gas guzzler. Marks VW wont be so expensive to run. They havent planned their route yet, but theyll no doubt hit Idaho because Marks best friend lives there, and a few nights lodging and a few free meals wont be unwelcome. The boys will be gone a month or maybe longer if theyre lucky enough to find jobs. Their aim is to see whether theyd like to settle in the West and also just to see a part of the country they havent seen before.

Proofreading Exercise

In this brief student paper you will find errors from all the material you have studied so far. See if you can correct all six errors before checking with the answers at the back of the book.

RUG CLEANER

I wanted a summer job, but its hard to find summer jobs. One day I answered a newspaper ad and went to a meeting where their were about 20 others looking for jobs. We learned that salespeople were needed by a manufacturing company to demonstrate vacuum cleaners in peoples homes. We could chose between working for a salary or working for a commission. But the fellows who chose a salary got sent home and were never called again. Those of us who chose a commission were sent out to demonstrate the vacuum cleaners.

In the next two weeks I must of cleaned a hundred rugs, but no one wanted to buy. That meant I didnt make a cent. So finally I quit. I had cleaned a lot of rugs for nothing, but I had also broadened my education. I had learned how some companies operate.

WORDS THAT CAN BE BROKEN INTO PARTS

Breaking words into their parts will often help you spell them correctly. Each of the following words is made up of two shorter words:

over run	. . . overrun	room mate	. . . roommate
over rate	. . . overrate	with hold	. . . withhold

Becoming aware of prefixes such as *dis*, *inter*, *mis*, and *un* is also helpful. Then when you add a word to the prefix, the spelling will be correct.

dis appear	disappear	mis spell	misspell
dis appoint	disappoint	mis step	misstep
dis approve	disapprove	un natural	unnatural
dis satisfied	dissatisfied	un necessary	unnecessary
dis service	disservice	un nerve	unnerve
inter racial	interracial	un noticed	unnoticed
inter related	interrelated		

Notice that no letters are dropped, either from the prefix or from the word added to it.

Have someone dictate the above list for you to write and then mark any words you miss. Memorize the correct spellings by noting how each word is made up of a prefix and a word.

RULE FOR DOUBLING A FINAL CONSONANT

Most spelling rules have so many exceptions that they aren't much help. But here's one that has almost no exceptions and is really worth learning.

> **Double a final consonant when adding an ending that begins with a vowel (such as *ing, ed, er*) if all three of the following are true:**
>
> **1. the word ends in a single consonant,**
> **2. the final consonant is preceded by a single vowel (the vowels are *a, e, i, o, u*),**
> **3. and the accent is on the last syllable (or the word has only one syllable).**

We'll try the rule on the following words to which we'll add *ing*, *ed*, or *er*.

begin 1. It ends in a single consonant—*n*,
2. preceded by a single vowel—*i*,
3. and the accent is on the last syllable—*be gin'*.
Therefore we double the final consonant and write *beginning, beginner.*

stop 1. It ends in a single consonant—*p*,
2. preceded by a single vowel—*o*,
3. and the accent is on the last syllable (there is only one).
Therefore we double the final consonant and write *stopping, stopped, stopper.*

motor 1. It ends in a single consonant—*r*,
2. preceded by a single vowel—*o*,
3. but the accent isn't on the last syllable. It's on the first—*mo' tor.*
Therefore we don't double the final consonant. We write *motoring, motored.*

sleep 1. It ends in a single consonant—*p*,
2. but it isn't preceded by a single vowel. There are two *e*'s.
Therefore we don't double the final consonant. We write *sleeping, sleeper.*

kick 1. It doesn't end in a single consonant. There are two—*c* and *k*.
Therefore we don't double the final consonant. We write *kicking, kicked, kicker.*

Note that *qu* is really a consonant because *q* is almost never written without *u*. Think of it as *kw*. In words like *equip* and *quit*, the *qu* acts as a consonant. Therefore *quit* does end in a single consonant preceded by a single vowel, and the final consonant is doubled—*quitting.*

Also note that *bus* may be written either *bussing* or *busing*. The latter is more common.

EXERCISES

Add *ing* to these words. Correct each group of ten by the perforated answer sheet at the back of the book.

□EXERCISE 1

1. put
2. control
3. admit
4. mop
5. plan
6. hop
7. jump
8. knit
9. mark
10. creep

□EXERCISE 2

1. return
2. swim
3. sing
4. benefit
5. loaf
6. nail
7. omit
8. occur
9. shop
10. interrupt

□EXERCISE 3

1. begin
2. spell
3. prefer
4. fish
5. hunt
6. excel
7. wrap
8. stop
9. wed
10. scream

□EXERCISE 4

1. feel
2. murmur
3. turn
4. add
5. subtract
6. stream
7. expel
8. miss
9. get
10. stress

□EXERCISE 5

1. forget
2. misspell
3. fit
4. plant
5. pin
6. trust
7. sip
8. flop
9. reap
10. cart

Progress Test

This test covers everything you have studied so far. One sentence in each pair is correct. The other is incorrect. Read both sentences carefully before you decide. Then write the letter of the correct sentence in the blank.

_____ 1. A. The Graham's cottage has just been painted.
B. My dad's principal hobby is fishing.

_____ 2. A. It dosen't matter whether she comes or not.
B. Her coming won't have any effect on my plans.

_____ 3. A. I'm going to chose my clothes with care this fall.
B. The Scotts have invited us to their barbecue.

_____ 4. A. I know it's important to cut out desserts.
B. But he past me a piece of cake, and I accepted it.

_____ 5. A. He submited his application for the job.
B. I wonder whether I should apply too.

_____ 6. A. Is this passbook yours or hers?
B. She's quiet sure that she won't lose any money.

_____ 7. A. Of coarse I know you're doing all your exercises.
B. I omitted the fourth sentence in our test.

_____ 8. A. I've all ready saved quite a large sum of money.
B. I'd like to save an even greater sum than that.

_____ 9. A. She wasn't conscious that he hadn't voted.
B. She should of asked him for his personal opinion.

_____ 10. A. It's an honor to know the principal of the academy.
B. And I like belonging to the mens' athletic club.

_____ 11. A. Our puppy got loose from it's leash and ran away.
B. I already knew what they wanted to hear.

_____ 12. A. Your going to their beach party, aren't you?
B. I'm not sure whether it's too rainy to go.

_____ 13. A. Who's car is that in the Millers' driveway?
B. Won't they be through with their new project soon?

_____ 14. A. If I ever lose my keys, I won't know where to look for them.
B. Of course Kellys advice surprised me.

_____ 15. A. He lead his class in math and got a compliment from the prof.
B. Now he's studying harder than ever before.

A LIST OF FREQUENTLY MISSPELLED WORDS

Have someone dictate this list of commonly misspelled words to you and mark the ones you miss. Then memorize the correct spellings, working on ten words each week.

Be sure to pronounce the following words correctly so that you won't misspell them: *athlete*, *athletics*, *environment*, *mathematics*, *nuclear*, *probably*, *sophomore*, *studying*. Also try to think up memory devices to help you remember correct spellings. For example, you *labor* in a *laboratory*; the two *l*'s in *parallel* are parallel; and the *r* separates the two *a*'s in *separate*.

1. absence
2. across
3. actually
4. a lot
5. amateur
6. among
7. analyze
8. appearance
9. appreciate
10. argument
11. athlete
12. athletics
13. awkward
14. becoming
15. beginning
16. belief
17. benefit
18. buried
19. business
20. certain
21. college
22. coming
23. committee
24. competition
25. complete
26. consider
27. criticism
28. decision
29. definitely
30. dependent
31. development
32. difference
33. disastrous
34. discipline
35. discussed
36. disease
37. divide
38. dying
39. eighth
40. eligible
41. eliminate
42. embarrassed
43. environment
44. especially
45. etc.
46. exaggerate
47. excellent
48. exercise
49. existence
50. experience
51. explanation
52. extremely
53. familiar
54. February
55. finally
56. foreign
57. government
58. grammar
59. grateful
60. guarantee
61. guard
62. guidance
63. height
64. hoping
65. humorous
66. immediately
67. independent
68. intelligence
69. interest
70. interfere
71. involved
72. knowledge
73. laboratory
74. leisure
75. length
76. library
77. likely
78. lying
79. marriage
80. mathematics
81. meant
82. medicine
83. necessary
84. neither
85. ninety
86. ninth
87. nuclear
88. occasionally
89. opinion
90. opportunity
91. parallel
92. particular
93. persuade
94. physically
95. planned
96. pleasant
97. possible
98. practical
99. preferred
100. prejudice
101. privilege
102. probably

103. professor
104. prove
105. psychology
106. pursue
107. receipt
108. receive
109. recommend
110. reference
111. relieve
112. religious
113. repetition
114. rhythm
115. ridiculous
116. sacrifice
117. safety
118. scene
119. schedule
120. secretary
121. senior
122. sense
123. separate
124. severely
125. shining
126. significant
127. similar
128. sincerely
129. sophomore
130. speech
131. straight
132. studying
133. succeed
134. success
135. suggest
136. surprise
137. thoroughly
138. though
139. tragedy
140. tried
141. tries
142. truly
143. unfortunately
144. until
145. unusual
146. using
147. usually
148. Wednesday
149. writing
150. written

USING YOUR DICTIONARY

By working through the following 13 exercises, you'll become familiar with what you can find in an up-to-date desk dictionary.

1. PRONUNCIATION

Look up the word *longevity* and copy the pronunciation here.

Now under each letter with a pronunciation mark over it, write the key word having the same mark. You'll find the key words at the bottom of one of the two dictionary pages open before you. Note especially that the upside-down *e* (ə) always has the sound of *uh* like the *a* in *ago* or *about*. Remember that sound because it's found in many words.

Next, pronounce the key words you've written, and then slowly pronounce *longevity*, giving each syllable the same sound as its key word.

Finally note which syllable has the heavy accent mark. (In most dictionaries the accent mark points to the stressed syllable, but in one dictionary it's in front of the stressed syllable.) The stressed syllable is *jev*. Now say the word, letting the full force of your voice fall on that syllable.

When two pronunciations are given, the first is the more common. If the complete pronunciation of a word isn't given, look at the word above it to find the pronunciation.

Look up the pronunciation of these words, using the key words at the bottom of the page to help you pronounce each syllable. Then note which syllable has the heavy accent mark, and say the word aloud.

condolence comparable koala mischievous

2. DEFINITIONS

The dictionary may give a number of meanings for a word. Read through all the meanings for each italicized word and then write a definition appropriate to the sentence.

1. When he didn't come to work, we suspected he was *malingering.* ______

____

2. She felt *apathetic* about her new job. ______________

____

3. His *sedentary* occupation gave him no opportunity for exercise. ______

____

4. Her lack of experience was an *insuperable* barrier to her promotion at that time. ______________

5. The orchestra conductor always maintained his *equanimity* even under the most trying circumstances. ______________

3. SPELLING

By making yourself look up each word you aren't sure how to spell, you'll soon become a better speller. When two spellings are given in the dictionary, the first one (or the one with the definition) is the more common.

Underline the more common spelling of each of these words.

ax, axe

dialog, dialogue

encyclopaedia, encyclopedia

gray, grey

4. COMPOUND WORDS

If you want to find out whether two words are written separately, written with a hyphen between them, or written as one word, consult your dictionary. For example:

half sister	is written as two words
brother-in-law	is hyphenated
stepson	is written as one word

Write each of the following correctly.

non conformity ______________ short order ______________

runner up ______________ south paw ______________

self contained ______________ week end ______________

5. CAPITALIZATION

If a word is capitalized in the dictionary, that means it should always be capitalized. If it isn't capitalized in the dictionary, then it may or may not be capitalized, depending on how it's used (see p. 183). For example:

Indian is always capitalized

college is capitalized or not, according to how it's used
She's attending college.
She's attending Chabot College.

Write these words as they're given in the dictionary (with or without a capital) to show whether they must always be capitalized or not.

Chickadee ______________ Halloween ______________

Democrat ______________ Spanish ______________

Senator ______________ Muslim ______________

6. USAGE

Because a word is in the dictionary is no indication that it's in standard use. The following designations indicate whether a word is used today and, if so, where and by whom.

obsolete	no longer used
archaic	not now used in ordinary language but still found in some biblical, literary, and legal expressions
colloquial informal	used in informal conversation but not in formal writing
dialectal regional	used in some localities but not everywhere
slang	popular but nonstandard expression
nonstandard substandard	not used by educated people

Look up each italicized word and write the designation that indicates its usage. Dictionaries differ. One may list a word as slang whereas another will call it colloquial. And still another may give no designation, thus indicating that that particular dictionary considers the word in standard use.

1. That restaurant is a *clip joint.* ______________________

2. He's *uptight* about the new regulations. ______________________

3. Why so pale and wan, fond lover?
   Prithee, why so pale? ______________________

4. He came to the party with a *far-out* haircut. ______________________

5. Add just a *smidgen* of salt to the recipe. ______________________

6. He had no worries because his parents were *well heeled.* ____________

7. He did a *snow job* in convincing the boss. ______________________

8. We were told not to go but went *anyways.* ______________________

7. DERIVATIONS

The derivations or stories behind words will often help you remember the current meanings. For example, if you read that someone had a laconic style, and you consulted your dictionary, you would find that *laconic* comes from the ancient province of Laconia in Greece. The Laconians were so well known for their concise way of speaking that *laconic* came to mean "brief and pithy." The story is told that Philip of Macedon, at war with the Laconians, sent word to them that if he came within their borders, he would leave not one stone of their capital city, Sparta. The Laconians sent back the laconic reply, "If." And so today anyone who writes or speaks briefly and to the point is said to have a laconic style.

Look up the derivation of each of these words. You'll find it in square brackets either just before or just after the definition.

aster ____________________

metropolis ____________________

apathy ____________________

sandwich ____________________

euthanasia ____________________

8. SYNONYMS

At the end of a definition, a list of synonyms is sometimes given. For example, at the end of the definition of *beautiful*, you'll find several synonyms. And if you look up *handsome* or *pretty*, you'll be referred to the synonyms under *beautiful.*

List the synonyms for the following words.

new ____________________

acknowledge ____________________

doubtful ____________________

gaudy ____________________

9. ABBREVIATIONS

Find the meaning of the following abbreviations.

ibid. ______________________ km ______________________

i.e. ______________________ Ph.D. ______________________

10. NAMES OF PEOPLE

The names of people will be found either in the main part of your dictionary or in a separate Biographical Names section at the back.

Identify the following.

Thoreau ______________________

Geronimo ______________________

Hippocrates ______________________

Beatrix Potter ______________________

11. NAMES OF PLACES

The names of places will be found either in the main part of your dictionary or in a separate Geographic Names section at the back.

Identify the following.

Agra ______________________

Georgian Bay ______________________

Karnak ______________________

Mauna Loa ______________________

12. FOREIGN WORDS AND PHRASES

Give the language and the meaning of the italicized expressions.

1. As I left, he waved and shouted, "*Auf Wiedersehen.*" ______________
2. The foreign government announced that the U.S. diplomat was *persona non grata* and must leave the country within 24 hours. ______________
3. The ability to care is the *sine qua non* of any friendship. ______________
4. I had a feeling of *déjà vu* when I read his paper. ______________

13. MISCELLANEOUS INFORMATION

Find these miscellaneous bits of information in your dictionary.

1. When was Pompeii destroyed? ______________
2. How long is the Suez Canal? ______________
3. What is the capital of Manitoba? ______________
4. A kilometer is equal to what portion of a mile? ______________
5. What is the population of Provo, Utah? ______________
6. When did Nebuchadnezzar die? ______________
7. What is the plural of *cupful*? ______________
8. What is the source of penicillin? ______________
9. Near what country is the Great Barrier Reef? ______________
10. What is the meaning of the British term *petrol*? ______________

2

Sentence Structure

2 Sentence Structure

The most common errors in freshman writing are fragments and run-together sentences. Here are some fragments:

> Having decided to drive to the mountains that afternoon
> Although we had never been on that road before
> The problem that bothered her the most
> Because I couldn't decide what to do

They don't make complete statements. They leave the reader wanting something more.

Here are some run-together sentences:

> I phoned Wendy she wasn't in.
> No one was in everybody had gone to the game.
> I finished my paper then I had a snack.
> It was almost time for dinner I was hungry.

Unlike fragments, they make complete statements, but the trouble is they make *two* complete statements, which shouldn't be run together into one sentence. The reader has to go back to see where there should have been a pause.

Both fragments and run-together sentences bother the reader. Not until you can get rid of them will your writing be clear and easy to read. Unfortunately there is no quick, easy way to learn to avoid them. You have to learn a little about sentence structure—mainly how to find the subject and the verb in a sentence so that you can tell whether it really is a sentence.

FINDING SUBJECTS AND VERBS

When you write a sentence, you write about *something* or *someone*. That's the subject. Then you write what the subject *does* or *is*. That's the verb.

> Birds fly.

The word *Birds* is the something you are writing about. It's the subject, and we'll underline it once. *Fly* tells what the subject does. It shows the action in the sentence. It's the verb, and we'll underline it twice. Because the verb often shows action, it is easier to spot than the subject. Therefore always look for it first. For example, in the sentence

> Pat drives a delivery truck on Saturdays.

which word shows the action? Drives. It's the verb. Underline it twice. Now ask yourself who or what drives. Pat. It's the subject. Underline it once.

Study the following sentences until you understand how to pick out subjects and verbs.

> Last night the rain flooded the playing field. (Which word shows the action? Flooded. It's the verb. Underline it twice. Who or what flooded? Rain. It's the subject. Underline it once.)
>
> Yesterday my brother ran in the five-mile relay. (Which word shows the action? Ran. And who or what ran? Brother.)
>
> This year my sister plays the cello in the high school orchestra. (Which word shows the action? Plays. Who or what plays? Sister.)

Often the verb doesn't show action but merely tells what the subject *is* or *was*. Learn to spot such verbs (*is, are, was, were, seems, appears . . .*).

> Dan is a trapeze artist. (First spot the verb is. Then ask who or what is. Dan is.)
>
> That guy in the blue shirt is a juggler. (First spot the verb is. Then ask who or what is. Guy is.)
>
> Allison seems content in her new job. (First spot the verb seems. Then ask who or what seems. Allison seems.)
>
> She appears happy. (First spot the verb appears. Then ask who or what appears. She appears.)

Sometimes the subject comes after the verb.

> In the stands were 5,000 spectators. (Who or what were? Spectators were.)
>
> Where is the fire? (Who or what is? Fire is.)
>
> There was a large crowd at the game. (Who or what was? Crowd was.)

There were not nearly enough seats for everybody. (Who or what were? Seats were.)
Here are my reasons. (Who or what are? Reasons are.)

Note that *there* and *here* (as in the last three sentences) are never subjects. They simply point out something.

In commands the subject often is not expressed. It is *you* (understood).

Come here. (You come here.)
Give me a hand. (You give me a hand.)

As you pick out subjects in the following exercises, you may wonder whether, for example, you should say the subject is *trees* or *redwood trees.* It makes no difference so long as you get the main subject, *trees,* right. In the answers at the back of the book, usually—but not always—the single word is used. Don't waste your time worrying about whether to include an extra word with the subject. Just make sure you get the main subject right.

EXERCISES

Underline the subject once and the verb twice. Find the verb first, and then ask **Who** or **What.** When you've finished ten sentences, compare your answers carefully with those on the perforated answer sheet.

□EXERCISE 1

1. Redwood trees are enormous.
2. They grow to over 300 feet.
3. They are the largest living things in the world today.
4. Redwoods grow in a limited area along the coast of California.
5. They resist decay.
6. And their bark resists fire.
7. Therefore redwood trees live a long time.
8. Many were here at the time of Columbus.
9. Thus many are about 500 years old.
10. Their wood varies in color from light cherry to dark mahogany.

□EXERCISE 2

1. From the top of a small hill we saw the prairie fire.
2. The fire swept across the dry land.

3. First there was only smoke.
4. Then there were a few flames.
5. Higher and higher rose the flames.
6. Fortunately a motorist saw the fire.
7. Minutes later he alerted the fire department in a nearby town.
8. Fire fighters spread out across the prairie.
9. They soon had the fire under control.
10. Only a small cabin on the edge of the prairie burned.

☐EXERCISE 3

1. My instructor stresses the importance of concentration.
2. One's attitude is important too.
3. I keep a study schedule these days.
4. I worked until midnight on my paper.
5. My paper now has a logical development.
6. Finally I typed my paper.
7. Typed papers make a good impression.
8. My paper satisfies me now.
9. I really worked hard.
10. Give me credit for that.

☐EXERCISE 4

1. The koala is popular in every zoo.
2. It is a native of Australia.
3. The koala looks a bit like a teddy bear.
4. No other plant-eating animal has such a restricted diet.
5. Its food consists almost exclusively of leaves of the eucalyptus tree.
6. And it eats only from certain types of eucalyptus trees.
7. Leaves from other types of eucalyptus trees are often fatal.
8. A newborn koala is about an inch long.
9. It crawls into its mother's pouch for further development.
10. At six months the fully developed koala rides on its mother's shoulders.

☐EXERCISE 5

1. There was not a cloud in the sky.
2. A lizard darted from cactus to cactus.
3. Locusts swarmed over the prairie like a thundercloud.
4. Louder and louder grew the sound of the insects.
5. Here and there we saw prairie flowers.
6. The wind shifted the prairie soil constantly.
7. In the distance rose the majestic mountains.

8. The sun sank rapidly below the horizon.
9. Then the prairie suddenly became cold.
10. We were glad for the warmth of our car.

☐EXERCISE 6

1. The Persians built the first windmill in the seventh century.
2. Today windmills meet some energy needs.
3. But windpower provides less than one percent of U.S. energy.
4. The future of windpower, however, looks bright.
5. The government supports the design and testing of large wind generators.
6. It also encourages residential windmills for individual homeowners.
7. It gives income-tax credits for such additions to property.
8. Residential windmills at $5,000 to $10,000 are hardly cheap.
9. Furthermore, they provide only part of a household's electrical needs.
10. Yet windpower has possibilities for the future.

☐EXERCISE 7

1. Every state in the Union now has a state bird.
2. The cardinal is the most popular.
3. Seven states chose it as their state bird.
4. Those states are Kentucky, Illinois, Indiana, Ohio, North Carolina, Virginia, and West Virginia.
5. The second most popular bird is the western meadowlark.
6. It belongs to Kansas, Wyoming, Nebraska, Montana, North Dakota, and Oregon.
7. The Hawaiian nene is on the endangered species list.
8. The smallest state bird is the black-capped chickadee of Maine and Massachusetts.
9. The cactus wren was a natural choice for Arizona.
10. Perhaps the most beautiful state bird is the ring-necked pheasant of South Dakota.

☐EXERCISE 8

1. Oceans cover 71 percent of the surface of the earth.
2. The five oceans are the Pacific, Atlantic, Indian, Arctic, and Antarctic.
3. The waters of all five oceans join.
4. Therefore they really make one great ocean.
5. The sea is actually a part of each of us.
6. Our body fluids are chemically similar to seawater.
7. This is probably an inheritance from our sea-living ancestors.

EXERCISES

Cross out the prepositional phrases. Then underline the subject once and the verb twice. Correct each group of ten sentences before going on.

□EXERCISE 1

1. Some of my friends went to the game with me.
2. Most of the bleachers were full.
3. But all of us found good seats in the middle of the bleachers.
4. During the game the atmosphere was tense.
5. Three of the players were on probation.
6. Neither of the teams scored during the first half.
7. Some of the spectators left at the end of the first half.
8. The most exciting part of the entire game was the last quarter.
9. In the last two minutes our team made a touchdown.
10. But the outcome of the game was a tie between the two teams.

□EXERCISE 2

1. All of my classes are on the top floor of Garwood Hall.
2. Most of my courses require a lot of homework.
3. Most of my professors give true-false tests.
4. But one of my professors gives essay tests.
5. All of us find the true-false tests easier.
6. One of the requirements of my economics course is a term paper.
7. Much of my time goes into that term paper.
8. In most classes an ability in writing helps.
9. A term paper with good organization gets a higher grade.
10. And writing without errors is also a plus.

□EXERCISE 3

1. Two of my friends went with me on a vacation.
2. All of us wanted to see more of California.
3. Above all, we wanted to see Muir Woods.
4. The road to the woods is long and winding.
5. But all of us were enchanted with the cathedral-like woods.
6. The quietness of the scene among the big trees was breathtaking.
7. All of us learned a great deal that day about redwoods.
8. The next place on our list was Golden Gate Park.
9. With its aquarium, arboretum, and museums, it kept us busy for an entire day.
10. Finally the three of us had tea in the Oriental Tea Garden.

Underline the subject once and the verb twice. If you aren't sure, cross out the prepositional phrases first.

☐EXERCISE 4

1. Hibernation differs from sleep.
2. In sleep animals merely relax.
3. In hibernation, however, their life almost stops.
4. The breathing of the animals becomes very slow.
5. And the beating of their hearts becomes irregular.
6. During hibernation, a woodchuck's body is only a little warmer than the air in its burrow.
7. Some kinds of insects freeze solid.
8. Mammals generally prepare for hibernation by eating large amounts of food.
9. They store the food in thick layers of fat.
10. Groundhogs, for example, become very plump before hibernation.

☐EXERCISE 5

1. The national bird of the United States is the bald eagle.
2. With its white head and white tail feathers, it is easy to identify.
3. But bald eagles are now an endangered species.
4. Cedar Glen along the Mississippi River in Illinois is a haven for these birds.
5. After their breeding season in the northern states and Canadian provinces, they gather here for the winter.
6. For five or six months each winter they stay in this protected place.
7. An area of about 580 acres around Cedar Glen is now an eagle sanctuary.
8. On frigid winter nights the eagles perch side by side on the branches of large sycamore trees.
9. More bald eagles spend the winter at Cedar Glen than at any other place in the Midwest.
10. Havens like this ensure a future for our national bird.

☐EXERCISE 6

1. One of my hobbies is the restoration of furniture.
2. In my spare time I pursue my hobby.
3. For example, a rung in one of our chairs was loose.
4. From some old wood I made a new rung.
5. After a good sanding, the rung was ready to glue in place.
6. A coat of dull varnish finished the job.

7. One of my next projects was an antique barrel-top trunk.
8. The embossed metal on the top was grimy with age.
9. With the help of an electric sander, I cleaned the metal.
10. Then a coat of dull varnish made it look antique again.

☐EXERCISE 7

1. Of the original Seven Wonders of the World, only the Great Pyramid exists today.
2. Between the huge blocks of the pyramids, the Egyptians used no mortar.
3. The Hanging Gardens of Babylon were another of the Seven Wonders.
4. The gardens, on a series of rising terraces, were not really "hanging."
5. A pump near the Euphrates watered the gardens.
6. Another one of the Seven Wonders was the Colossus of Rhodes.
7. The meaning of *colossus* is huge statue.
8. It stood beside, but not across, the harbor at Rhodes in the third century B.C.
9. During an earthquake it toppled to the ground.
10. Later, in A.D. 653 someone sold it for scrap.

☐EXERCISE 8

1. There are wonders in our country too.
2. In Virginia one of the most striking natural phenomena is the Natural Bridge over Cedar Creek.
3. The 27-meter stone arch spans the gorge 60 meters above the stream.
4. A still larger natural bridge is Rainbow Bridge in southern Utah.
5. A former tributary of the Colorado River carved it out of salmon-pink sandstone.
6. With an 85-meter span, it arches to a height of 94 meters.
7. It is high enough to straddle the national Capitol.
8. Its width is some 13 meters.
9. Therefore it is wide enough to accommodate an average highway.
10. It is the largest natural stone arch in the world.

☐EXERCISE 9

1. Making maple syrup is an important industry in Vermont.
2. The sap rises in the maple trees from late February through April.
3. The Indians taught the early settlers the secret of gathering the sap.
4. The farmer bores a half-inch hole into the tree trunk to a depth of about two inches.
5. He then inserts a wooden or metal spout.
6. The sap drips into a trough.

7. Sap ferments quickly.
8. Therefore the farmer sends the sap immediately to the boilers.
9. Each tree yields from 10 to 25 gallons of sap.
10. But it takes about 35 gallons of sap to make one gallon of maple syrup.

□EXERCISE 10

1. On a backpacking trip to Alaska, we visited Admiralty Island National Monument.
2. With no changes since the end of the last Ice Age, the island stands in its original grandeur.
3. In the center of the island, rugged snowcapped peaks rise 5,000 feet above the magnificent forests.
4. The natives call the island "The Fortress of the Bears."
5. It is home to about 1,000 Alaskan brown bears or grizzlies.
6. And along the shores are havens for young salmon and king crab.
7. Admiralty Island is one of the few totally natural areas still in existence.
8. But now a logging firm wants to cut 23,000 acres of virgin timber on the island and to build a logging transfer terminal on the shore.
9. The U.S. government passed the Alaska Lands Act in 1980 to protect such areas.
10. But it often takes years of legal battles to halt the developers.

JOURNAL WRITING

As you write in your journal about things that are happening, note the subject and verb of each sentence you write so that you'll be sure it is a complete sentence.

MORE ABOUT VERBS AND SUBJECTS

Sometimes the verb is more than one word. Here are a few of the many forms of the verb *drive*:

I drive	I will be driving	I may drive
I am driving	I will have been driving	I could drive
I have driven	I will have driven	I might drive
I have been driving	I am driven	I should drive
I drove	I was driven	I would drive
I was driving	I have been driven	I must drive
I had driven	I had been driven	I could have driven
I had been driving	I will be driven	I might have driven
I will drive	I can drive	I should have driven

Note that words like the following are never part of the verb even though they may be in the middle of the verb:

already	even	never	only
also	ever	not	really
always	finally	now	sometimes
before	just	often	usually

Stephanie is not going far. She has never driven a car before.

Two other verb forms—*driving* and *to drive*—look like verbs, but neither can ever be the verb of a sentence. No *ing* word by itself can ever be the verb of a sentence; it must have a helping verb in front of it.

Derek driving home. (not a sentence because there is no proper verb)
Derek was driving home. (a sentence)

And no verb with *to* in front of it can ever be the verb of a sentence.

To drive north along the coast. (not a sentence because there is no proper verb and no subject)
I like to drive north along the coast. (a sentence with *like* as the verb)

These two forms, *driving* and *to drive*, may be used as subjects, or they may have other uses in the sentence.

Driving costs a lot. To drive costs a lot.

But neither of them can ever be the verb of a sentence.

Not only may a verb be composed of more than one word, but also there may be more than one verb in a sentence:

Kevin painted the house and planted trees in the yard.

Also there may be more than one subject.

Kevin and Natalie painted the house and planted trees in the yard.

EXERCISES

Underline the subject once and the verb twice. Be sure to include all parts of the verb. Also watch for more than one subject and more than one verb. It's a good idea to cross out the prepositional phrases first.

☐EXERCISE 1

1. There always have been periodic forest fires.
2. Before the coming of people, fires were started by lightning.
3. Conditions must be right for vegetation to burn.
4. Vegetation usually contains too much water and will not burn.
5. During dry seasons, fires start easily and spread rapidly.
6. Fire can race across a forest at express-train speed.
7. The land can change in minutes from an area of life to an area of ashes.
8. Sometimes only heavy rain will extinguish a fire.
9. With the coming of people, the number of forest fires has increased.
10. Constant vigilance is necessary to save our forests.

☐EXERCISE 2

1. For years she had been collecting shells.
2. She would identify each one carefully.
3. Then she would place it in a cabinet with a neatly typed label.
4. Limpets had always been her favorites.
5. Those shells could be found only at low tide.
6. Others could be found only on the ocean floor.
7. That morning she awoke at sunrise and scanned the lake below.
8. She went to the shore and wandered for several miles.
9. She gathered shells and took them home to identify.
10. In the evening she and her friends went for a boat ride on the lake and later had their supper on the shore under the stars.

☐EXERCISE 3

1. Harvesting wild rice is like harvesting jewels.
2. It sells for between $9 and $10 a pound on supermarket shelves.
3. Wild rice is a species of grass and is unrelated to white rice.
4. The Indians used wild rice for 300 years before the coming of the Europeans.
5. Minnesota produces 70 percent of the total world supply and has strict laws about harvesting.
6. Mechanical harvesting leaves no rice for seed and is therefore illegal.
7. Indians now harvest only 25 percent of Minnesota's crop.
8. Independent ricers must obtain a license and then may harvest the rice under strict rules.
9. They row through the rice paddies and tap the grains off into their boats during strictly regulated hours.
10. The ricers must cope with mosquitoes and horseflies and also must beware of the needle-sharp grains and their bristly "beards."

☐EXERCISE 4

1. The Library of Congress is probably the world's largest library.
2. In its holdings are included over 74 million items.
3. And over 7,000 new items are added to the collection every working day.
4. All forms of preserved thought from papyrus to microfilm are included.
5. It was established in 1800 as a reference library for Congress.
6. Today it has become a library for all Americans.
7. Libraries in all parts of the country can borrow from it.
8. Or people can go to the Library of Congress and use the materials there.
9. Besides books there are manuscripts, photographs, recordings of folklore, and reels of motion pictures.
10. It also houses the world's largest collection of maps, with 3½ million maps and atlases.

☐EXERCISE 5

1. The papers of 23 American Presidents are stored in the Library of Congress.
2. And four million pieces of music from classical to rock may be found there.
3. A collection of rare Stradivarius violins is also included in the library.
4. Two-thirds of the 18 million books are in 470 different foreign languages.
5. Perhaps the most famous book is the Gutenberg Bible.
6. This volume is one of three surviving copies in the world.

7. The vast collections are housed in a complex of buildings on Capitol Hill.
8. The main building, of course, is the ornate Library of Congress Building.
9. In that main building the sculptures, paintings, and murals were produced by 50 American artists.
10. Visitors are given free tours through the building.

□EXERCISE 6

1. I have been reading about volcanoes.
2. The most famous volcanic explosion in history was that of Mount Vesuvius in A.D. 79.
3. It buried Pompeii and Herculaneum and killed at least 2,000 people.
4. The 1980 blast of Mount St. Helens was of about the same magnitude but occurred in a less populated area.
5. It was the first volcanic explosion in the continental United States since the eruption of Mount Lassen, 400 miles to the south, in 1914.
6. The Mount St. Helens blast blew down 150 square miles of timber and caused millions of dollars' worth of damage to crops and streams.
7. About 5,900 miles of roads were buried under ash.
8. The largest volcanic eruption in North American history occurred at remote Mount Katmai in Alaska in 1912.
9. That blast had a magnitude ten times that of Mount St. Helens but caused no fatalities.
10. Today there are 600 active volcanoes on the earth's surface.

□EXERCISE 7

1. Galileo made the first telescope in 1609.
2. Improvements have been made on that first crude instrument ever since.
3. But astronomers have never been able to see the stars clearly through their telescopes.
4. The atmosphere of the earth has always interfered.
5. In 1983 a $180 million space telescope was put into orbit to send back information without the interference of the earth's atmosphere.
6. The space telescope was operated under radio control from earth.
7. At an altitude of 310 miles, it orbited the earth once every 100 minutes.
8. It made discoveries about our solar system and about new galaxies.
9. It could detect a speck of dust two miles away.
10. That would be the same as someone in New York seeing a baseball in Los Angeles.

☐EXERCISE 8

1. He opened the cabin door and looked into the semidarkness.
2. At that time of year in Alaska days were short.
3. Night came in midafternoon and lasted until late morning.
4. Only the tracks of rabbits and wolves could be seen around the cabin.
5. But sometimes the tracks of bears and deer could also be seen.
6. The nearby mountains and ice-covered cliffs looked menacing.
7. And after a heavy fall of snow, the cabin was inaccessible.
8. Soon the northern lights appeared low in the sky.
9. Perhaps the cause of these lights is a leakage of radiation particles from the Van Allen belts.
10. The Van Allen belts are the doughnut-shaped radiation belts around the earth.

☐EXERCISE 9

1. Yellow has always been the favorite color for pencils.
2. Pencils in other colors simply have not sold.
3. Over two billion pencils are sold in the United States annually.
4. An ordinary pencil can draw a line 35 miles long.
5. America could conserve huge amounts of energy by recycling steel cans.
6. Steel cans can be separated magnetically from waste and can be put back to work.
7. Many cities are recovering billions of steel cans in modern recovery plants.
8. Aluminum cans are being recycled also.
9. America is finally realizing the wealth in waste products.
10. And environmentalists are happy with the outcome.

☐EXERCISE 10

1. I have been learning the derivations of some flower names.
2. The roots of heliotrope (HELIO and TROP) mean "sun" and "to turn."
3. And the heliotrope flowers do turn to follow the sun from morning to evening.
4. The roots of nasturtium (NAS and TORT) mean "nose" and "to twist."
5. The pungent odor of the nasturtium gave it the name "nose twister."
6. A daisy is simply a "day's eye."
7. And tulip comes from a Turkish word and means "turban."
8. Dandelion has come to us from the French *dent de lion* or "tooth of a lion."

9. Perhaps the sharp points of the dandelion leaf do look a bit like a lion's teeth.
10. I am really enjoying the stories behind words and want to learn more.

WRITING ASSIGNMENT

Turn to the section that begins on page 196 for your writing assignment.

CORRECTING RUN-TOGETHER SENTENCES

Any group of words having a subject and verb is a clause. The clause may be independent (able to stand alone) or dependent (unable to stand alone). Every sentence you have worked with so far has been an independent clause because it has been able to stand alone. It has made a complete statement.

If two such independent clauses are written together with no punctuation or with merely a comma, they are called a run-together sentence. We noted some run-together sentences on page 54. Here are some more:

He cooked the dinner she washed the dishes.
He cooked the dinner, she washed the dishes.
I like science fiction therefore I enjoyed the movie.
I like science fiction, therefore I enjoyed the movie.

Such run-together sentences can be corrected in one of three ways:

1. Make the two independent clauses into two sentences.

He cooked the dinner. She washed the dishes.
I like science fiction. Therefore I enjoyed the movie.

2. Separate the two independent clauses with a semicolon.

He cooked the dinner; she washed the dishes.
I like science fiction; therefore I enjoyed the movie.
I turned my paper in; then I began to review.
I worked hard; thus I passed the test.

When a connecting word such as *therefore, thus, then, finally, however, furthermore, also, nevertheless, consequently, likewise, moreover, otherwise* comes between two independent clauses, that word must have a semicolon before it. It may also have a comma after it, especially if there seems to be a pause between the word and the rest of the clause.

The book was interesting; however, I didn't finish it.
I'll enjoy the job; furthermore, I need the money.
I want to go; also, I think it's my duty.
The attendance was small; nevertheless, a lot was accomplished.

The semicolon before the connecting word is required. The comma after it is a matter of choice.

3. Connect the two independent clauses with a comma and one of the following words: *and, but, for, or, nor, yet, so.*

He cooked the dinner, and she washed the dishes.
I don't want to go, but I think it's my duty.
I couldn't go to the movie, for I had no money.
I must hurry, or I'll never finish.
I haven't seen that movie, nor do I want to.

But be sure there are two independent clauses. The first sentence below has two independent clauses. The second sentence is merely one independent clause with two verbs, and therefore no comma should be used.

He jogged two kilometers, and then he went for a swim.
He jogged two kilometers and then went for a swim.

THE THREE WAYS TO PUNCTUATE INDEPENDENT CLAUSES

I went to the library. I needed to study.
I went to the library; I needed to study.
I went to the library, for I needed to study.

Learn these three ways, and you'll avoid run-together sentences.

You may wonder when to use a period and capital letter and when to use a semicolon between two independent clauses. In general, use a period and capital letter. Only if the clauses are closely related in meaning should you use a semicolon. But either way is permissible. Therefore your punctuation of the sentences that follow may differ from the answers at the back of the book.

EXERCISES

In each independent clause underline the subject once and the verb twice. Then be ready to give a reason for the punctuation.

□EXERCISE 1

1. Pronunciations change over the years, and new words are constantly being added to the language.
2. Read with your dictionary beside you; then you will learn interesting new words.
3. Note derivations, for they will help you to remember words.

4. Keeping a vocabulary list is a good idea too; then you can review your words.
5. Use the new words. It's a good way to fix them in your memory.
6. Use a new word three times, and you won't forget it.
7. Forty million handguns circulate in this country, and two and a half million are sold annually.
8. Half of all suicides and murders are committed with handguns.
9. Some people believe in their right to own guns and resent any effort to curb that right.
10. But others enumerate the hazards of gun ownership; they are working for gun control.

☐EXERCISE 2

1. I'm writing a term paper on Arthur Erickson; he's a famous Canadian architect.
2. He has designed universities and public buildings, and at Japan's Expo '70 he won the top architectural award over entries from 78 countries.
3. He has now designed a three-block complex in downtown Vancouver. His achievement has restored vitality to the downtown area.
4. The complex consists of buildings and plazas, and it has the most extensive urban plantings of trees, shrubs, and vines of any North American city.
5. A luxurious office building for the local government and a seven-story courthouse are included in the complex.
6. The courthouse is more open and less forbidding than most courthouses, and its glass roof is one of the biggest in the world.
7. Robson Square is the greatest attraction, for it is a place for outdoor lunches, shows, and theater groups.
8. Robson Square also has an outdoor ice- or roller-skating rink as well as indoor theaters, restaurants, and an exhibition hall.
9. An energy tank for the complex is heated or cooled during cheaper off-peak hours, and the buildings are then heated or cooled from the tank.
10. I've learned a lot about Erickson, and I hope to see his work someday.

Most—but not all—of the following sentences are run-together. If the sentence is run-together, separate the two clauses with the correct punctuation —comma, semicolon, or period with a capital letter. In general, use the period with a capital letter rather than the semicolon. But either way is correct. Thus your answers may differ from those at the back of the book.

☐EXERCISE 3

1. The day dawned clear not a cloud was in the sky.
2. My pals and I decided to go to the lake it was too nice a day to stay at home.
3. We first went for a swim in the lake then we started to fish.
4. We fished all afternoon but we had no luck.
5. Then finally I caught a tiny fish we had it for supper.
6. We gathered firewood from the nearby woods and built a fire.
7. After supper we broke camp and started home.
8. All of us lived in a small town in the heart of the mining country and the hills were full of deserted mine shafts.
9. My pals and I explored a few of them we didn't realize the dangers.
10. Luckily our parents didn't know about our explorations or we would have been in trouble.

☐EXERCISE 4

1. Grizzly bears are causing problems and conservationists are worried about them.
2. In the 1800s there were 50,000 grizzlies in the West now there are fewer than 1,000.
3. About 200 of those grizzlies live in and near Yellowstone National Park and formerly they caused no trouble.
4. But in 1960 the Park Service decided to keep the park natural and the garbage dumps were closed.
5. Hotelkeepers were no longer allowed to put out food to attract the bears and the bears had to fend for themselves.
6. The Park Service meant well but the new rules had unexpected consequences.
7. The bears began to look for food in campgrounds and they killed sheep on nearby farms.
8. They began prowling in mining camps and near vacation homes and maulings and even deaths occurred.
9. The Park Service refuses to reopen the old dumps but they are going to leave food out for the bears in certain places.
10. The grizzlies won't change their habits therefore humans must change theirs.

☐EXERCISE 5

1. A strong wind was blowing our boat nearly capsized.
2. The rain fell in torrents consequently we abandoned our boat and swam ashore.

3. We were grateful to get to shore we should not have ventured out in such weather.
4. We saw a cabin nearby and knocked on the door.
5. All was quiet only the wind could be heard.
6. We went inside but found no traces of recent occupants.
7. The cabin was cold moreover there was no firewood.
8. The wind blew through the cracks and the shutters rattled.
9. Even so we were grateful for shelter and stayed there until the storm was over.
10. The next day we found our boat downstream it had been a wild adventure.

□EXERCISE 6

1. Clement had grown up on the family farm he had played under the old sycamore trees in the yard.
2. In his day there was no TV he had had to make his own entertainment.
3. He read books then he read more books.
4. He was determined to succeed he worked far into the night on his studies.
5. Furthermore he made his own way he never had help from anyone.
6. Later he was successful in his career.
7. His success was due to his hard work and also it was due to his belief in his work.
8. Now he had returned and was looking once more at the sycamore trees.
9. The old house and the trees had shared that yard for more than a hundred years but now the trees were being cut down.
10. He would have liked to save them but they were his no longer.

□EXERCISE 7

1. Of all the kinds of winds, tornadoes are the most violent they do millions of dollars worth of damage each year.
2. Tornadoes consist of winds with speeds of 30 or 40 miles an hour some have speeds even higher and they cause the most deaths.
3. These winds rotate in a counterclockwise direction and look like a funnel at the bottom of a cloud.
4. Tornadoes are usually only a quarter of a mile wide and not more than 15 miles long furthermore they don't last very long.
5. Their coverage is small and their time is short yet in a few seconds they can leave a path of destruction.
6. A few safety tips are worth knowing they could save lives.
7. Stay away from windows, doors, and outside walls shield your head.

8. Go to a basement, or the interior part of a first floor. closets or interior halls are the best places.
9. In the outdoors go to a sturdy shelter, or lie in a ditch with your hands protecting your head.
10. Spring is the tornado season, but tornadoes can strike at any time.

□EXERCISE 8

1. The 856-mile border between East Germany and West Germany is a heavily fortified wire mesh fence.
2. Watchtowers can see every yard of the fence and the crossing spots are heavily guarded.
3. At places the fence goes three feet underground to prevent tunneling furthermore the top is sharpened mesh to prevent a fingerhold.
4. East Germany claims the fence is for protection against the West but many of the watchtowers don't even have a view of West Germany.
5. The fence was first fortified in 1961 to stop the flood of East Germans to the West more than 200,000 a year were leaving.
6. In the first year 5,761 people escaped across the fence but few make it today.
7. In 1979 two families made a balloon out of bedsheets and curtains and sailed across the fence at night but most are not so lucky.
8. It is safer to try to get out through a neighboring country only the desperate risk the "death strip" today.
9. Many West Germans have relatives on the other side but communication is difficult.
10. East Germany has spent an estimated $7 billion on the barrier and more is being spent.

□EXERCISE 9

1. One of the most popular museums in Washington, D.C., is the National Air and Space Museum it portrays the age of the airplane from the flight of the Wright brothers to the landing on the moon 66 years later.
2. Here may be seen the Wright brothers' first plane and Lindbergh's *Spirit of St. Louis* here too is the command module for the first voyage to the moon.
3. In all there are more than 200 original airplanes and spacecraft they are housed in a three-block-long marble building.
4. Each of the largest galleries is more than six stories high and three times larger than a basketball court.
5. Three of these galleries house historic aircraft such as the linked *Apollo-Soyuz Spacecraft* and the *Skylab Orbital Workshop* here also are historic commercial airliners.

6. The exhibits are either suspended from the glass-roofed ceiling or else they seem to rise from below the floor level.
7. Smaller galleries show examples of vertical flight, balloons, combat flying in World War I, air traffic control, and man-made satellites.
8. A motion picture *To Fly* is sensational it begins with a balloon ascension in 1831 and ends with a voyage to outer space.
9. In the film the viewer feels the thrill of flying upside down or of sailing along in a tiny hang glider.
10. The Air and Space Museum is part of the Smithsonian Institution it would take weeks to see all of that great institution.

Punctuate the following paragraphs so there will be no run-together sentences.

☐EXERCISE 10

1. Last spring we were driving through Arizona and decided to see the Petrified Forest therefore we took the 27-mile drive through that strange landscape trees have turned to stone and thousands of great stone logs lie on the ground we learned a great deal about petrified wood and were glad for the experience we had seen a new part of our country the National Park Service is preserving the area for future generations.
2. The most striking feature of the oceans is their vast size the next most striking feature is the constant motion of their surfaces one cause of the motion is the wind it may make waves from an inch to over 60 feet in height another cause of waves is geologic disturbances such as earthquakes and volcanic eruptions below the surface of the oceans waves from geologic disturbances are sometimes incorrectly called tidal waves but they have no relation to the tides.

JOURNAL WRITING

In your journal write three sentences, each containing two independent clauses, and punctuate them correctly.

WRITING ASSIGNMENT

Continue with your writing assignments that begin on page 196. Are you listing all your misspelled words on the inside back cover?

CORRECTING FRAGMENTS

There are two kinds of clauses: independent, which we have just finished studying, and dependent. A dependent clause has a subject and a verb just like an independent clause, but it can't stand alone because it begins with a dependent word such as

after	since	whereas
although	so that	wherever
as	than	whether
as if	that	which
because	though	whichever
before	unless	while
even if	until	who
even though	what	whom
ever since	whatever	whose
how	when	why
if	whenever	
in order that	where	

Whenever a clause begins with one of the above dependent words (unless it's a question, which would never give you any trouble), it is dependent. If we take an independent clause such as

We finished the game.

and put one of the dependent words in front of it, it becomes dependent:

After we finished the game
Although we finished the game
As we finished the game
Before we finished the game
Since we finished the game
That we finished the game
When we finished the game
While we finished the game

Now the clause can no longer stand alone. As you read it, you can hear that it doesn't make a complete statement. It leaves the reader expecting something more. It's a fragment and must not be punctuated as a sentence. To correct such a fragment, simply add an independent clause:

After we finished the game, we went to the clubhouse.
We went to the clubhouse after we finished the game.
We were happy that we finished the game early.
While we finished the game, the others waited.

In other words **EVERY SENTENCE MUST HAVE AT LEAST ONE INDEPENDENT CLAUSE.**

Note in the examples that when a dependent clause comes at the beginning of a sentence, it is followed by a comma. Often the comma prevents misreading, as in the following sentence:

When he entered, the room became quiet.

Without a comma after *entered*, the reader would read *When he entered the room* before realizing that that was not what the author meant. The comma prevents misreading. Sometimes if the dependent clause is short and there is no danger of misreading, the comma is omitted, but it's safer simply to follow the rule that a dependent clause at the beginning of a sentence is followed by a comma.

Note that sometimes the dependent word is the subject of the dependent clause:

I took the highway that was finished last month.

Sometimes the dependent clause is in the middle of the independent clause:

The highway that was finished last month goes to Kalamazoo.

And sometimes the dependent clause is the subject of the entire sentence:

What I was doing was not important. (Here no comma is necessary after the dependent clause because it flows right into the rest of the sentence.)

Also note that sometimes the *that* of a dependent clause is omitted:

This is the house that Jack built.
This is the house Jack built.
I thought that you were coming with me.
I thought you were coming with me.

And finally the word *that* doesn't always introduce a dependent clause. It may be a pronoun (That is my book) or a describing word (I like that book).

EXERCISES

Underline the subject once and the verb twice in both the independent and the dependent clauses. Then put a broken line under the dependent clause.

□EXERCISE 1

1. I refused to go because I had homework to do.
2. I could make good grades if I studied.
3. After I finish college, I'll get a job.
4. They were out playing Frisbee while he was studying.
5. Her essay would have been better if she had rewritten it.
6. Unless you return your library book today, you'll have to pay a fine.
7. A large vocabulary is the characteristic that most often accompanies outstanding success.
8. He was searching for the money that he had dropped in the snow.
9. Although he looked a long time, he couldn't find it.
10. Until you understand subjects and verbs, you cannot understand clauses.

Underline each dependent clause.

□EXERCISE 2

1. If you are too busy for a vacation, at least get some exercise.
2. Although I studied, I still found the exam difficult.
3. If you want to learn to write, you must rewrite and rewrite.
4. After I rewrite, I'm more satisfied with my papers.
5. When the sun went down, the air became cool.
6. As it became dark, we looked at the stars through our telescope.
7. Astronomers have located a quasar that may be the largest object in the universe.
8. Whereas the Earth's diameter is about 8,000 miles, the diameter of the newly discovered quasar is 468,000,000 miles.

9. If you stood on the moon and looked back toward Earth, you could see with the naked eye only one man-made structure.
10. That structure is the Great Wall of China, which was built in the third century B.C.

If the clause is independent and therefore a sentence, put a period after it. If the clause is dependent and therefore a fragment, add an independent clause either before or after it to make it into a sentence. Remember that if the dependent clause comes first in the sentence, it should have a comma after it.

☐EXERCISE 3

1. As he ran to catch the ball
2. Then he finally caught it
3. She couldn't find the necessary reference material
4. Because no one had told me about the new ruling
5. When I finally decide to really work
6. Therefore I'm going to stay at home tonight
7. If I can just spend a couple of hours on my math
8. Moreover I should study my psychology
9. When I'm finished with both of them
10. I'll feel confident about those tests

☐EXERCISE 4

1. The people flocked around the injured man
2. As the ambulance came racing down the street
3. When a book is really interesting
4. Come into the office
5. As we learned more about the problem

6. Because I had so much homework that evening

7. Unless something goes wrong

8. While everyone else was studying

9. Therefore I decided to go

10. The hills in the distance are green

On pages 71–72 you learned three ways of correcting run-together sentences. Now that you are aware of dependent clauses, you may use a fourth way. In the following run-together sentence

> The snow was melting we canceled our ski trip.

you can make one of the two independent clauses into a dependent clause:

> Since the snow was melting, we canceled our ski trip.
> We canceled our ski trip because the snow was melting.
> If the snow begins to melt, we'll cancel our ski trip.

This fourth way is often the best way to correct a run-together sentence because it subordinates one of the two ideas and makes the more important one stand out.

Correct the following run-together sentences by making one of the clauses dependent. In some sentences put the dependent clause first, and in others put it last. Since various dependent words can be used to make a dependent clause, your answers may differ from those suggested at the back of the book.

☐EXERCISE 5

1. The afternoon was hot we decided to go to the woods.

2. There was no breeze in the woods it was cool under the trees.

3. We sat under a large oak we listened to the sounds of the forest.

4. We could not see any birds we could hear a chickadee not far away.

5. And two yellowthroats were calling to each other they hopped from tree to tree.

6. Some bees were buzzing around a flower we knew there must be a bee tree not far away.

7. We didn't want to get stung we decided not to investigate.

8. We sat there quietly a downy woodpecker lit on the tree trunk in front of us.

9. We watched in delight it circled the trunk in search of insects.

10. I made a slight movement it flew off to another part of the woods.

☐EXERCISE 6

1. We think of apples as food for people animals like apples too.

2. Bears are led by their sense of smell they'll travel miles to find juicy apples.

3. Apple leaves are eaten by deer apple seeds are eaten by squirrels and birds.

4. Birds also eat young apple buds this has perturbed apple growers.

5. Now most apple growers accept the debudding actually it improves the size and quality of the remaining fruit.

6. Some trees hold their fruit all winter most let their fruit fall to the ground.

7. The apples on the ground rot they then enrich the soil.

8. Worms flourish in the enriched soil birds then gather to hunt the worms.

9. John Chapman was a nineteenth-century missionary from Massachusetts he traveled across the country and planted and gave away apple seeds and seedlings.

10. The news of his work spread he became known as Johnny Appleseed.

☐EXERCISE 7

1. This course is difficult I refuse to give up.
2. I've been working on spelling I now catch most of my errors.
3. Even my letters to my parents have fewer errors my dad has commented on the fact.
4. I like writing papers I like hearing them read aloud in class.
5. I like to hear other students' papers read I mainly like to hear my own.
6. They sometimes sound terrible other times I think they're great.
7. I do all the exercises then I always pass the test.
8. Occasionally I don't do all the exercises then I find the test difficult.
9. I'm not really sure of myself still I know more than I did at first.
10. Learning all this has been a struggle I'm finding it of value.

WRITING YOUR OWN SENTENCES

Now that you are aware of independent and dependent clauses, you can vary the sentences you write. On a separate sheet write eight sentences, **each containing two independent clauses** connected by one of the following words. Be sure to use the correct punctuation—comma or semicolon.

consequently	and
but	or
therefore	nevertheless
however	then

Now make up eight sentences, **each containing one independent and one dependent clause,** using the following dependent words. If you put the dependent clause first, put a comma after it.

although	unless
after	until
while	because
since	if

MORE ABOUT FRAGMENTS

We have seen that a dependent clause alone is a fragment. Any group of words that does not have a subject and verb is also a fragment.

> Was beginning to take an interest in astronomy (no subject)
> Scott turning his telescope skyward every night (no adequate verb. Although *ing* words look like verbs, no *ing* word by itself can ever be the verb of a sentence. It must have another verb in front of it.)
> Thinking about the big bang (no subject and no adequate verb)
> That every part of the universe is receding from every other part (no independent clause)

To change these fragments into sentences, we must give each a subject and an adequate verb:

> He was beginning to take an interest in astronomy. (We added a subject.)
> Scott was turning his telescope skyward every night. (We put a helping verb in front of the *ing* word to make an adequate verb.)
> He was thinking about the big bang. (We added a subject and a helping verb.)
> He realized that every part of the universe is receding from every other part. (We added a subject and a verb to make an independent clause.)

Sometimes you can simply tack a fragment onto the sentence before or after it.

> Wondering why she had not come. I finally phoned her.
> Wondering why she had not come, I finally phoned her.

Or you can change a word or two in the fragment and make it into a sentence.

> Wondering why she had not come.
> I wondered why she had not come.

Are fragments ever permissible? Increasingly, fragments are being used in advertising and in other kinds of writing. In Exercises 6 and 7 you'll find advertisements that make use of fragments effectively to give a dramatic pause between individual parts of a sentence. But such fragments are used by writers who know what they're doing. The fragments are used intentionally, never in error. Until you're an experienced writer, stick with complete sentences. Especially in college writing, fragments should not be used.

EXERCISES

Put a period after each sentence. Make each fragment into a sentence either by adding an independent clause before or after it or by changing some words in it. Sometimes changing just one word will change a fragment into a sentence.

☐EXERCISE 1

1. After answering the telephone and taking the message
2. Having washed my only pair of jeans, I crawled into bed
3. After falling on the ice and breaking his leg
4. The announcement that there would be no classes on Friday
5. Perspiration is often more needed than inspiration
6. Whether I should continue my education
7. My parents wanting desperately to give me more than they had
8. Not wanting to disappoint them
9. My father being a man of very decided opinions
10. Having always done his best in school

☐EXERCISE 2

1. Having walked through the forest all day without even a break for lunch
2. Where no man had ever set foot before
3. Trying to keep the fire burning
4. Weakened by lack of food and sleep, we were glad to go home
5. Having traveled almost 200 miles
6. A boring evening in which we did nothing but watch TV
7. Not having anything to do all day but wait for the phone to ring
8. The gracious home that they had so carefully planned
9. A place where the puppy would feel secure
10. Finishing the day by vacuuming and doing the washing

☐EXERCISE 3

1. Facts that no educated person could deny
2. My hobby being one that is not expensive
3. At a time when I was too busy to be bothered
4. Although neither of us was eager to undertake the job
5. Each of us hoping the other would volunteer
6. Being a fellow who was always ready to help
7. Even though we were told that the game might be postponed
8. Since I was sure I'd get there on time if I maintained my present speed
9. Keep to the right
10. The audience applauding wildly and calling for more

Get rid of the fragments in the following paragraphs. Each of these particular fragments can be tacked onto the sentence before it. Just change the punctuation and the capital letter. To change a capital letter to a small letter or to remove a period, simply put a diagonal line through it.

☐EXERCISE 4

Individuals can help save our forests. Americans waste vast amounts of paper. Because they don't think of paper as forests. They think nothing of wasting an envelope. Because an envelope is only a tiny piece of paper. But it takes two million trees to make the yearly supply of 112 billion envelopes. Even small savings can encourage others to save. Until finally the concerted efforts of enough individuals can make a difference.

☐EXERCISE 5

Future historians will probably call our age the time when humans began the exploration of space. Some historians say that space exploration marks a turning point in the history of the world. Some people criticize space exploration. Saying that the money should have been spent on the poor here on earth. Others say, however, that we wouldn't have spent the money on anything of greater human value. The annual space budget is less than one percent of federal spending. Whereas the bulk of federal spending goes to defense and to health, education, and welfare. There have been practical payoffs from space exploration. One is the transoceanic television broadcasts that can be relayed by communications satellites. Another payoff is the daily weather picture. That appears on television screens. Still another payoff is the earth-resource satellites. That circle the earth and help map remote regions, search for water and minerals, and monitor crops and timber. And the final payoff is military reconnaissance. That helps make possible arms limitation agreements among nations.

In the following excerpts from advertisements, the writers have chosen to use a number of fragments. Although the fragments are effective in the ads, they would not be acceptable in formal writing. On a separate sheet rewrite each ad, turning it into acceptable college writing.

☐EXERCISE 6

Welcome to Stouffer's Lasagna. And more than 40 delicious entrees. Food that good cooks appreciate. And appreciate even more because we've done the work.

Set yourself free. With Stouffer's.

—Stouffer Foods Corporation

☐EXERCISE 7

Hartmann has an interesting angle on luggage. The right angle.

When we make Hartmann luggage, we never cut corners. We keep them nice and square.

And for good reason.

There's less wasted space in square corners. So you can pack more.

And you can pack more neatly too. Because your clothes fit snugly right against the corner.

But Hartmann is more than right angles. (If that weren't so, we'd just be an overpriced box.)

There are lots of other ways we don't cut corners.

Our master craftsmen tailor each exquisite detail of our luggage. Stitch by stitch. From the handle to the inside lining. . . .

You'll never find a production shortcut—or a cut corner in a Hartmann. Which is why Hartmann isn't the cheapest luggage you can buy. It's simply the best.

—Hartmann

Review of Run-together Sentences and Fragments

SIX SENTENCES THAT SHOW HOW TO PUNCTUATE CLAUSES

I gave a party. Everybody came. I gave a party; everybody came.	(two independent clauses)
I gave a party; moreover, everybody came.	(two independent clauses connected by a word such as *also, consequently, finally, furthermore, however, likewise, moreover, nevertheless, otherwise, therefore, then, thus*)
I gave a party, and everybody came.	(two independent clauses connected by *and, but, for, or, nor, yet, so*)
When I gave a party, everybody came.	(dependent clause at beginning of sentence)
Everybody came when I gave a party.	(dependent clause at end of sentence) The dependent words are *after, although, as, as if, because, before, even if, even though, ever since, how, if, in order that, since, so that, than, that, though, unless, until, what, whatever, when, whenever, where, whereas, wherever, whether, which, whichever, while, who, whom, whose, why*

If you remember these six sentences and understand the rules for their punctuation, most of your punctuation problems will be taken care of. It is essential that you learn the italicized words in the above table. If your instructor reads some of the words, be ready to tell which ones come between independent clauses and which ones introduce dependent clauses.

Make the necessary changes in these paragraphs so that there will be no run-together sentences or fragments.

1. In the 1960s Lake Erie was so polluted that experts feared there wouldn't be a single living organism in it within 20 years strict antipollution laws in the United States and Canada, however, have eliminated much of the industrial pollution also better sewage-treatment methods have reduced the flow of phosphorus into the lake now the waters are teeming with fish again and the beaches are crowded with swimmers.

2. How to dispose of hazardous chemical wastes is one of the greatest environmental problems society has benefited from the chemicals that control pain and disease and those that create new industrial products but almost 35,000 chemicals used in the United States are classified as possibly hazardous to human health the Environmental Protection Agency estimates that the United States is generating more than 77 billion pounds of hazardous chemical wastes a year and that only 10 percent are being handled safely at least half of the wastes are being dumped indiscriminately, poisoning the earth and the underground water supplies toxic chemicals are adding to disease according to the Surgeon General and virtually the entire population is carrying some body burden of these chemicals.

3. The science of medicine has had a long history it began with superstitions and illness was attributed to evil spirits the ancient Egyptians were among the first to practice surgery anesthesia was, of course, unknown therefore the patient was made unconscious by a blow on the head with a mallet surgery was also practiced in early Babylonia and the Code of Hammurabi lists the penalties that an unsuccessful surgeon had to pay for example, if a patient lost an eye through poor surgery, the surgeon's eye was put out.

4. In 1598 the famous Globe Theater was built across the Thames from London Shakespeare became a shareholder and his plays were produced there the theater was octagonal and held about 1,200 people the "groundlings" stood on the floor and watched the play but the wealthier patrons sat in the two galleries those paying the highest fees could sit upon the stage the stage jutted out into the audience thus the players and the audience had a close relationship.

5. The pronghorn has one of the shortest "childhoods" of any mammal within three or four days after birth it can outrun a man in a year it becomes the fastest long-distance runner on this continent.

Proofreading Exercise

Four errors have been put into this selection from *Comfortable Words* by Bergan Evans. They are errors in contractions, possessives, and the punctuation of dependent clauses. See if you can correct all four before checking with the answers at the back of the book.

DRIVE SLOW(LY)

DRIVE SLOW is perfectly good English. DRIVE SLOWLY is equally good, but since it requires a little more of the taxpayer's paint and the drivers attention the shorter form is preferable.

Many people object to DRIVE SLOW, apparently on the assumption that *slow* is an adjective and *slowly* the adverb. But slow has been used as an adverb (that is, has been an adverb)—as well as an adjective—for almost five hundred years. "How slow this old moon wanes," Shakespeare wrote. Milton spoke of the curfew bell "swinging slow with sullen roar," and Byron of a ship that "glided slow."

So that when you have Shakespeare, Milton, Byron, a hundred and fifty million or so Americans *and* the County Road Commissioners arrayed against you, you might as well give in. And when you realize that a form which you see on every roadside every day has been in universal use for more than five centuries its a little late to start getting upset about it.

USING STANDARD ENGLISH VERBS

This chapter and the next are for those who need practice in using standard English verbs. Many of us grew up speaking a dialect other than standard English, whether it was in a farm community where people said *I ain't* and *he don't* and *they was* or in a black community where people said *I be* and *it do* and *they has*. Such dialects are colorful and powerful in their place, but in college and in the business and professional world, the use of standard English is essential. Frequently, though, after students have learned to speak and write standard English, they go back to their home communities and are able to slip back into their community dialects while they are there. Thus they have really become bilingual, able to use two languages—or at least two dialects.

The following tables compare four verbs in one of the community dialects with the same four verbs in standard English. Memorize the standard English forms of these important verbs. Most verbs have endings like the first verb *walk*. The other three verbs are irregular and are important because they are used not only as main verbs but also as helping verbs. We'll be using them as helping verbs in the next chapter.

Don't go on to the exercises until you have memorized the forms of these standard English verbs.

REGULAR VERB: WALK

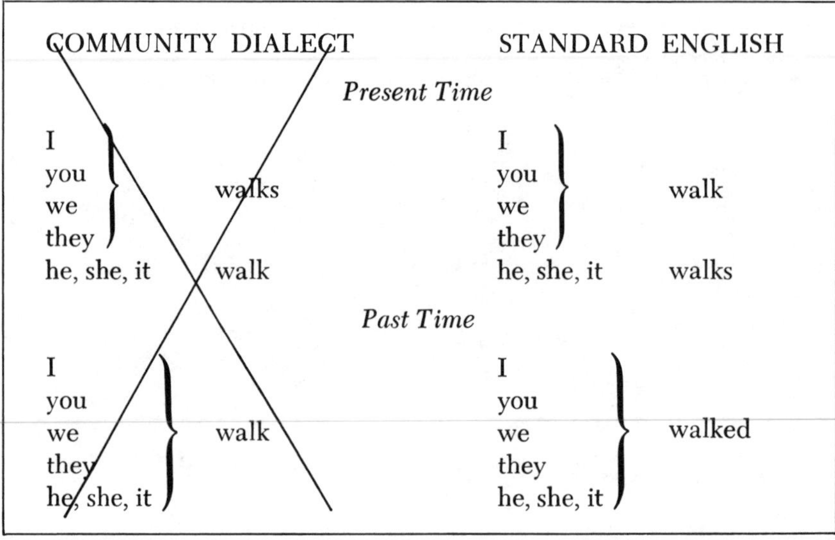

Present Time

COMMUNITY DIALECT		STANDARD ENGLISH	
I, you, we, they	walks	I, you, we, they	walk
he, she, it	walk	he, she, it	walks

Past Time

COMMUNITY DIALECT		STANDARD ENGLISH	
I, you, we, they, he, she, it	walk	I, you, we, they, he, she, it	walked

IRREGULAR VERB: HAVE

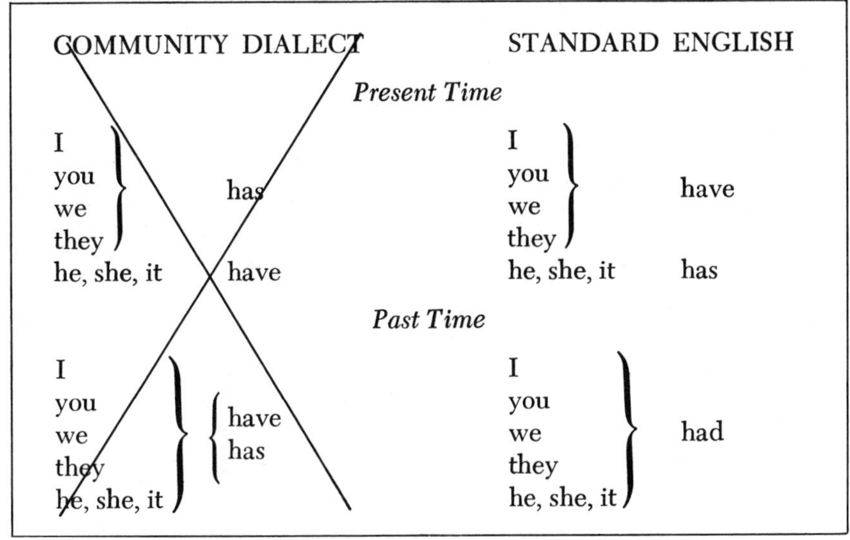

COMMUNITY DIALECT		STANDARD ENGLISH	
Present Time			
I, you, we, they	has	I, you, we, they	have
he, she, it	have	he, she, it	has
Past Time			
I, you, we, they, he, she, it	have / has	I, you, we, they, he, she, it	had

IRREGULAR VERB: BE

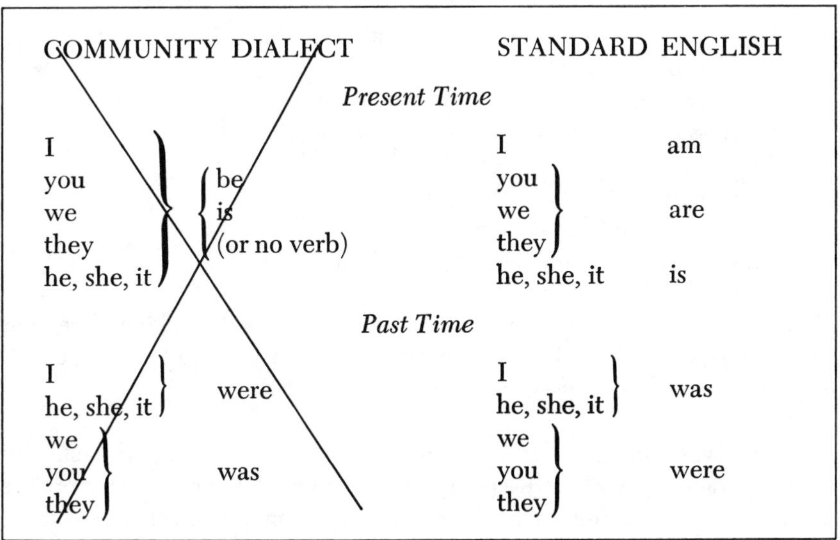

COMMUNITY DIALECT		STANDARD ENGLISH	
Present Time			
I, you, we, they, he, she, it	be / is / (or no verb)	I	am
		you, we, they	are
		he, she, it	is
Past Time			
I, he, she, it	were	I, he, she, it	was
we, you, they	was	we, you, they	were

IRREGULAR VERB: DO

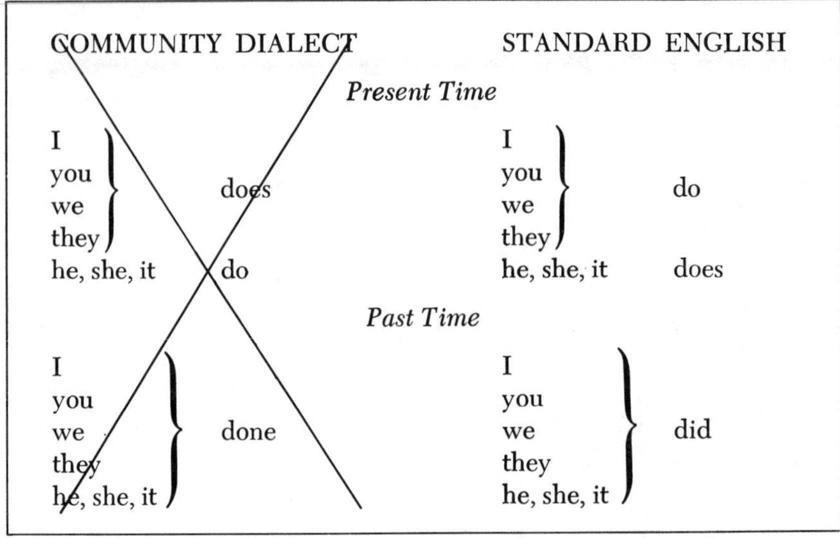

COMMUNITY DIALECT		STANDARD ENGLISH	
Present Time			
I, you, we, they	does	I, you, we, they	do
he, she, it	do	he, she, it	does
Past Time			
I, you, we, they, he, she, it	done	I, you, we, they, he, she, it	did

Sometimes students have difficulty with the correct endings of verbs because they don't hear the words correctly. As you listen to your instructor or to TV, note carefully the *s* sound and the *ed* sound at the end of words. Occasionally the *ed* is not clearly pronounced, as in *He asked me to go*, but most of the time you can hear it if you listen.

Try reading the following sentences aloud, making sure that you say every sound.

1. He seems to enjoy his two new friends.
2. He likes his job and hopes to stay with it.
3. It costs a dollar to go by bus, so she walks.
4. He rests for ten minutes before he starts again.
5. I was interested in his story.
6. He composed a piece for the piano.
7. She learned all I hoped she would.
8. I decided to jog a mile before I started to work.

Now read some other sentences aloud from this text, making sure that you sound all the *s*'s and *ed*'s. Listening to others and reading aloud will help you use the correct verb endings automatically.

A good way to learn to speak standard English is to make a pact with a friend that you will both speak only standard English when you are together. By correcting each other, you'll soon find yourselves speaking easily.

EXERCISES

In these pairs of sentences, use the present form of the verb in the first sentence and the past form in the second. All the verbs follow the pattern of the regular verb *walk* except the three irregular verbs *have*, *be*, and *do*. Keep referring to the tables if you're not sure which form to use. Correct your answers for each exercise before going to the next.

☐EXERCISE 1

1. (walk) I often ____________ to the park these days. I ____________ in the park yesterday.
2. (be) I ________________ happy now. I ________________ not happy last week.
3. (have) She ________________ a bike now. She ________________ a moped last year.
4. (do) I ________________ as I please. I ________________ as I pleased last year.
5. (need) He ________________ help right now. He ________________ help last fall.
6. (help) Her tutoring ____________ me now. Her tutoring ____________ me last semester.
7. (want) I ________________ help right now. I ________________ help yesterday.
8. (attend) He ________________ a four-year college now. Last year he ________________ a community college.
9. (talk) He ____________ with her frequently now. He ____________ with her last week.
10. (suppose) I ________________ I'm late. They ________________ that I had already gone.

☐EXERCISE 2

1. (be) I ________________ tired now. I ________________ tired last night too.
2. (do) I always ________________ my best now. I ________________ my best last year too.
3. (have) She ____________ a scholarship now. She ____________ a scholarship last year.

4. (ask) I ________________ for help if I need it. I ________________ for help last semester.
5. (enjoy) They ________________ their garden now. They ________________ their garden last summer.
6. (finish) She ________________ work at two now. She ________________ work at four last fall.
7. (learn) She ________________ when she tries. She ________________ a lot last year.
8. (work) He ________________ hard these days. He ________________ hard on his last job.
9. (listen) I ________________ to her now. I ________________ to her then.
10. (play) Now I ________________ the drums. Last year I ________________ the cello.

Underline the standard English verb form. All the verbs follow the pattern of the regular verb *walk* except the three irregular verbs *have*, *be*, and *do.* Keep referring to the tables if you are not sure which form to use.

☐EXERCISE 3

1. It (doesn't don't) matter to me what you (do does).
2. I (expect expects) to hear that she (change changed) her mind.
3. I (suggest suggests) that you (watch watches) your step.
4. It (bother bothers) me that I (miss missed) that play.
5. I (did done) what I (want wanted) to do.
6. They (was were) here a short while ago, but where (are is) they now?
7. I (did done) my best, but he (did done) still better.
8. Yesterday I (ask asked) her to a movie, but she (wasn't weren't) in the mood.
9. You (was were) there, (wasn't weren't) you?
10. All of us (was were) there, and we all (return returned) together last night.

☐EXERCISE 4

1. I (join joined) the college orchestra last fall and (like likes) it.
2. I (play played) the drums in high school, but I (play plays) the flute in the college orchestra.

3. The orchestra director (need needs) more players and (hope hopes) to get some.
4. It (doesn't don't) matter whether you (are be) a music major.
5. We (work works) hard at each practice and (learn learns) a lot.
6. The director (expect expects) perfection and (insist insists) on it.
7. We (practice practices) two hours and (has have) a short break in the middle.
8. Everyone (enjoy enjoys) those practices and (benefit benefits) from them.
9. We (watch watches) the director's baton and (do does) our best to follow.
10. Last night we (was were) pleased when the director (praise praised) us.

□EXERCISE 5

1. I never (like liked) English before, but now I (work works) hard at it.
2. Last week we (learn learned) about possessives and (discuss discussed) how to form them.
3. Our instructor (explain explained) what we (did done) wrong.
4. I (do does) my best in the course and (hope hopes) to pass.
5. Last semester I (like liked) the course in psychology, but I (drop dropped) chemistry.
6. I (check checked) into the possibilities and (decide decided) not to major in math.
7. I (pick picked) this college because it (did done) well in football last fall.
8. The athletic coach (encourage encouraged) me to enroll, and I (listen listened) to his advice at that time.
9. Now when the going (be is) rough, he always (be is) there.
10. He (advise advises) me and (treat treats) me like a friend.

□EXERCISE 6

1. I (start started) to collect stamps when I (was were) small.
2. I still (collect collects) them and (has have) quite a good collection.
3. Last year I (ask asked) all my friends to save foreign stamps, and they (was were) glad to.
4. At first I (want wanted) stamps from all countries; then I (decide decided) to specialize.
5. Now I (want wants) only stamps from the South Pacific.
6. I (dispose disposed) of my other stamps last winter and (receive received) good prices for them.
7. The South Pacific stamps (is are) pretty, and I (has have) quite a few.

8. The biggest stamps (be are) from Tonga; they (measure measures) more than two inches wide.
9. The stamps (help helps) me to learn about other countries; they also (impress impresses) me with their beauty.
10. I (intend intends) to go to the South Pacific some day.

☐EXERCISE 7

1. When I (finish finished) that book yesterday, I (return returned) it to the library.
2. Then I (ask asked) for another book by the same author, but the library (had have) none.
3. An accident (occur occurred) when I (was were) on my way home.
4. I (happen happened) to see the accident and (report reported) it to the police.
5. No one (expect expected) the police to arrive so soon, but they (appear appeared) in five minutes.
6. The driver of the truck (did done) the best he could to avoid the accident, but it (happen happened) in spite of him.
7. Three people (was were) involved, but they (wasn't weren't) hurt.
8. It (was were) lucky that it (wasn't weren't) more serious.
9. When I (arrive arrived) home later, I (rest rested) a while before dinner.
10. I always (enjoy enjoys) my dinner more if I (am be) rested.

In these sentences, cross out the community dialect expressions and write the standard English ones above.

☐EXERCISE 8

1. The lecture last night impress me and change my mind about capital punishment.

2. Cleaning the house always bore me, but I does it once in a while.

3. She need support, and I intends to give it to her.

4. When I asks him to help me yesterday, he do what he can.

5. He seal the letter and drop it in the mailbox last night.

6. I discover some violets this morning; they be early this year.

7. Yesterday I happen to see a horned lark in a field; it were the first of the season.

8. I ask for directions yesterday and walk to her house.
9. She seem glad to see me and ask me to stay for lunch.
10. My friends expects me to call them tonight.

☐EXERCISE 9

1. It please me that she come to our house last night.
2. I order a pizza last night and finish all of it.
3. I hand my paper in yesterday when I finish it.
4. She loan me a dollar yesterday, and I wants to return it now.
5. No one complain about the meal last night, but I dislike it.
6. He drop the course because he have no interest in it.
7. It occur to me now that I needs a haircut before the wedding tomorrow.
8. I observe all the traffic rules when I start to drive last year.
9. He want to speak standard English and refuse to give up now.
10. Speaking standard English be important for everyone.

JOURNAL WRITING

In your journal write about something that interests you at the moment using verbs you may formerly have had trouble with.

STANDARD ENGLISH VERBS (compound forms and irregular verbs)

In the last chapter we talked about the present and past forms of the regular verb *walk.* Other forms of the regular verb may be used with helping verbs. Here is a table showing all the forms of some regular verbs and the various helping verbs they are used with.

REGULAR VERBS

BASE FORM (Use after *can, may, shall, will, could, might, should, would, must, do, does, did.*)	PRESENT	PAST	PAST PARTICIPLE (Use after *have, has, had.* Or use after some form of *be* to describe the subject or to make a passive verb.)	*ING* FORM (Use after some form of *be.*)
ask	ask (*s*)	asked	asked	asking
dance	dance (*s*)	danced	danced	dancing
decide	decide (*s*)	decided	decided	deciding
enjoy	enjoy (*s*)	enjoyed	enjoyed	enjoying
finish	finish (*es*)	finished	finished	finishing
happen	happen (*s*)	happened	happened	happening
learn	learn (*s*)	learned	learned	learning
like	like (*s*)	liked	liked	liking
need	need (*s*)	needed	needed	needing
open	open (*s*)	opened	opened	opening
start	start (*s*)	started	started	starting
suppose	suppose (*s*)	supposed	supposed	supposing
walk	walk (*s*)	walked	walked	walking
want	want (*s*)	wanted	wanted	wanting

Sometimes a past participle is used after some form of the verb *be* (or verbs that take the place of *be* like *appear, seems, look, feel, get, act, become*) to describe the subject.

He is satisfied
He was confused.
He has been disappointed.
He appeared pleased. (He was pleased.)
He seems interested. (He is interested.)
He looked surprised. (He was surprised.)
He feels frightened. (He is frightened.)
He gets bored easily. (He is bored easily.)
He acts concerned. (He is concerned.)

Usually these past participles are called describing words that describe the subject rather than being called part of the verb of the sentence. What you call them doesn't matter. The only important thing is to be sure you use the correct form of the past participle (*ed* for regular verbs).

Sometimes the subject of the sentence neither *does* nor *is* anything. It just stays there passive in the sentence and is acted upon.

The birthday cake was eaten by the children.

The subject is *cake*. It doesn't do anything. It is passive. It is acted upon by the children. Thus we say that *was eaten* is a passive verb. All you really need to remember is that whenever a form of *be* is used with a past participle, you must be sure to use the correct past participle form (*ed* for regular verbs).

Note that when there are several helping verbs, it is the last one that determines which form of the main verb should be used: she *should* finish soon; she should *have* finished yesterday.

When do you write *ask, finish, suppose, use*? And when do you write *asked, finished, supposed, used*? Here's a rule that may help you decide.

Use *asked, finished, supposed, used* rather than *ask, finish, suppose, use*

1. **when it's past time:**
   He *asked* her for a date last night.
   She *finished* her paper yesterday.
   When I saw you, I *supposed* you had had lunch.
   I *used* to like her.

2. **when some form of *be* or *have* comes before the word:**
   He has *asked* her to go out with him.
   She is *finished* with her paper now.
   I am *supposed* to give you this note.
   I am *used* to getting up early.

IRREGULAR VERBS

All the verbs in the table on page 100 are regular. That is, they are all formed in the same way—with an *ed* ending on the past form and on the past participle. But many verbs are irregular. Their past and past participle forms change spelling instead of just adding an *ed*. Here is a table of some irregular verbs. (The present and the *ing* forms are not usually given in a list of principal parts because they are formed easily from the base form and cause no trouble.) Refer to this list when you aren't sure which verb form to use. Memorize all the forms you don't know.

BASE FORM	PAST	PAST PARTICIPLE
be	was, were	been
become	became	become
begin	began	begun
break	broke	broken
bring	brought	brought
buy	bought	bought
build	built	built
catch	caught	caught
choose	chose	chosen
come	came	come
cost	cost	cost
do	did	done
draw	drew	drawn
drink	drank	drunk
drive	drove	driven
eat	ate	eaten
fall	fell	fallen
feel	felt	felt
fight	fought	fought
find	found	found
fit	fit	fit
forget	forgot	forgotten
forgive	forgave	forgiven
freeze	froze	frozen
get	got	got *or* gotten
give	gave	given
go	went	gone
grow	grew	grown
have	had	had

BASE FORM	PAST	PAST PARTICIPLE
hear	heard	heard
hold	held	held
hurt	hurt	hurt
keep	kept	kept
know	knew	known
lay (to place)	laid	laid
lead	led	led
leave	left	left
lie (to rest)	lay	lain
lose	lost	lost
make	made	made
meet	met	met
pay	paid	paid
read	read	read
ride	rode	ridden
ring	rang	rung
rise	rose	risen
run	ran	run
say	said	said
see	saw	seen
sell	sold	sold
shake	shook	shaken
shine (to give light)	shone	shone
shine (to polish)	shined	shined
sing	sang	sung
sleep	slept	slept
speak	spoke	spoken
spend	spent	spent
stand	stood	stood
steal	stole	stolen
strike	struck	struck
swim	swam	swum
swing	swung	swung
take	took	taken
teach	taught	taught
tear	tore	torn
tell	told	told
think	thought	thought
throw	threw	thrown
wear	wore	worn
win	won	won
write	wrote	written

EXERCISES

Write the correct form of the verb. Refer to the tables and explanations on the preceding pages if you aren't sure which form to use after a certain helping verb. Do no more than ten sentences at a time before checking your answers.

☐EXERCISE 1

1. (finish) I should ________________ my paper today, but I may not be ________________ until tomorrow.
2. (finish) I could ________________ in a few hours if I worked hard.
3. (finish) I have often ________________ a paper rapidly, and I might ________________ this one rapidly.
4. (finish) I am ________________ it so that I can hand it in on Monday.
5. (finish) I wish that I had ________________ it earlier.
6. (finish) It was ________________ yesterday, but then I made some changes in it.
7. (finish) Now I must ________________ it all over again.
8. (finish) When my paper is ________________, I'll be glad.
9. (finish) I always ________________ whatever I start.
10. (finish) Most students have ________________ their papers by now.

☐EXERCISE 2

1. (speak, begin) Newscasters always ________________ standard English, and I now have ________________ to imitate them.
2. (seem, want) That ________________ to be a good way to learn standard English, and I now ________________ to learn it as fast as possible.
3. (know, become) I ________________ that it will help me in my job; in fact it has ________________ a requirement in my field.
4. (imitate, use) I am ________________ my teachers too because they all ________________ standard English.
5. (teach, begin) I must ________________ my ears to hear the standard endings of verbs, and I now am ________________ to hear them.

6. (like) I ________________ the feeling now of knowing two dialects.

7. (speak, learn) We had ________________ to our son's teacher and had ________________ that our son needs extra help.

8. (intend, begin) We now ________________ to help him; in fact we ________________ last night.

9. (be, realize) Last night as we ________________ helping him, we ________________ how much we can do.

10. (help, be, began) As we ____________ him last night, we ____________ impressed with how quickly he was ____________ to catch on.

☐EXERCISE 3

1. (be, see) We ________________ delighted when we ________________ our nephew's car turn into the driveway yesterday.

2. (see, begin) We hadn't ________________ him for a year, and we had ________________ to miss his visits.

3. (drive, eat) He had ________________ 500 miles that day and had ________________ very little.

4. (offer, do) We ________________ him some food immediately and ________________ what we could to make him comfortable.

5. (eat, ask) He sat down then and ________________ ravenously and ________________ for more.

6. (write, ask, receive) Then he said he had ________________ to us and ________________ whether we had ________________ his letter.

7. (come, begin) The letter hadn't ________________, and we told him we had ________________ to think he had forgotten us.

8. (see, suggest) We ____________ that he was tired and ____________ that he go to bed.

9. (go, wash, prepare) After he had ____________ to bed, we ____________ the dishes and ________________ for the next day.

10. (see, be, drive) I ________________ then that we ________________ low on food and ________________ to the grocery for more supplies.

☐EXERCISE 4

1. (decide, see) Last winter I ________________ to go to the annual ice carnival at the college because I had never ________________ one before.
2. (freeze, reach) I was almost ____________ by the time I ____________ the rink.
3. (be, come) As I watched, however, I ________________ glad I had ________________.
4. (observe, see) A friend of mine was competing in the figure skating, and as I ________________ her, I ________________ that she was good.
5. (announce, win) Finally when the judges' decision was ______________, she had ______________ first place.
6. (smile, receive) She ________________ through her tears then as she ________________ the trophy.
7. (be, do) All her friends that night ________________ pleased that she had ________________ so well.
8. (be, accept) ________________ you there when she ________________ her trophy?
9. (discuss, impress) That book that we ________________ in class yesterday really ________________ me.
10. (analyze, quote) Our instructor ________________ it yesterday and ________________ from it.

☐EXERCISE 5

1. (say, visit) Our friends from Texas had ________________ that they would ________________ us when they came east.
2. (hope, come) We were ______________ they would ______________ last weekend.
3. (be, drive) We ________________ delighted, therefore, when they ________________ in Friday evening.
4. (see, grow) We had not ________________ them for years, and their children had ________________ tall.

5. (take, take) Their son has ________________ up skiing, and their daughter is ________________ ballet lessons.
6. (be, stay) I ________________ impressed with their good family relationship and was pleased that they would ________________ for two days.
7. (occupy, take) Our time was ________________ mainly with talking, but we ________________ a few excursions.
8. (see, be) They had never ______________ our lake and ______________ eager to sail on it.
9. (ask, like) Also we ______________ them if they would ______________ to see our local antique museum.
10. (be, collect) They ________________ interested because they have ________________ antiques for years.

Avoiding Dialect Expressions

Although verbs cause the most trouble for those who have grown up speaking a dialect other than standard English, certain other expressions, more common in speech than in writing, should be avoided. Some (such as *he don't* and *you was*) are discussed elsewhere in the book. A few others are listed here.

DIALECT	STANDARD ENGLISH
anywheres, nowheres, somewheres	anywhere, nowhere, somewhere
anyways	anyway
hisself, theirselves	himself, themselves
this here book, that there book, those there books	this book, that book, those books
them books	those books
he did good, she sang good	he did well, she sang well
my brother he plays ball	my brother plays ball
haven't none, haven't got none	have none, haven't any
haven't no, haven't got no	have no, haven't any
haven't never	have never, haven't ever
haven't nothing	have nothing, haven't anything
wasn't no	was no, wasn't any
wasn't never	was never, wasn't ever
(These are called double negatives.)	
ain't	am not, isn't, aren't, hasn't, haven't

Change the following sentences into standard English.

□EXERCISE 1

1. My brother he did good in the track meet last week.

2. I wasn't never any good at sports, and anyways I ain't got time for them.

3. He rather fix his car hisself than take it to a garage.

4. We look and look for our pup last night but can't find him anywheres.

5. This here book be the best I ever read.

6. She done her best, but she still didn't get no trophy.

7. Last night I want a pizza, but I didn't have no money.

8. I ain't read none of them books.

9. Where you find all them cookies?

10. She sings good now that she's taking lessons.

WRITING ASSIGNMENT

As you continue your writing assignments that begin on page 196, are you keeping a list of your misspelled words on the inside back cover of this book?

Proofreading Exercise

See if you can correct all five errors in this student paper before you check with the answer sheet. The errors are in the first and third paragraphs.

THE HAIRCUT

Like all college students, we were always broke. We constantly tried to save money in every way possible, and that lead to cutting out luxuries like barbers and hair stylists.

There we were—three fellows with no money—all needing haircuts, so we agreed to cut each other's hair. I took first turn at doing the cutting on my not-too-confident friend while our third friend watched and provided encouragement.

It seemed like it should be easy but after about ten minutes with scissors and comb, it wasnt going well. In another five minutes of trying to correct my mistakes, it was even worse. The protests were growing and I managed only a few more snips before my friends insisted that I stop while their was any hair left. I must admit my handiwork looked terrible, and I suppose it was only natural that my offer to even it out a little was refused.

We pooled all our change and came up with just enough for one haircut—by a real barber—to fix up the damage I'd done.

Progress Test

This test covers everything you have studied so far. One sentence in each pair is correct. The other is incorrect. Read both sentences carefully before you decide. Then write the letter of the correct sentence in the blank.

_____ 1. A. It don't really matter to me whether you come or not.
B. Your new suit is sharper than your old one.

_____ 2. A. I chose this course because I need it.
B. I'm jogging every morning it's good exercise.

_____ 3. A. Wondering how I'd ever get back home again.
B. Don't you find your apartment too far from work?

_____ 4. A. Their trip into the city took two days.
B. They was dissatisfied with the new ruling.

_____ 5. A. When my husband came home, he ask me where I'd been.
B. What you think is important to me.

_____ 6. A. I've all ready finished writing my paper.
B. It's the best one I've ever written.

_____ 7. A. If you can write a good paper, it's a help in college.
B. I studied for four hours, then I went to bed.

_____ 8. A. I bought a new table; then I bought a rug.
B. He seem happy when I saw him last night.

_____ 9. A. I'm taking a course of study that will lead to a degree.
B. Wondering all the time how I'll make it through four years.

_____ 10. A. I'm surprise that you didn't get an *A*.
B. I don't know whether to go to the play or whether to study.

_____ 11. A. I'd rather have a incomplete than a *D* in that course.
B. But of course I'd rather have a *C* than either of them.

_____ 12. A. When I write my paper a week ahead then I can revise it.
B. And revising is important for a good grade.

_____ 13. A. I invited her to go with me to see the play and afterward to have a snack.
B. I enjoyed the play however I was tired afterward.

_____ 14. A. Who's bike is that in our yard?
B. I mowed the lawn and then settled down to study.

_____ 15. A. I hear that Brians car has faulty brakes.
B. I'd advise him to get them adjusted immediately.

MAKING SUBJECTS, VERBS, AND PRONOUNS AGREE

All parts of a sentence should agree. In general if the subject is singular, the verb should be singular; if the subject is plural, the verb should be plural.

Each of the boys has his own room.

Both have their own rooms.

He and I were there.

Many of the class were absent.

Some of the students were late.

There were vacant seats in the front row.

The following words are singular and take a singular verb:

(*one* words)	(*body* words)	
one	nobody	each
anyone	anybody	either
someone	somebody	neither
everyone	everybody	

One of my friends is a freshman.

Each of the students is responsible for one report.

Either of the girls is a good choice.

The following "group" words take a singular verb if you are thinking of the group as a whole, but they take a plural verb if you are thinking of the individuals in the group:

group	band	heap
committee	flock	lot
crowd	class	audience
team	dozen	jury
family	kind	herd
number	public	none

My family *is* behind me. . . . . My family *are* all scattered.
The number present *was* small. . . . A number *are* going to the rally.
A dozen *is* enough. . . . . A dozen *are* going.
A lot *was* accomplished . . . . A lot *were* late to class.

Here are some subject-verb pairs you can *always* be sure of. No exceptions!

you were	(*never* you was)
we were	(*never* we was)
they were	(*never* they was)
he doesn't	(*never* he don't)
she doesn't	(*never* she don't)
it doesn't	(*never* it don't)

Not only should subject and verb agree, but a pronoun also should agree with the word it refers to. If the word referred to is singular, the pronoun should be singular; if the word referred to is plural, the pronoun should be plural.

Each of the boys has *his* own car.

The pronoun *his* refers to the singular subject *Each* and therefore is singular.

Both of the boys have *their* own cars.

The pronoun *their* refers to the plural subject *Both* and therefore is plural.

Today many people try to avoid sex bias by writing sentences like the following:

> If anyone wants a ride, he or she can go in my car.
> If anybody calls, tell him or her that I've left.
> Somebody has left his or her textbook here.

But those sentences are wordy and awkward. Therefore some people, especially in conversation, turn them into sentences that are not grammatically correct.

> If anyone wants a ride, they can go in my car.
> If anybody calls, tell them that I've left.
> Somebody has left their textbook here.

Such ungrammatical sentences, however, are not necessary. It just takes a little thought to revise each sentence so that it avoids sex bias and is also grammatically correct:

> Anyone who wants a ride can go in my car.
> Tell anybody who calls that I've left.
> Somebody has left a textbook here.

Another good way to avoid the awkward *he or she* and *him or her* is to make the words plural. Instead of writing, "Each of the students was in his or her place," write, "All of the students were in their places," thus avoiding sex bias and still having a grammatically correct sentence.

EXERCISES

Underline the correct word. Check your answers ten at a time.

□EXERCISE 1

1. Everybody in our family (are is) planning a trip this summer.
2. Each of us (are is) going to a different part of the country.
3. One of my brothers (are is) going fishing in the Far North.

4. My other brother (doesn't don't) know yet where he'll go.
5. Each of them (are is) taking (his their) own motorcycle.
6. My sister and I (was were) planning to go to Wyoming.
7. But my sister decided she (doesn't don't) want to go.
8. No one in our family (has have) ever been to California.
9. So my sister and one of her friends (think thinks) they'll go there.
10. My parents (intend intends) to drive to Pennsylvania.

□EXERCISE 2

1. Each member of the family (are is) sure to have a good experience.
2. One of my friends (has have) just come back from Jersey City.
3. Nobody in our family (has have) been in the New York area.
4. Each of us (hope hopes) someday to go there.
5. Everybody in our family (like likes) to travel.
6. It has been two years since we (was were) at my grandfather's farm.
7. Both of my cousins (live lives) near his farm.
8. They (was were) expecting us to visit them last summer.
9. But not one of us (was were) able to go then.
10. Each of us (was were) busy doing other things.

□EXERCISE 3

1. Each of these rules (are is) important.
2. And doing the exercises (help helps) me to remember the rules.
3. Some of the rules (are is) harder than others.
4. Each of the rules (has have) been a challenge to me.
5. A few of them (was were) familiar, but most of them (was were) new.
6. Every one of the rules (depend depends) on the previous rule.
7. It (doesn't don't) do any good to learn one isolated rule.
8. All of them (work works) together.
9. For example, the punctuation of sentences (require requires) a knowledge of subjects and verbs.
10. Each of the rules (are is) going to be of value in my writing.

□EXERCISE 4

1. Each of my sisters (has have) (her their) own apartment.
2. Both of them (like likes) independence.
3. One of them (live lives) in the center of the city.
4. She (doesn't don't) like to have far to walk to work.
5. The other one of my sisters (has have) her apartment in the suburbs.
6. Each of them (has have) (her their) own car.

7. It (doesn't don't) take either of them long to drive to our house.
8. Both of them (was were) over here last night.
9. Two of their friends (was were) with them.
10. All of them (spend spends) an evening with us now and then.

□EXERCISE 5

1. The hours spent on my hobby (are is) the best part of my day.
2. Routine tasks and studying of course (take takes) up some time.
3. But a good many hours (are is) devoted to photography.
4. Both of my parents (is are) interested in taking pictures.
5. They (was were) always buying me little cameras when I was young.
6. So now I (spend spends) a lot of time working with cameras.
7. Several hours each week (are is) spent in the dark room.
8. The job of developing and printing pictures (take takes) time.
9. But a few of my photos (has have) been excellent.
10. Last month two of them (was were) published in a magazine.

□EXERCISE 6

1. All of the buildings on our campus (are is) modern Gothic.
2. Each one (exhibit exhibits) a slightly different style of architecture.
3. Each of the buildings (was were) built to conform to the master plan.
4. Every one of the buildings (are is) fireproof.
5. Most of the students (come comes) to the free movie each week.
6. All of them (like likes) a break from studying.
7. You (was were) there too, (wasn't weren't) you?
8. There (was were) 50 people in line, and we (was were) at the end.
9. Both of us (was were) able to get in though.
10. Each of us (feel feels) the movie was worth the long wait.

□EXERCISE 7

1. A number of women (are is) going to the conference.
2. Each of the women (has have) to make (her their) own reservation.
3. A few of them (has have) made (her their) reservations already.
4. It (doesn't don't) matter when they are made.
5. The conference planners (expect expects) a good attendance.
6. Some of the women (hope hopes) to go by car, but most of them (intend intends) to go by plane.
7. My friend and I (enjoy enjoys) going to the country to ski.
8. We (spend spends) many weekends that way.
9. Some of our friends usually (go goes) with us too.
10. Each of us (take takes) ski equipment and food for the weekend.

☐EXERCISE 8

1. Each of the boys (are is) working on (his their) own project.
2. All of the boys (are is) going to finish (his their) work by Christmas.
3. Most of the boys (intend intends) to give their projects as gifts.
4. Each of the chapters (present presents) a different problem.
5. One of my friends (expect expects) to be here tomorrow.
6. Everyone on the team (admire admires) the coach.
7. Each of the candidates (promise promises) to work for lower taxes.
8. My aunt and uncle (send sends) me a check each Christmas.
9. The price of the set of encyclopedias (are is) too high.
10. She and my brother (play plays) tennis every morning.

☐EXERCISE 9

1. Neither of my coats (are is) warm enough for this weather.
2. A box of macadamia nuts (was were) sent to our house by mistake.
3. I'm sure she (doesn't don't) believe all those compliments.
4. (Wasn't Weren't) you surprised at her answer?
5. Here (are is) the hammer and nails you asked for.
6. There (was were) two reasons why I sold my car.
7. We (was were) delighted to see our old friends.
8. There (remain remains) a number of insoluble problems.
9. It (doesn't don't) matter what you decide.
10. You (was were) the best player on the team.

☐EXERCISE 10

1. Each of those guys (think thinks) (he is, they are) going to make the relay team.
2. Ice skating takes strong muscles, (doesn't don't) it?
3. Everybody on the committee (are is) in favor of the proposal.
4. (Doesn't Don't) she like her new position?
5. There (has have) been many reasons for my inability to concentrate.
6. You (was were) on my mind all day yesterday.
7. Each of us (have has) been at fault.
8. Both of us (has have) made mistakes.
9. All of us (sleep sleeps) late on Saturday mornings.
10. We slept late this morning because we (was were) up late last night.

JOURNAL WRITING

Write about something that interests you using at least four words from your Spelling List on the inside back cover.

CHOOSING THE RIGHT PRONOUN

Of the many kinds of pronouns, the following cause the most difficulty:

SUBJECT GROUP	NONSUBJECT GROUP
I	me
he	him
she	her
we	us
they	them

A pronoun in the Subject Group may be used in two ways:

1. **as the subject of a verb:**

He is my brother. (*He* is the subject of the verb *is.*)
We gave a party. (*We* is the subject of the verb *gave.*)
He is taller than *I.* (The sentence is not written out in full. It means "He is taller than *I* am." *I* is the subject of the verb *am.*) Whenever you see *than* in a sentence, ask yourself whether a verb has been left off. Add the verb, and then you'll automatically use the correct pronoun. In both speaking and writing, always add the verb. Instead of saying, "She's smarter than (I, me)," say, "She's smarter than I am." Then you can't fail to use the correct pronoun.

2. **as a word that means the same as the subject:**

That boy in the blue jeans is *he.* (*He* is a word that means the same as the subject *boy.* Therefore the pronoun from the Subject Group is used.)
It was *she* all right. (*She* means the same as the subject *It.* Therefore the pronoun from the Subject Group is used.)

Modern usage allows some exceptions to this rule however. *It is me* and *it is us* (instead of the grammatically correct *it is I* and *it is we*) are now established usage; and *it is him, it is her*, and *it is them* are widely used, particularly in informal speech.

Pronouns in the Nonsubject Group are used for all other purposes. In the following sentence, *me* is not the subject, nor does it mean the same as the subject. Therefore it comes from the Nonsubject Group.

He came with Julie and me.

A good way to tell which pronoun to use is to leave out the extra name. By leaving out *Julie*, you will say, *He came with me*. You would never say, *He came with I.*

We saw Loretta and *him* last night. (We saw *him* last night.)
He gave *us* boys a pony. (He gave *us* a pony.)
The firm gave my wife and *me* a trip. (The firm gave *me* a trip.)

EXERCISES

Underline the correct pronoun. Remember the trick of leaving out the extra name to help you decide which pronoun to use. Use the correct grammatical form even though an alternate form may be acceptable in conversation.

☐EXERCISE 1

1. It cost Dave and (I me) a dollar apiece to make that long-distance call.
2. Dave is smarter than (I me), but he doesn't work as hard.
3. Consequently I usually get better grades than (he him).
4. This time, though, (he him) and (I me) studied together.
5. No one could be better prepared for this exam than (we us).
6. We expect that both (he him) and (I me) will pass.
7. An invitation came to (her she) and her husband.
8. It invited (she her) and her husband to a wedding.
9. I hope that Dave and (I me) will be invited too.
10. Dave and (I me) would love to go.

☐EXERCISE 2

1. (Me and my sister, My sister and I) share an apartment.
2. My aunt asked my sister and (I me) to visit her.
3. My aunt asked whether my sister and (I me) would like to see the carnival.
4. Of course my sister and (I me) were eager to go.
5. That's a problem for you and (he him) to solve.
6. No one knows all the angles except you and (he him).
7. You and (he him) will just have to sit down and work it out.
8. Both you and (he him) must compromise.
9. I know it can be worked out to suit both you and (he him).
10. Let me know when you and (he him) have reached an agreement.

☐EXERCISE 3

1. The director asked (we us) girls to plan the party for the cast.
2. (We Us) girls did most of the decorating.

3. The food was left up to (we us) girls too.
4. It was a close game of chess between my friend and (I me).
5. Did you watch (he him) and (I me) playing?
6. No one could be more of a clown than (he him).
7. There's always good feeling between (we us) two.
8. While we were traveling in Nevada, time went fast for Lou and (I me).
9. (Lou and I, Me and Lou) were gone three weeks.
10. It was one of the best trips Lou and (I me) ever took.

□EXERCISE 4

1. (He and I, Him and me) went skiing last weekend.
2. It was the first ski trip (he and I, him and me) had taken.
3. Several others joined (we us) two.
4. I sent an invitation to his brother and (he him).
5. You should have heard the conversation between (he him) and (I me).
6. Mom asked Dad and (I me) what we intended to do about the dented fender.
7. No one could decide that problem except Dad and (I me).
8. (Me and Dad, Dad and I) sat down to talk it over.
9. My dad and (I me) now have a standing agreement.
10. We may disagree, but there are never hard feelings between (we us) two.

□EXERCISE 5

1. The bus rolled away leaving Don and (I me) standing there.
2. We were going to miss (she her) and Joan a lot.
3. Between you and (I me), I think we have the best coach in the state.
4. The coach has left it to Robert and (I me) to arrange the rides.
5. It's no big job for Robert and (I me).
6. The president of the firm invited my wife and (I me) to a reception.
7. (Me and my wife, My wife and I) will enjoy going.
8. (David and I, Me and David) have always been the best of friends.
9. Don't you think you should leave that for David and (I me) to decide?
10. Don't you think that David and (I me) should decide that?

JOURNAL WRITING

Write three sentences using pronouns you may have formerly used incorrectly.

MAKING THE PRONOUN REFER TO THE RIGHT WORD

When you write a sentence, *you* know what it means, but your reader may not. What does this sentence mean?

> Joe told his father he would have to take the car to the garage.

Who would have to take the car? We don't know whether the pronoun *he* refers to Joe or to his father. The sentence might mean

> Joe said that his father would have to take the car to the garage.

or

> Joe told his father that he was taking the car to the garage.

The simplest way to correct such a faulty reference is to use a direct quotation:

> Joe said to his father, "I'll have to take the car to the garage."

Here is another sentence with a faulty reference:

> I've always been interested in nursing and finally have decided to become one.

Decided to become a nursing? There's no word for *one* to refer to. We need to write

> I've always been interested in nursing and finally have decided to become a nurse.

Another kind of faulty reference is a *which* clause that doesn't refer to any specific word, thus making it difficult to tell what part of the sentence it refers to.

> No one could tell him where the bike had been left which made him angry.

Was he angry because no one could tell him or because the bike had not been left in its proper place? The sentence should read

> It made him angry that the bike had not been left in its place.

or

> It made him angry that no one could tell him where the bike had been left.

EXERCISES

Most—but not all—of these sentences aren't clear because we don't know what word the pronoun refers to. Revise such sentences, making the meaning clear. Remember that using a direct quotation is often the easiest way to clarify what a pronoun refers to. Since there are more ways than one to rewrite each sentence, yours may be as good as the one on the answer sheet. Just ask yourself whether the meaning is clear.

☐EXERCISE 1

1. I put the omelet on the table, took off my apron, and began to eat it.
2. They offered me a job which pleased me.
3. I've been trying to decide what trip to take which isn't easy.
4. She told her sister that her room was a mess.
5. I have a pair of glasses, but my eyes are so good that I don't use them except for reading.
6. The president told the dean he had been too lenient.
7. When I praised the child's finger painting, it was pleased.
8. I thought he would phone, and I waited all evening for it to ring.
9. The teachers arranged for a play center where they can play on swings, slides, and jungle gyms.
10. Felipe told the professor that his watch was wrong.

☐EXERCISE 2

1. When I picked up the dog's dish, it began to whine.
2. I have always been interested in coaching football ever since I was in high school, and now I have decided to become one.
3. I decided not to accept the summer job which annoyed my family.

4. She asked her sister why she wasn't invited to the party.

5. Jay's father let him take his new tennis racket to school.

6. I have always liked French Provincial furniture and have finally decided to buy one.

7. She told her instructor she didn't understand what she was saying.

8. She likes to swim; in fact she spends most of her summer doing it.

9. She is good in her studies although not very good in sports. This is why she was chosen student body president.

10. When the boss talked with Ed, he was really despondent.

□EXERCISE 3

1. His motorcycle swerved into the side of a house, but it wasn't damaged.

2. As I approached the baby's playpen, it began to cry.

3. As soon as the fender was repaired, I drove it home.

4. I stopped at the old Wiley Schoolhouse, which has been designated a state historical site.

5. The instructor told him his typewriter needed a new ribbon.

6. He told his father he ought to wash the car.

7. I walked into the room, climbed on the ladder, and began to paint it.

8. I'm taking lessons in golf, which is my favorite sport.

9. She told her mother she needed to be positive before making such a big decision.

10. We couldn't find a single bottle and blamed Rudy for drinking all of them.

☐EXERCISE 4

1. Andy told his brother that his car had a flat tire.
2. It would be cold in New England at this time of year which I don't like.
3. He asked the mechanic why he was having trouble.
4. When her sister came in at 4 A.M., she was crying.
5. As I tried to attach the dog's leash, it ran away.
6. Yesterday I turned in a paper that came back with an *A* grade.
7. The cars whizzed past, but they didn't even look my way.
8. As soon as I approached the robin's nest, it flew away.
9. I've decided to save all my money for a trip which won't be easy.
10. She told her daughter that she had missed her appointment.

☐EXERCISE 5

1. He told his dad he needed a new suit.
2. We couldn't find the cake plate and realized the children must have eaten it.
3. She served me a pizza, which was cold.
4. When I moved the child's tricycle, it screamed.
5. I have adjusted the steering wheel, and you can take it home.
6. After I read about Lindbergh's life, I decided that's what I want to be.
7. He asked the man to come back when he had time to talk.
8. When Jerome talked to his father, he was very angry.
9. Ben told his father he ought to get a refund for the faulty tire.
10. When I opened the door of the kennel, it ran away.

CORRECTING MISPLACED OR DANGLING MODIFIERS

A modifier gives information about some word in a sentence, and it should be as close to that word as possible. In the following sentence the modifier is too far away from the word it modifies to make sense:

Chewing on an old shoe, we sat and watched the puppy.

Was it *we* who were chewing on an old shoe? That's what the sentence says because the modifier *Chewing on an old shoe* is next to *we*. Of course it should be next to *puppy*.

We sat and watched the puppy chewing on an old shoe.

The next example has no word at all for the modifier to modify:

At the age of six my family moved to South Carolina.

Obviously the family was not six when it moved. The modifier *At the age of six* is dangling there with no word to attach itself to, no word for it to modify. We must change the sentence so there will be such a word:

At the age of six I moved to South Carolina with my family.

Now the modifier *At the age of six* has a proper word—*I*—for it to modify. Or we could get rid of the dangling modifier by turning it into a dependent clause.

When I was six, my family moved to South Carolina.

Here the clause has its own subject—*I*—and there's no chance of misunderstanding the sentence.

Here's another dangling modifier:

After a quick lunch, the bus left for Fort Lauderdale.

Did the bus have a quick lunch? Who did?

After a quick lunch, I took the bus for Fort Lauderdale.

EXERCISES

Most—but not all—of these sentences contain misplaced or dangling modifiers. Some you may correct simply by shifting the modifier so it will be next to the word it modifies. Others you'll need to rewrite. Since there is more than one way to correct each sentence, your way may be as good as the one at the back of the book.

□EXERCISE 1

1. While talking on the phone, the cake burned.
2. Sound asleep on the front porch, I came across my grandfather.
3. Crawling across the dusty road, I saw a furry little caterpillar.
4. Taking her in his arms, the moon hid behind a cloud.
5. You will enjoy looking at the pictures that you took years later.
6. By concentrating intently, I at last understood the meaning of the paragraph.
7. Lincoln Park is the most interesting park in the city that I have seen.
8. She was engaged to a man with a Cougar named Smith.
9. At the age of 14 my sister was born.
10. We gave all the food to the dog that we didn't want.

□EXERCISE 2

1. After cleaning my room, my dog wanted to go for a walk.
2. A son was born to Mr. and Mrs. N. L. Dixon weighing eight pounds.
3. Being a bore, I don't enjoy his company.
4. Except when pickled, I don't care for cucumbers.
5. Screaming and kicking, I tried to quiet the child.
6. I bought a car from a used-car dealer with a leaky radiator.

7. Leaning against the barn, I saw the broken ladder.

8. After watching TV all evening, the dirty dishes were still on the table.

9. At the age of six my grandfather paid us a visit.

10. Slamming the door he marched out of the house.

☐EXERCISE 3

1. Badly in need of a bath, I brought the dog into the laundry room.

2. Quietly munching hay, I watched the horses in the pasture.

3. Having been born and raised in the country, the old cookstove naturally appeals to me.

4. Excited and eager to go, the bus was waiting for us.

5. The house is surrounded by a grove of catalpa trees where I was born.

6. Crying pitifully, I stopped and talked to the child.

7. Unwrapping gift after gift, the puppy had a great time playing with all the tissue paper.

8. I decided to give the clothes to a charity that I had no use for.

9. Although almost eight years old, he refused to turn his car in on a newer model.

10. She put the sandwiches back in the bag that she had not eaten.

☐EXERCISE 4

1. At the age of ten my father became manager of his company.

2. Falling from the top of the Empire State Building, we could see little white pieces of paper.

3. While on a two-week vacation, the office had to take care of itself.

4. I saw that the murderer had been captured in the evening paper.
5. After playing Frisbee all evening, my English paper did not get finished.
6. Consulting the Lost and Found section of the paper, the dog was soon safe at home again.
7. The youngster went careening down the driveway just as we arrived on a skateboard.
8. After eating lunch hurriedly, the two taxis then started for the airport.
9. Moving slowly down the street, we saw the parade.
10. We bought a duck decoy in a store that had been refinished.

□EXERCISE 5

1. While tobogganing down the hill, a huge bear came into view.
2. The class made me aware of little speech habits I have while speaking with my friends which I got rid of very soon.
3. I watched a monkey running up a coconut tree.
4. The monkey watched us peeling a banana in the cage.
5. I saw a cute little rabbit on the way to school.
6. Dressed in a long blue evening gown, he thought she had never looked prettier.
7. Being a small town, one doesn't have to worry about crime.
8. You can read in the paper about someone having an accident every day.
9. Because of going to too many parties, my term paper was late.
10. We are having a series of lectures on religions of the world which will end May 30.

USING PARALLEL CONSTRUCTION

Your writing will be clearer if you use parallel construction. That is, when you make any kind of list, put the items in similar form. If you write

He's good at skiing, skating, and plays basketball.

the sentence lacks parallel construction. The items don't all have the same form. But if you write

He's good at skiing, skating, and playing basketball.

then the items are parallel. They all have the same form. They are all *ing* words. Or you could write

He skis, skates, and plays basketball.

Again the sentence has parallel construction because the items all use the present form of the verb. Here are some more examples. Note how much easier it is to read the sentences with parallel construction.

LACKING PARALLEL CONSTRUCTION	HAVING PARALLEL CONSTRUCTION
She liked to work hard, to save her money, and then she would spend it all on a trip.	She liked to work hard, to save her money, and then to spend it all on a trip. (All three items start with *to* and a verb.)
They were looking for a house with eight rooms, a two-car garage, and in a good location.	They were looking for a house with eight rooms, a two-car garage, and a good location. (All three items can be read smoothly after the preposition *with*.)
The interviewer wanted to know what college I had attended, whether I could use a word processor, and my experience.	The interviewer wanted to know what college I had attended, whether I could use a word processor, and what experience I had had. (All items are dependent clauses.)
She was brainy, a hard worker, attractive, and liked a good time.	She was brainy, industrious, attractive, and vivacious. (All four words describe her.)

The supporting points for a thesis statement (see p. 204) should always be parallel. For the following thesis statements, the supporting points in the left-hand column are not all constructed alike. Those in the right-hand column are; they are parallel.

NOT PARALLEL	**PARALLEL**
Belonging to a drama group was valuable.	Belonging to a drama group was valuable.
1. Dramatic training.	1. I got training in dramatics.
2. Speech improved.	2. It improved my enunciation.
3. Friendships.	3. I made good friends.
I've quit watching soaps.	I've quit watching soaps.
1. Wasting time.	1. I was wasting too much time.
2. All the same.	2. Soaps are all the same.
3. Compared with reading.	3. Reading does more for me.

Using parallel construction will make your writing more effective. Note the effective parallelism in these well-known quotations:

> Some books are to be tasted, others to be swallowed, and some few to be chewed and digested.
>
> —Francis Bacon

> Let every nation know, whether it wishes us well or ill, that we shall pay any price, bear any burden, meet any hardship, support any friend, oppose any foe to assure the survival and success of liberty.
>
> —John F. Kennedy

> Go back to Mississippi, go back to Alabama, go back to South Carolina, go back to Georgia, go back to Louisiana, go back to the slums and ghettos of our northern cities, knowing that somehow this situation can and will be changed.
>
> —Martin Luther King, Jr.

> Every right implies a responsibility, every opportunity an obligation, every possession a duty.
>
> —John D. Rockefeller, Jr.

EXERCISES

Most—but not all—of these sentences lack parallel construction. Cross out the part that is not parallel and write the correction above.

☐EXERCISE 1

1. I like staying up late at night and to sleep late in the morning.

2. She taught her preschool son by reading to him, by teaching him songs, by giving him constructive toys, and she took him on neighborhood excursions.

3. Each student was given a choice of writing a term paper, taking a written exam, or an oral report could be given.

4. She wants a house near the city and having modern conveniences.

5. I had read the textbook, read the reference books, written the term paper, and I had studied for the exam.

6. After we had eaten our supper, we put water on the fire, washed the dishes, and we packed the car for an early morning start.

7. Among the advantages of my new job are the short hours, the boss is pleasant, and the good salary.

8. I enjoy hiking, mountain climbing, and love camping out.

9. I have learned to adapt myself to new environments and how to get along with other people.

10. My small brother likes candy, popcorn, and chewing bubble gum.

☐EXERCISE 2

1. He washed the dishes, tidied the house, and was waiting for Sue to return.

2. He wrote his paper, had a friend read it, rewrote it, read it aloud, and rewrote it once more.

3. By careful planning, by smart shopping, and cooking economy meals, she stayed within their budget.

4. The driver warned us against littering, picking plants, or feeding the animals during our eight-hour drive through Denali National Park.

5. At the auction she bought a victrola, two old chairs, and she also bought an old popcorn popper.

6. If you want to create a beautiful room, it is more essential to have a knowledge of decorating than having a great deal of money.

7. The speaker was interesting, inspiring, and entertained the audience too.

8. I'm learning to read more rapidly, to improve my vocabulary, and I'm also reading better books.

9. He spoke with authority, illustrated his talk with personal incidents, and then he concluded with a poem.

10. He suggested doing all the exercises and that we rewrite all our papers.

□EXERCISE 3

1. With tact, kindness, and having understanding, one can usually help a disturbed child.

2. They chose a house in the country because they wanted to grow their own vegetables, to give their children a country environment, and to enjoy the quiet of rural life.

3. A coaching career offered him a good salary, enjoyable work, and he would have security.

4. Her garden included evergreens, deciduous trees, bushes, and there were all kinds of flowers.

5. She weeded them, pruned them, watered them, and sometimes she even sat and enjoyed them.

6. We tried to teach our puppy to sit up, to beg, and come when called.

7. I finished studying, had a snack, and then I went to bed.

8. The box is six inches long and five inches in width.

9. Radiation is something you can't see, can't feel, and you can't even smell it.

10. I like taking a leisurely walk to campus, getting to class a few minutes early, and then I get myself organized to take notes before the lecture begins.

☐EXERCISE 4

1. She took her children to art classes, skating classes, and to judo lessons.

2. The preschool gave Justin experience in working with his hands, in developing rhythm, and in getting along with others.

3. When Justin started kindergarten, however, he was shy, frightened, and he was unhappy.

4. A concerned teacher and children who were friendly soon changed his attitude.

5. He lost his shyness and his being afraid.

6. He became outgoing, happy, and he was interested in all that was going on.

7. His father bought him a paint set, wrapped it in fancy paper, and then he placed it at Justin's place at the table.

8. Justin's father was even-tempered, kind, and thought of others before himself.

9. He showed Justin how to root a plant, how to plant it, and finally the way fertilizer should be added.

10. That we give our children too many material things, that we don't develop values, and that we don't help them become creative were his main beliefs.

☐EXERCISE 5

1. Michelle has wanted a new job for a long time, has been offered several, and finally has accepted one in a dress shop.

2. She has previously worked as a secretary, a bookkeeper, and she has worked as a bank teller too.

3. Now she is responsible for checking the new shipments, pricing the clothes, and then she has to make the window displays.

4. The rest of the clerks merely have to keep the racks in order, the display counters should be kept neat, and of course wait on customers.

5. Her job is demanding, but she feels satisfied with what she is accomplishing; it's really challenging.

6. She likes a job where she meets people, where she can help people, and have some job security.

7. Her supervisor reports that she knows the stock well, is pleasant with customers, and that she gets along well with the other employees.

8. Last winter she went to Phoenix to attend a convention and for a vacation.

9. She brought back from Arizona turquoise beads, some Indian baskets, and she also brought back an Indian blanket.

10. She traveled by car, by bus, and train.

□EXERCISE 6

1. When our family went on a camping trip, we had rain, sleet, and it was cold the first day.

2. After we had set up camp, we cooked our supper, walked down to the beach, and watched the children playing in the water.

3. Then we went to a lecture that taught us the names of flowers and trees, the songs of birds, and to recognize the sounds of insects.

4. The lecture was informative and good entertainment.

5. The next morning on our walk through the woods, we saw the buds on the maple trees opening, the tightly rolled leaves of the May apples showing their heads above ground, and the anemone blossoms were waving in the wind.

6. We watched the waxwings eating berries, the starlings pecking in the grass, and a redheaded woodpecker was tapping away on a tree trunk.

7. Walking along the stream, looking for wild flowers, and to watch for birds fascinated me.

8. I enjoy living on a beach because I can sunbathe, sail, or I can go in swimming without driving miles to a resort.

9. I waxed my car, vacuumed the interior, and polished the chrome.

10. We found the summer camp challenging, enjoyable, and it taught us some things as well.

☐EXERCISE 7

1. My chief objectives in this course are to learn to spell, to learn to write good sentences, and being able to write a clear composition.

2. His talk was about law enforcement, gun control laws, and that crime is increasing.

3. He had traveled by land, by sea, and air.

4. She is a woman with infinite charm and who always says the tactful thing.

5. By then I had learned how to change the oil, how to check the battery, and the way to change a tire.

6. I must now do the laundry, buy some groceries, and I need to get some gas.

7. I'm going to quit studying, take a walk, have a snack, and go to bed.

8. For their dinner she planned to have fish, two vegetables, salad, and probably she'd also make a dessert.

9. Whether we'll go, when we'll go, and when we'll come back are still big questions.

10. With a lot of studying, a little tutoring, and a bit of luck, I may pass this course.

Review the thesis statements on page 130, and then make the supporting points of these thesis statements parallel.

☐EXERCISE 8

1. Every college student should know how to type.

    1. Some instructors require typed papers.

    2. Saves time.

    3. Get higher grades.

2. Going home every weekend is unwise.

    1. I spend too much time on the bus.

    2. I get behind in my college work.

    3. Expensive.

    4. Miss out on weekend activities at college.

3. Commercial billboards along highways should be prohibited.

    1. They often cause accidents.

    2. Mar scenery.

4. Learning to sew is valuable.

    1. Sewing your own clothes saves money.

    2. Creative.

Underline the examples of parallelism in these paragraphs. No answers are provided at the back of the book for this exercise.

☐EXERCISE 9

Every night from early April to early June on the beaches of St. Croix in the U.S. Virgin Islands, gravid female leatherback turtles crawl out of the sea to deposit their eggs in the sand. Each turtle digs with her smaller rear flippers a neat pit as deeply as she can reach and lays in it 80–85 eggs ranging from ping-pong ball to tennis ball size. She gently covers the eggs with sand, kicks up surrounding sand to disguise the nest, and heads back into the sea. Two months later the baby turtles hatch, spend a few days underground gaining energy by absorbing their yolk sacs, and then, again at night, scramble collectively to the sea.

For millions of years this reproductive cycle has been the leatherbacks' common practice. But no longer. Today leatherbacks are threatened by pollution of the seas, continued turtle hunting, and run-ins with fishermen. Their nesting beaches are poached for turtle eggs, are altered or destroyed by human development, are populated by both natural and exotic predators, and are washed away by erosion. The leatherbacks' survival is in jeopardy.

—*Earthwatch News*, December 1981

JOURNAL WRITING

Write two sentences with parallel construction, one telling the qualities you look for in a friend and the other telling your reasons for wanting a college education.

CORRECTING SHIFT IN TIME

If you begin writing a paper in past time, don't shift now and then to the present; and if you begin in the present, don't shift to the past. In the following paragraph the writer starts in the present and then shifts to the past.

> In *The Old Man and the Sea*, the Old Man has to fight not only the marlin and the sharks but also the doubts in his own mind. He wasn't sure that he still had the strength to subdue the giant marlin.

It should be all in the present:

> In *The Old Man and the Sea*, the Old Man has to fight not only the marlin and the sharks but also the doubts in his own mind. He isn't sure that he still has the strength to subdue the giant marlin.

Or it could be all in the past:

> In *The Old Man and the Sea*, the Old Man had to fight not only the marlin and the sharks but also the doubts in his own mind. He wasn't sure that he still had the strength to subdue the giant marlin.

EXERCISES

These sentences have shifts in time, either from past to present or from present to past. Make all the verbs in each sentence agree with the first verb used. Cross out the incorrect verb and write the correct one above it.

□EXERCISE 1

1. In my excitement I stumbled over rocks and dirt and then finally I see what looks like a path.
2. We hiked to the end of the trail, and then we come back.
3. We rented a boat, went out on the lake, and watched the sunset before we come in for supper on the beach.
4. In the short story "The Secret Life of Walter Mitty," Mr. Mitty is first driving his car, but then in his mind the car became an airplane.
5. When Mr. Mitty's wife asks him why he isn't wearing his gloves, he suddenly thought of surgeon's gloves and became a doctor performing an operation on a millionaire banker.

6. I heard a knock, and then in comes my old high school friend.
7. I went to my room to dress but suddenly remember that my clothes were all in the washer.
8. The heroine was rescued after the speedboat turns over.
9. He tells us he'll write, but he never wrote.
10. Berne's book lists the games people play and told why they play them.

☐EXERCISE 2

1. The candidate gave his speech, answered questions, and then came down from the stage and goes around shaking hands with everyone.
2. We worked the entire summer at the camp, and then at the end the director surprises us with an extra week's pay.
3. The bad guy shoots at the good guy, but of course the good guy escaped.
4. The heroine gives up her right to the fortune, but she got it finally anyway.
5. I wanted to do my best in that course; I give it all I have.
6. I finished the dishes, set the table for morning, and crawl into bed.
7. Friends are important to me, especially because I had no close relatives.
8. She loved that little house and goes back to see it again and again.
9. I took one look at the clock and run for the bus.
10. The book gave an account of Freud's work, but it doesn't tell much about his life.

The following paragraphs from student papers shift back and forth between past time and present. Change the verbs to agree with the first verb used, thus making the entire paragraph read smoothly.

☐EXERCISE 3

As I traveled down the highway, I signal to turn left. I start the turn, and all of a sudden I heard a braking noise that could be heard for miles. A man had tried to pass me and had not seen my signal, probably because of the glaring sunlight. The man stopped finally. Really not knowing what I was doing, I pull off the road. Then it hit me, a sick feeling that reached all parts of my body. I stop the truck and get out, stunned but relieved.

☐EXERCISE 4

That summer I decided to buy a radio receiver with the money I had earned mowing lawns. I set it up in my bedroom, and then I spent an afternoon putting an antenna on the roof. My mother stands down there on the lawn hollering advice at me because she's afraid I'm going to fall off the roof. In spite of her I finally get it up, and then I went inside and connected the antenna to the receiver. Presto! I am listening to radios all over the world. Eventually I decide I want a ham radio operator's license too so I could transmit back to some of the stations I was hearing. I got the license all right, but being young and shy, I never did much talking. Mostly I just listen and work on my equipment. After a few months I tired of my new toy and never did any more with it. The challenge of striving for the set was more fun than actually having it.

☐EXERCISE 5

The astronomer Carl Sagan says that life elsewhere in the cosmos is probable. He said there are many places where life could develop. In the Milky Way, for example, there are 400 billion suns, and most may have planetary systems. Sagan says that the building blocks of life form readily and that there are billions of years of time for evolution. He said it's likely that life has emerged in a large number of places and that intelligence has emerged in a smaller number of places.

☐EXERCISE 6

Early people had to find shelter in nature. In warm climates trees provide shelter, but in cold climates caves were the best protection. The people built a fire at the mouth of the cave to keep fierce animals away, and they live near the fire rather than in the damp, chill interior of the cave. Several families live together in a cave and hunted together. This was the beginning of group living.

☐EXERCISE 7

Even though Robert Frost eventually became the most beloved of New England poets, his early career was not promising. After a few months in college, he decides that the routine of study is too much for him, and he became a bobbin boy in a mill. Later he married and once more tried college at Harvard but gave up after two years. Then followed a period in which he tramps, teaches school, makes shoes, and edits a weekly paper. Finally his grandfather took pity on him and bought him a farm. For eleven years he tried with scant success to wrest a living from the stony hills. During all this time he is writing poetry, but no magazine wanted it. Not until he sold his farm and went to England, where his first book of poems was published, did he become known. When he returned to America three years later, he finds himself famous.

JOURNAL WRITING

Write a brief paragraph describing an accident you once had. Then write another paragraph describing the same accident as if it is happening at this moment.

CORRECTING SHIFT IN PERSON

You may write a paper in

First person—*I, we*
Second person—*you*
Third person—*he, she, they, one, anyone, a person, people*

but do not shift from one group to another.

Wrong: In painting a room, one should prepare the surface carefully. Otherwise you won't get a smooth finish.

Right: In painting a room, one should prepare the surface carefully. Otherwise one won't get a smooth finish.

Right: In painting a room, you should prepare the surface carefully. Otherwise you won't get a smooth finish.

Wrong: Few *people* get as much enjoyment out of music as *they* could. *One* need not be an accomplished musician to get some fun out of playing an instrument. Nor do *you* need to be very far advanced before joining an amateur group of players.

Right: Few *people* get as much enjoyment out of music as *they* could. *One* need not be an accomplished musician to get some fun out of playing an instrument. Nor is it necessary to be very far advanced before joining an amateur group of players.

Too many *one*'s in a paper make it sound stilted and formal. Often a sentence can be revised (as in the last sentence of the last example) to avoid using either *one* or *you*.

Also, too frequent use of the expressions *he or she* and *him or her* can make a paper sound awkward. Turn back to page 114 to see how a sentence can be revised to avoid sex bias without using those expressions.

Wrong: A student should get to class on time; otherwise you may miss something.

Right (but awkward): A student should get to class on time; otherwise he or she may miss something.

Better: Students should get to class on time; otherwise they may miss something.

Often students write *you* in a paper when they don't really mean *you, the reader.*

You could tell that no one had been there in weeks.

Such sentences are always improved by getting rid of the *you.*

Obviously no one had been there in weeks.

Sometimes, though, a shift to *you* is permissible. The brief article on page 91 shifts quite logically to *you* in the last paragraph because the writer wants to talk directly to the reader. The essay on page 220 shifts to *you* in the first sentence of paragraph 3 for humorous effect. And the essay on page 222 uses *you* in the first sentence to catch the reader's attention. These are all special cases. As a rule, a shift to *you* should be avoided.

EXERCISES

Change the pronouns (and verbs when necessary) so that there will be no shift in person. Cross out the incorrect words and write the correct ones above. Sometimes you may want to change a sentence from singular to plural to avoid using too many *one's* or the awkward *he or she* (see p. 114). Sentence 5 below is an example.

☐EXERCISE 1

1. If you do all these exercises, one should be able to get an *A.*
2. I like the feeling that comes when you have reviewed thoroughly and feel ready for any exam.
3. We used to fight a lot when we were kids, but as you grow up you become more friendly.
4. I'm learning to spell, but I find you really have to work at it.
5. A student should have a study schedule. Otherwise you won't get all your work finished.
6. I studied until midnight; after that your brain just doesn't function well.
7. I discovered when I got to college that you can't take it easy the way you did in high school.

8. If parents expect their children to be unselfish, you have to set the example.
9. To improve your reading ability, one should read a great deal.
10. Those who want to go on the field trip should get your equipment now.

☐EXERCISE 2

1. In high school I took a course called General Woods in which you made a piece of furniture. You did this on your own with a little help from the teacher. I made a coffee table, which my teacher encouraged me later to enter in a state contest.
2. Mr. Martin was one of the best teachers I ever had. He would give you two work sheets every day, and if you didn't do them, he would keep after you until you did. And he was the kind of teacher you could tell your problems to. I'll never forget the talks I had with him.
3. The part of the accounting course I liked best was the practice sets. We did four sets during the semester. Doing them made you feel you were getting the experience of working for a company because we wrote checks, filed papers, and wrote in journals and ledgers. The practice sets prepared you for the business world.

When students write *you* in a paper, they usually don't mean *you, the reader.* Eliminate the *you* in these sentences. Getting rid of the *you* will usually get rid of wordiness too.

☐EXERCISE 3

1. You should have seen the mountain of presents she received.
2. You'll find that jogging is good for your health.
3. One should get some exercise every day if you want to stay healthy.
4. You can imagine how upset I was when I heard about the accident.

5. As the plane took off, you could see the entire city below.

6. You can imagine how delighted I was to receive his letter.

7. You've never seen such a mess as my desk was in.

8. When we had gone a hundred miles, you could hear a thumping in the engine.

9. You ought to see how we've improved our garden.

10. Anyone who wants to lose weight has to cut out sugar, and you have to stick to some rigid diet.

Revise these student papers so there will be no shift in person.

☐EXERCISE 4

FREEDOM COSTS FREEDOM

I had worked all summer to save money for my first car. For months I'd kept at my job every day and saved every penny I earned. I'd never buy donuts at coffee break or dessert at lunch because every dollar saved brought me closer to the car I wanted so much. Finally for a few hundred dollars I bought a car that was just right for me.

A car is more than just a means of getting around. It's a status symbol. It's your sign of independence. It's your ticket to freedom. You don't have to ask to borrow the family car, and you don't have to explain where you are going or when you'll be back. Now I could drive where I wanted when I wanted.

The one thing I hadn't counted on, though, was how much it cost to keep a car running. With insurance, gas, and repairs, I found myself working just to support my car. My paychecks went for new wheel rims, car stereo components, and every accessory you could think of. I worked extra evenings to buy plush seatcovers and overtime on weekends to buy new tires.

Funny how it costs so much of your freedom to support your freedom.

☐**EXERCISE 5**

FLOATING ON A CLOUD

Ever since I'd seen pictures of hot air balloons, I knew I'd have to try one. They looked so beautiful and peaceful as they floated along. Finally I made arrangements for a flight, and today was the day.

Driving to a field outside the city, I joined the pilot and some friends. Together we unloaded the balloon from a trailer, spread it on the grass, and inflated it. It was amazing to watch a bundle of fabric expand to such an enormous size, its bright yellow and red colors lit up by the morning sun.

When a balloon is inflated with hot air, it really wants to fly, so I hopped in the basket with the pilot, and he turned up the gas burner until the others outside couldn't hold us down. As we rose silently and slowly into the morning sky, you could see the people below getting smaller and smaller. The serenity was marred only by the noise from the burner that the pilot turned on periodically to keep the air in the balloon hot.

Flying in a balloon is about as close to floating on a cloud as you can get. You can't feel the wind, of course, because you are drifting with it, but you can see the ground moving along beneath you. We rose higher by running the burner and then drifted lower as the air cooled off. When we went low, a dog in a yard barked wildly at us; when we went high, you could see for miles. Then sometimes we just hung there quietly in the sky.

After a couple of hours the pilot carefully let the balloon cool off, and we descended gently into a field. The landing was so soft it almost seemed as if we were still in the air. Our friends drove up, and as we deflated the balloon and loaded it back on the trailer, they congratulated us on a beautiful flight.

Few experiences you could have could compare with floating on a cloud.

JOURNAL WRITING

1. Write a brief paragraph—three sentences will do—telling a friend how to develop good study habits. It will, of course, be a "you should" paragraph.
2. Then write the same paragraph to yourself—an "I should" paragraph.
3. Finally write the same paragraph using "students should" and using the pronoun *they.*

CORRECTING WORDINESS

Good writing is concise writing. Don't say something in ten words if you can say it as well, or better, in five. "In this day and age" is not as effective as simply "today." "At the present time" should be "at present" or "now."

Another kind of wordiness comes from saying something twice. There is no need to say "in the month of July" or "7 A.M. in the morning" or "my personal opinion." July *is* a month, 7 A.M. *is* the morning, and my opinion obviously *is* personal. All you need to say is "in July," "7 A.M.," and "my opinion."

Still another kind of wordiness comes from using expressions that add nothing to the meaning of the sentence. "The fact of the matter is that I'm tired" says no more than "I'm tired."

Here are more examples of wordiness.

WORDY WRITING	CONCISE WRITING
at that point in time	then
there is no doubt but that	no doubt
he is a person who	he
a person who is honest	an honest person
there are many boys who	many boys
he was there in person	he was there
personally I think	I think
my father he	my father
surrounded on all sides	surrounded
during the winter months	during the winter
brown in color	brown
refer back	refer
repeat again	repeat
two different kinds	two kinds
free complimentary copy	complimentary copy
free gift	gift
very unique	unique
past history	history
end result	result
and etc.	etc.
usual custom	custom
new innovation	innovation
the field of electronics	electronics
no money at all	no money
each and every	each
final outcome	outcome

EXERCISES

Cross out words or rewrite parts of each sentence to get rid of the wordiness. Doing these exercises can almost turn into a game to see how few words you can use without changing the meaning of the sentence.

□EXERCISE 1

1. I woke up at 4 A.M. in the morning.
2. We were considering the question as to whether we should charge admission.
3. There are many people who never read a book from one end of the year to the other.
4. After our lengthy hike that lasted over eight hours, we were hungry for food.
5. He had tried several different sports. These sports included football, basketball, and hockey.
6. He is a man who can be depended upon to do what he says he will do.
7. I had an unexpected surprise yesterday when the guy who had roomed with me in college stopped in to see me.
8. I think, if I am not mistaken, that she is really planning to go.
9. I found that I had no money at all by the end of the year.
10. All of the three different kinds of stones we found were very unique.

□EXERCISE 2

1. There is no doubt but that our team will win.
2. They carried him to his place of residence in an intoxicated condition.
3. At this point in time there is a lot more permissiveness than there used to be in years gone by.
4. In my personal opinion there is no doubt but that justice is too slow in this country of ours.
5. What I am trying to say is that in my opinion justice should be swift and sure.
6. He is a man who has worked hard all his life.

7. It is his height that makes him such a good basketball player.
8. The melons were large in size and sweet in taste.
9. The great percentage of students do not leave the campus on weekends.
10. The last point that I will try to make in this paper is the idea that one should learn more at college than just what is learned from one's courses.

☐EXERCISE 3

1. There were a lot of people there.
2. At the present time thousands of acres of land are under water along the river.
3. Personally I think something should be done to prevent all this flooding.
4. It is my opinion that no one seems to be working on the problem.
5. Finally the doctor arrived on the scene, but absolutely nothing could be done for her.
6. The plane circled around the airport for half an hour and then disappeared from view.
7. I was unaware of the fact that she had arrived.
8. The reason he left college was that he wanted some experience in the world of business.
9. In this modern day and age, it is important for the wealthier countries to help the developing countries all over the world by giving them aid.
10. In the year of 1981 my brother accepted a new job with the Bell and Howell Company, which is located in the city of Chicago.

☐EXERCISE 4

1. It is my personal opinion that most people these days are spending entirely too much of their leisure time watching programs presented on TV.
2. The fact of the matter is that I completely forgot about the meeting that was scheduled for last night.

3. Most writers use too many words, repeating themselves and saying things over and over again.
4. When driving a new car for the first time, one must take care not to drive too fast for the first 500 miles.
5. With reference to your letter, I may say that I really appreciate your kind invitation and am happy that I am able to accept.
6. What I intend to do is to finish my year here and then look for a job that will bring in some money.
7. Most people, you will find, want a business form that is clear, concise, and easy to understand.
8. It seems to me that the president should take it upon herself to see that the motion comes to a vote of the members of the organization.
9. I couldn't help but think that she was just pretending to be ill.
10. I am making an effort to try to get rid of wordiness in my papers.

On a separate sheet rewrite this paragraph from a university publication, cutting its 117 words to about 47 and see how much more effective it will be.

☐EXERCISE 5

One of the main problems of a student entering university is how to find his way around the twelve floors of the Library and how to use the materials. The students are confronted by rows of books, journals, complicated indexes, abstracts and ponderous reference works, and need help in finding the information they seek amid the mass of material. The Library staff recognizes its responsibility to help them utilize all this material. Orientation programs are given to all new students. Many faculty members bring their classes to a particular subject area or to the Government Publications for an orientation. Short printed handouts are available, such as special subject bibliographies, how to use periodical indexes or psychological abstracts.

AVOIDING CLICHÉS

A cliché is an expression that has been used so often it has lost its originality and effectiveness. Whoever first said "light as a feather" had thought of an original way to express lightness, but today that expression is outworn and boring. Most of us use an occasional cliché in speaking, but clichés have no place in writing. The good writer thinks up fresh new ways to express ideas.

Here are a few clichés. Add some more to the list.

all work and no play
apple of his eye
as luck would have it
as white as snow
better late than never
blue in the face
bright and early
by leaps and bounds
by the skin of our teeth
center of attention
cool as a cucumber
die laughing
easier said than done
few and far between
heavy as lead
last but not least
last straw
quick as a flash
sadder but wiser
short but sweet
sigh of relief
slick as a whistle
slowly but surely
thank my lucky stars
too funny for words
work like a dog

Clichés are boring because the reader always knows what's coming next. What comes next in these expressions?

beat a hasty . . .
burning the midnight . . .
cold as . . .
fit as a . . .
frightened out of . . .
goes without . . .
have a nice . . .
pretty kettle of . . .
raining cats and . . .
ripe old . . .
save wear and . . .
smart as a . . .
throw caution to the . . .

On a separate sheet rewrite these sentences to get rid of the clichés.

☐EXERCISE 1

1. I hadn't cracked a book all weekend, so I decided to do a little studying before I hit the hay.
2. But then quick as a flash I had a better idea.
3. Studying is a pain in the neck, and I decided I'd rather dabble in the culinary art.
4. Therefore I went to the kitchen and slowly but surely got out all my equipment.
5. But as luck would have it, there were no eggs in the fridge and no cake mix in the cupboard.
6. I was at loose ends. You'd have died laughing if you'd seen me.
7. Since I couldn't find ingredients for anything, I decided to give the kitchen a cleaning to end all cleanings.
8. I worked like a dog and had everything clean as a whistle in no time at all.
9. But all good things must come to an end, and I finally decided that I'd better hit the books.
10. I studied that night until I was blue in the face, but the next morning I was up bright and early and all ready to ace that exam.

☐EXERCISE 2

One way to become aware of clichés so you won't use them in your writing is to see how many you can purposely put into a paragraph. Write a paragraph describing your first morning on campus or on a job, using all the clichés possible while still keeping your account smooth and clear. You might start something like this: "I was up at the crack of dawn, fresh as a daisy, and raring to go . . . ." What title will you give your paper? Why a cliché of course! Writing such a paragraph should make you so aware of clichés that they'll never creep into your writing again.

Review of Sentence Structure

One sentence in each pair is correct; the other is incorrect. Read both sentences carefully before you decide. Then write the letter of the *correct* sentence in the blank. You may find any one of these errors:

run-together sentence
fragment
wrong verb form
lack of agreement between subject and verb and pronoun
wrong pronoun
faulty reference of pronoun
dangling modifier
lack of parallel construction
shift in time or person

_____ 1. A. You're right this can't go on.
B. My sister and I planned the program.

_____ 2. A. The tutor helped both Renée and me.
B. It don't matter if you're a little late.

_____ 3. A. One of my friends is getting a job for the summer.
B. I intended to study, but I watch a TV program instead.

_____ 4. A. Laughter is an indication of mental health some people never laugh.
B. She had lost her camera but hoped she would find it.

_____ 5. A. If one wants a thrill, you should try waterskiing.
B. Our team won the first game but lost in the finals.

_____ 6. A. We was planning a get-together after the game.
B. I worked for hours but didn't get my paper finished.

_____ 7. A. Each of my sisters has her own car now.
B. Getting that *A* pleases me and gave me new confidence.

_____ 8. A. He had worked as a farmhand, a chauffeur, and in a mine.
B. That sports car belongs to my fiancé and me.

_____ 9. A. Hoping for years that I could go to college and then finally making it.
B. I liked his good humor, his easygoing way, and his generosity.

_____ 10. A. He was surprise to hear from her.
B. They invited my boyfriend and me to their cottage.

_____ 11. A. The professor told my friend and I that we had passed.
B. One of us is making a mistake.

_____ 12. A. Each of the candidates is well qualified for the job.
B. Bright red and steaming, I took the lobster from the boiling water.

_____ 13. A. The group leader asked my wife and me to canvass our block.
B. Because he wanted people he could depend on.

_____ 14. A. You was certainly the best runner we had.
B. We freshmen were entertained by the upperclassmen.

_____ 15. A. They invited Nan and me to dinner.
B. An invitation which of course pleased us.

_____ 16. A. She ask me to help her with the refreshments.
B. Drive carefully.

_____ 17. A. When I entered the cottage, you could see that someone had been there.
B. I've finished mowing the lawn and now am going to rest.

_____ 18. A. The president asked Karen and me to be on the nominating committee.
B. I can't decide whether to become a teacher, a secretary, or go into social work.

_____ 19. A. Having finished all my homework, I went to bed.
B. He told his dad that his car needed a tune-up.

_____ 20. A. Every one of my plants are withering.
B. They expected us students to keep our rooms tidy.

_____ 21. A. One of my cousins is getting married in the spring.
B. Which is what we had been expecting her to do.

_____ 22. A. Running to catch the bus, she slipped and fell.
B. I had finish my paper before it was due.

_____ 23. A. Because most of us intend to get jobs during vacation.
B. Having finished play practice, they went out for some food.

_____ 24. A. A list of readings was posted in the library.
B. He always comes late therefore he often misses the assignment.

_____ 25. A. You can improve your vocabulary it just takes determination.
B. Winning that trophy was the best thing that ever happened to him.

3

Punctuation and Capital Letters

3 Punctuation and Capital Letters

PERIOD, QUESTION MARK, EXCLAMATION MARK, SEMICOLON, COLON, DASH

Every mark of punctuation should help your reader. Just like Stop and Go signals at an intersection, marks of punctuation will keep the reader, like the traffic, from getting snarled up.

Here are the rules for six marks of punctuation. The first three you have known for a long time and have no trouble with. The one about semicolons you learned when you studied independent clauses (p. 71). The one about the colon may be less familiar.

Put a period at the end of a sentence and after most abbreviations.

Mr.	Ms.	Dr.	Wed.	sq. ft.
Mrs.	etc.	Jan.	P.M.	lbs.

Put a question mark after a direct question (but not after an indirect one).

Shall we go? (the exact words of the speaker)
He asked whether we should go. (not the exact words)

Put an exclamation mark after an expression that shows strong emotion.

Great! You're just in time!

Put a semicolon between two closely related independent clauses unless they are joined by one of the connecting words *and, but, for, or, nor, yet, so.* (Refer to pp. 71–72 for more information about the semicolon.)

The rain came down in torrents; we ran for shelter.
I have work to do; therefore I must leave.

Actually you can write acceptably without ever using semicolons because a period and capital letter can always be used instead of a semicolon.

The rain came down in torrents. We ran for shelter.
I have work to do. Therefore I must leave.

Put a colon after a complete statement when a list or long quotation follows.

We took the following items: hot dogs, potato chips, and coffee. (*We took the following items* is a complete statement. You can hear your voice fall at the end of it. Therefore we put a colon after it before adding the list.)

We took hot dogs, potato chips, and coffee. (Here *We took* is not a complete statement; it needs the list to make it complete. Therefore, since we don't want to separate the list from the first part of the sentence, no colon is used.)

The speaker closed with a quotation from Emerson: "The only true gift is a portion of thyself." (*The speaker closed with a quotation from Emerson* is a complete statement. Therefore we put a colon after it before adding the quotation.)

Emerson said, "The only true gift is a portion of thyself." (*Emerson said* is not a complete statement. Therefore we don't put a colon after it.)

Use a dash when there is an abrupt change of thought.

A mother's role is to deliver children—by labor once and by car forever after.

EXERCISES

Add the necessary punctuation to these sentences (period, question mark, exclamation mark, semicolon, colon). Not all sentences require additional punctuation. Also, your answer may not always agree with the one at the back of the book because independent clauses can be separated either with a semicolon or with a period and capital letter. In general, use a period and capital letter. Only if the clauses are closely related in meaning should a semicolon be used.

☐EXERCISE 1

1. Hurry We've only two minutes until the bus leaves.
2. He asked whether we had seen his wife.
3. She was late however she still made the bus.
4. It was an hour's trip to Lake Placid we'd never been there before.
5. The snow was deep and crusty it was a perfect day for skiing.
6. That was the beginning of a good week I'll never forget it.
7. I couldn't decide what I liked best the skiing, the scenery, or the food.

8. That was only the first of our trips it made us want more.
9. We visited the following national parks Yellowstone, Glacier, and Yosemite.
10. We visited Yellowstone, Glacier, and Yosemite.

☐EXERCISE 2

1. Henry Ford built his first car in a shed behind his home, using the following materials scrap metal, four bicycle wheels, and a doorbell for a horn.
2. By 1906 he was ready to try it out he was too excited, however, to wait until morning.
3. At 3 A.M. he cranked it and rode out of the shed America has never been the same since.
4. In 1908 his first Model T appeared by 1913 he was turning out over 200,000 Model T's a year.
5. A model T cost $290 in 1924 that would be equivalent to $1,680 today.
6. By 1930 there were 23 million cars on the road in the United States that was one for every five people.
7. For years the U.S. auto companies had no competition then came the gasoline shortage.
8. People turned from the big gas guzzlers to the compacts American companies could not keep up.
9. The Japanese could because they had three advantages more efficiently operated plants, teamwork between labor and management, and devoted employees.
10. American companies are learning from the Japanese therefore they are now making a comeback.

☐EXERCISE 3

1. Ervin has been collecting fossils for years he now has a large collection.
2. He finds the fossils in various places creek beds, gulleys, ravines.
3. He has found most of them in the surrounding countryside a few he has bought.
4. His practiced eye can always spot a likely rock he's always on the lookout for them.
5. Fossils are the hardened remains or traces of prehistoric plants or animals they were embedded in the earth's crust in past geological ages.
6. Some fossils are on the surface of rocks others appear only when the rock is broken open.
7. One fossil may show the fronds of a fern another may show the skeleton of a small fish.

8. Still another may be the imprint of a leaf another may reveal the outline of a worm.
9. Fossils reveal much about the age of the earth, about prehistoric plants and animals, and about the evolution of the species.
10. Ervin is now giving his collection to a state park it will be an exhibit worth seeing.

□EXERCISE 4

1. Ancient civilizations had no clocks they did, however, have simple devices for measuring time.
2. The early timekeepers were sundials, notched candles, and hourglasses.
3. No one knows the date of the first hourglass it was probably invented about 2,000 years ago.
4. A huge mechanical clock was installed in the Cathedral of Strasbourg in France in 1354 it was far from accurate however.
5. In 1656 a Dutch scientist invented the pendulum his invention revolutionized timekeeping.
6. By 1800 pocket watches became popular not until 1914, however, were wristwatches accurate enough to compete with pocket watches.
7. The early Egyptians divided their nights into 12 parts each part represented the rising of a certain star.
8. They divided their days into 12 parts too the length of the hours varied, however, according to the season.
9. In winter the hours were short in summer they were long.
10. Today we still follow the Egyptian custom of dividing our days into 24 parts the parts, though, have now become of equal length.

□EXERCISE 5

1. Lincoln at six-feet-four was our tallest president Taft at 332 pounds was our heaviest.
2. Nine presidents never attended college three had been college or university presidents.
3. Among those who never went to college were the following Washington, Lincoln, and Truman.
4. The three who had been college or university presidents were Garfield, Wilson, and Eisenhower.
5. Ronald Reagan at 69 became the oldest elected president John Fitzgerald Kennedy at 43 was the youngest elected president.
6. Theodore Roosevelt became president at 42 he was not, however, elected president but merely moved up from the vice-presidency at the death of William McKinley.

7. Four presidents were assassinated Lincoln, Garfield, McKinley, and Kennedy.
8. Richard Nixon was the only president to resign he was also the first to visit all 50 states while in office.
9. Eisenhower was the first president to appear on national television he appeared during his election campaign.
10. Franklin D. Roosevelt was the only president to serve more than two terms he served twelve years, one month, and eight days.

☐EXERCISE 6

1. Did you know that horses are making a comeback on farms.
2. For years horses were considered an outmoded source of energy now they are the latest thing.
3. On many farms giant draft horses are being used for the following jobs planting, plowing, mowing, and hay-loading.
4. Horses don't compact the soil thus they are better in that way than tractors.
5. They have no trouble starting on a cold morning tractors sometimes do.
6. They will work for 15 or 20 years the average life of a tractor is about half that.
7. Horses are a source of power that reproduces itself other kinds of power deplete the source.
8. But of course the main advantage of horses is that they are fueled by homegrown food furthermore they add fertilizer to the soil.
9. It is true that a tractor can move more than three times as many logs in a day as horses can however the horses don't tear up tree roots or skim away the bark of other trees.
10. Horses will never take the place of tractors on huge farms they are useful, however, as an alternate energy source for smaller jobs.

☐EXERCISE 7

1. Have you ever been to Greenfield Village in Dearborn, Michigan.
2. It's not only a reconstructed historical village it's almost an autobiography of Henry Ford.
3. In his early years Ford wasn't interested in the past then in 1919 he began to reconstruct the old Ford family farm.
4. Later he moved the buildings to Dearborn then he began to add other buildings.
5. He reconstructed the shop where he had built his first horseless carriage next he added the first factory of the Ford Motor Company.
6. No expense was too great he spent half a million, for example, to restore an old country inn.

7. The 107 houses and shops in the village span 300 years of American history and include a toy store, drugstore, barbership, baker's shop, milliner's shop, and locksmith's shop.
8. Ford scoured the country to find furniture and china to refurnish the buildings he wanted an example of every article that had been used in America from the days of the first settlers to his own day.
9. Nothing was too small or insignificant for his museum one collection, for example, shows the evolution of the clothespin.
10. His Model T Ford had just about abolished the old way of life Ford tried, however, to reconstruct that way of life in Greenfield Village.

□EXERCISE 8

1. Why is the U.S. so slow in adopting metric.
2. In Canada speed limits are posted in metric gas is measured in liters.
3. But the U.S. still clings to miles, gallons, pounds, and ounces.
4. Only four other nations in the world have not converted to metric Brunei, Burma, Yemen Arab Republic (North), and People's Democratic Republic of Yemen (South).
5. But the U.S. still resists change a Gallup Poll in 1977 showed that Americans opposed metric by more than two to one.
6. And now, unfortunately, funds to promote metric have been cut therefore any change in attitude will be slow.
7. There are, however, a few hopeful signs industry is finding it difficult to sell nonmetric goods abroad and may promote metric.
8. And a few large corporations have switched furthermore even some government agencies, including NASA, have converted.
9. But the most hopeful sign is that more than half the states now require metric instruction in the schools thus the next generation will not have metric phobia.
10. Soon the new generation will take over management then maybe they will bring the U.S. into line with the rest of the world.

□EXERCISE 9

1. Terry Fox was an outstanding Canadian soccer and basketball player then he lost his right leg to cancer.
2. But he refused to give up he decided to run a "marathon of hope" across Canada to aid cancer research.
3. He started in Newfoundland in April 1980 his goal was to finish in Vancouver.
4. Terry ran with a kind of hop and skip on his artificial leg some days he ran as much as 30 miles.

5. He endured all kinds of weather rain, snow, hailstones, and blistering heat.
6. Everyone admired his pluck and perseverance they came out to see him and to give him money or pledges.
7. In Toronto 10,000 people greeted him he had become a national hero.
8. Then in September, halfway across Canada, he had to give up the disease had spread to his lungs.
9. In four and a half months he had run 3,317 miles furthermore he had collected over $20 million for the Canadian Cancer Society.
10. And he had made his point "I wanted to show people," he said, "that just because they're disabled, it's not the end."

□EXERCISE 10

1. Our friends have moved they live on the north side of town now.
2. We'd like a house and garden just like theirs it's our ideal.
3. Last week a flock of Bohemian waxwings descended on their garden all the pyracantha berries were gone in an hour.
4. A scrub jay has become tame it will hop on their patio table and accept bits of food.
5. Their house is small it's in a good neighborhood though.
6. And everything is within walking distance they seldom use their car.
7. That's a big advantage it saves both time and money.
8. I never used to worry about miles per gallon now I do.
9. I used to jump in my car for every small errand now I usually walk.
10. It's making a difference I now fill my gas tank less often.

JOURNAL WRITING

Write two sentences, the first requiring a colon and the second not requiring a colon, in which you list the things you have to do this coming weekend. Make sure, of course, that the items are parallel.

COMMAS

Students often sprinkle commas through their papers as if they were shaking pepper out of a pepper shaker. Don't use a comma unless you know a rule for it. But commas are important. They help the reader. Without them, a reader would often have to go back and reread a sentence to find out what the writer meant.

Actually you need only six comma rules. MASTER THESE SIX RULES, and your writing will be easier to read. The first rule you have already learned (p. 72).

1. Put a comma before *and, but, for, or, nor, yet, so* when they connect two independent clauses.

He found a quarter, and that was the end of his studying.
I may try to get a new job, or I may stick with this one.

But be sure such words do connect two independent clauses. The following sentence is merely one independent clause with one subject and two verbs. Therefore no comma should be used.

She wanted to go to college but didn't have enough money.

2. Put a comma between items in a series.

He ordered pie, cake, and ice cream.
She slammed the door, ran down the walk, and got in her car.

Some words "go together" and don't need a comma between them even though they do make up a series.

He wore a baggy old red sweater.
The bright blue morning sky gave her a lift.

The way to tell whether a comma is needed between two words in a series is to see whether *and* could be used naturally between them. It would sound all right to say *pie and cake and ice cream*; therefore commas are used. But it would not sound right to say *baggy and old and red sweater* or *bright and blue and morning sky*; therefore no commas are used. Simply put a comma where an *and* would sound right.

It's permissible to omit the comma before the *and* connecting the last two members of a series, but more often it's used.

If an address or date is used in a sentence, treat it as a series, putting a comma after every item, including the last.

> He was born on May 17, 1962, in Okmulgee, Oklahoma, and grew up there.
> She lived in Chicago Heights, Illinois, for two years.

When only the month and year are used in a date, the commas may be omitted.

> In May 1980 he moved to Macon, Georgia.

3. **Put a comma after an introductory expression or afterthought that doesn't flow smoothly into the sentence.** It may be a word, a group of words, or a dependent clause.

> Yes, I'll go.
> Well, that was the end of that.
> Moreover, the umpire agreed with me.
> It's cold this morning, isn't it?
> Running down the hill, she slipped and fell.
> When everyone had left, the auditorium was locked for the night.

When you studied dependent clauses, you learned that a dependent clause at the beginning of a sentence needs a comma after it. In the last example you can see that a comma is necessary. Otherwise the reader would read *When everyone had left the auditorium . . .* before realizing that that was not what the writer meant. A comma prevents misreading.

EXERCISES

Punctuate these sentences according to the first three comma rules. Correct your answers ten at a time.

☐EXERCISE 1

1. When I am going on a trip I plan long in advance.
2. I read travel brochures and I make lists of what I want to see.
3. If I have time I consult books in the library.
4. I also look at newspapers encyclopedias and travel magazines.

5. Yes planning is half the fun of travel.
6. Even if I'm not going far away the planning is enjoyable.
7. When I've done a lot of planning the entire trip goes more smoothly.
8. After I finish college I intend to take a really long trip.
9. I might go to Hawaii Tahiti or Australia.
10. Even if I don't go that far it's fun to think about it.

□EXERCISE 2

1. I've been having trouble concentrating lately and I have to do something about it.
2. Since I've been out of school for several years it's difficult to get back in the swing.
3. Although my professors aren't dull my mind still wanders.
4. I'll be listening to an interesting lecture and then suddenly my mind is miles away.
5. Just a word can ensnare me and I'm off.
6. Since I've got to quit this daydreaming I'm trying a new plan.
7. Whenever my mind drifts off I put down a mark on a sheet of paper.
8. Then I yank my mind back and concentrate for a while.
9. At the end of every period I have a lot of marks but each day they become fewer.
10. One of these days I'll have no marks at all and then I'll have arrived.

□EXERCISE 3

1. I write all my papers and do all my exercises without fail.
2. After I've finished ten sentences I check my answers.
3. If I miss an answer I go back and reread the rules.
4. When I've done all the exercises I start my paper.
5. As soon as I have a good thesis statement I begin to write.
6. I often work on my paper all evening and finish about midnight.
7. When I finish my paper is usually two or three pages long.
8. After I've finished I have a sense of accomplishment.
9. I've learned something about writing and I'm proud of the result.
10. Even though I don't always like writing I like having written.

□EXERCISE 4

1. More than any other animal the bison is a symbol of the West.
2. Nearly wiped out in the 1800s the bison are now making a comeback.
3. When Lewis and Clark explored the West there were about 60 million bison.

4. But in the 1800s they were slaughtered by the settlers by sportsmen and by hide and meat hunters.
5. Hoping to subdue the Indians by cutting off their food supply the U.S. Army also slaughtered the bison.
6. By 1889 only 551 bison were alive in the United States and of those a herd of 20 was almost wiped out by poachers.
7. Under careful management the bison have now made a comeback and there are at present about 25,000 in the United States and Canada.
8. They are kept in preserves such as Yellowstone National Park National Bison Range in Montana and Theodore Roosevelt National Park in North Dakota.
9. While they are not completely free they are given adequate space to roam.
10. These shaggy beasts are part of our national heritage and they must be helped to survive.

☐EXERCISE 5

1. Of the 39 national parks in the United States only five are in the East.
2. They are Acadia in Maine Shenandoah in Virginia Mammoth Cave in Kentucky Everglades in Florida and Great Smoky Mountains in Tennessee and North Carolina.
3. Perhaps the best known is Mammoth Cave in Kentucky.
4. When I was in the South last summer I decided to visit Mammoth Cave.
5. I had read about stalactites and stalagmites but I was not prepared for their amazing variety.
6. A stalactite projects downward from the ceiling of the cave and a stalagmite projects upward from the floor.
7. Both are formed by the dripping of mineral-rich water and both have taken many years to form.
8. Some are tinted with manganese or iron oxide and have a purple brown or reddish tint.
9. While I was in the cave I also saw gypsum and crystal formations in the shapes of flowers.
10. There are 150 miles of passages on five levels and I walked along a few of the passages.

☐EXERCISE 6

1. Some of the most striking formations in Mammoth Cave are Crystal River Frozen Niagara and Cathedral Domes.
2. Before I left I took a boat ride on the underground Echo River.
3. Now I want to see more national parks for they include the most striking natural scenery of our country.

4. Our national parks cover some 16 million acres and they have about 275 million visitors a year.
5. Yellowstone was the first national park to be created and no other park the same size has as many natural wonders.
6. In Yellowstone are geysers hot springs lakes rivers and cataracts.
7. Of the 200 active geysers in Yellowstone Old Faithful is the most famous.
8. Ever since it was discovered in 1870 it has been spouting on an average of every 65 minutes.
9. Since the intent of national parks is to preserve the balance of nature animal and plant life are disturbed as little as possible.
10. Hunting and lumbering are prohibited but fishing is allowed.

□EXERCISE 7

1. With a galloping speed of up to 35 miles an hour the giraffe is one of the swiftest animals.
2. The Arabs called it *zarafa* or "swift creature" and thus it got its name.
3. Few animals are so delicate yet giraffes have survived for 25 million years.
4. Of the 400,000 giraffes that exist today most are in East Africa.
5. Of those that have been measured the tallest was 19 feet and 3 inches.
6. Since a giraffe's eyes are set in sockets bulging from its head it has almost 360-degree vision.
7. Each giraffe may eat 100 pounds of leaves twigs and branches in a day.
8. The giraffe curls its one-and-a-half-foot tongue around a branch draws it between its thick lips and skims off a mouthful of twigs.
9. Its favorite tree is the acacia and some acacia seeds won't take root unless they've been through a giraffe's digestive system.
10. The female giraffe gives birth while standing and drops her calf five or six feet to the grass.

□EXERCISE 8

1. Since giraffes do little harm they are likely to survive.
2. They seldom molest anyone and they don't kill people as lions do.
3. They won't bend down for the grass that sheep and cattle eat and they don't trample crops as elephants do.
4. Among the most graceful of animals the giraffe adds to the interest of the African countryside.
5. In national parks throughout the world the feeding of wild animals is forbidden.
6. But the law is often ignored and people feed wild animals potato chips bread cheese anything.

7. Even though signs warn that such food is not good for animals the public cannot resist giving handouts.
8. The animals are thus lured to the highways and may be struck by trucks or cars.
9. Since there are never enough wardens to enforce the antifeeding laws hundreds of animals are killed in this way each year.
10. Through thoughtlessness the public is depleting the number of animals in national parks.

☐EXERCISE 9

1. When Phil Mahre won his third World Cup in skiing he didn't even seem excited.
2. He says he just skis for the fun of it and he thinks about the Cup later.
3. He was the first American ever to win a World Cup in skiing and now he has won three.
4. He excels in the three skiing disciplines: slalom giant slalom and downhill.
5. Phil and his twin brother Steve are the best skiers in the United States and they've always been competitors.
6. Sometimes Phil will win a race by a second or two and sometimes it will be Steve.
7. Steve was born four minutes after Phil and says that he's been trying to catch up ever since.
8. They used to time each other with stopwatches and try to improve their techniques.
9. Both have had broken bones to cope with but both have had the resilience to come back.
10. Instead of being tense or ambitious they both laugh and say that games are for fun.

JOURNAL WRITING

Write a few sentences telling about some valuable information you've gained from some course, and in your account make use of the first three comma rules.

COMMAS (continued)

4. Put commas around the name of a person spoken to.

I think, Melissa, that we're late.
Chris, how about a game of chess?
Are you about ready, Amy?

5. Put commas around an expression that interrupts the flow of the sentence (such as *however, moreover, finally, therefore, of course, by the way, on the other hand, I am sure, I think*).

I hope, of course, that they'll come.
We took our plates, therefore, and got in line.
It should, I think, take only an hour.

Read the preceding sentences aloud, and you'll hear how those expressions interrupt the flow of the sentence. Sometimes, however, such expressions flow smoothly into the sentence and don't need commas around them. Whether a word is an interrupter or not often depends on where it is in the sentence. If it's in the middle of a sentence, it's more likely to be an interrupter than if it's at the beginning or the end. The expressions that were interrupters in the preceding sentences are not interrupters in the following sentences and therefore don't require commas.

Of course I hope they'll come.
Therefore we took our plates and got in line.
I think it should take only an hour.

Note that when one of the above words like *however* comes between two independent clauses, that word always has a semicolon before it. It may also have a comma after it, especially if there seems to be a pause between the word and the rest of the clause.

The taxi was late; *however*, I still made the plane.
I didn't want to go; *furthermore*, I had no money.
I wanted a good grade; *therefore* I worked harder.
I spent hours on that course; *finally* I made an *A*.

Thus. a word like *however* or *therefore* may be used in three ways:

1. as an interrupter (commas around it)
2. as a word that flows into the sentence (no commas needed)
3. as a connecting word between two independent clauses (semicolon before it and often a comma after it).

6. Put commas around nonessential material.

Such material may be interesting, but the main idea of the sentence would be clear without it. In the following sentence

> Miriam Tilden, who heads the hospital volunteers, will speak tonight.

the clause *who heads the hospital volunteers* is not essential to the main idea of the sentence. Without it we still know exactly who the sentence is about and what she is going to do: Miriam Tilden will speak tonight. Therefore the nonessential material is set off from the rest of the sentence by commas to show that it could be left out. But in the following sentence

> The woman who heads the hospital volunteers will speak tonight.

the clause *who heads the hospital volunteers* is essential to the main idea of the sentence. Without it the sentence would read: The woman will speak tonight. We would have no idea which woman. The clause *who heads the hospital volunteers* is essential because it tells us which woman. It couldn't be left out. Therefore commas are not used around it. In this sentence

> *The Grapes of Wrath*, a novel by John Steinbeck, was a best-seller.

the words *a novel by John Steinbeck* could be left out, and we would still know the main meaning of the sentence: *The Grapes of Wrath* was a best-seller. Therefore the nonessential material is set off by commas to show that it could be left out. But in this sentence

> John Steinbeck's novel *The Grapes of Wrath* was a best-seller.

the title of the novel is essential. Without it the sentence would read: John Steinbeck's novel was a best-seller. We would have no idea which of John Steinbeck's novels was a best-seller. Therefore the title couldn't be left out, and commas are not used around it.

EXERCISES

Punctuate these sentences according to Comma Rules 4, 5, and 6.

☐EXERCISE 1

1. Bill who had almost fallen asleep jumped when the professor called on him.
2. She repainted the old chair that had once belonged to her grandmother.
3. The little cabin overlooking the river is over a hundred years old.

4. I'm hoping Elizabeth that you'll come with us.
5. The car it seems was parked on the wrong side of the street.
6. We have of course given no thought to that question.
7. Of course we'll come.
8. My wife who teaches kindergarten doesn't get home until four.
9. Isn't it odd Rosa that he never even called?
10. We tried nevertheless to persuade him to go with us.

☐EXERCISE 2

1. Yes Oswaldo there's a lot to be done.
2. It should not be imagined moreover that the job is an easy one.
3. Commas should not be used around expressions that are essential to the meaning of the sentence.
4. This is the house that my grandfather built.
5. Of course I was glad to see her.
6. She was beyond a doubt the most unselfish person I had ever known.
7. She should I think be going to see you shortly.
8. The house was filled with people who had come for the wedding.
9. We always take our vacation in Minnesota the land of a thousand lakes.
10. Kilauea which was active when we were in Hawaii is one of the world's largest volcanoes.

☐EXERCISE 3

1. The boy carrying the flag led the parade.
2. The two longest rivers in the world are the Amazon flowing into the South Atlantic and the Nile flowing into the Mediterranean.
3. The book that I told you about is now on the best-seller list.
4. Some of the adventures that he had last summer were breathtaking.
5. The entire country of course is concerned about the increase in crime.
6. What we need many think is stricter law enforcement.
7. Swifter and surer punishment they say is the solution.
8. The senator who spoke to our group last night is sure he has the solution.
9. The town where my parents were born is a special place to me.
10. Atchison where my parents were born is a special place to me.

☐EXERCISE 4

1. The antique picture frame that she had found in the basement now hung in her living room as a showpiece.
2. The company hired an engineer who had more experience than I had.
3. Of course I was happy to have them stay with me.
4. Mel could we finish that painting now?

5. I was positive however that I had locked the door before I left.
6. I've done all the exercises that I was supposed to do.
7. The zest for gardening it seems got a boost from climbing food prices.
8. He went to his favorite fishing spot which is in Wisconsin.
9. The Amos Place 30 acres of virgin timber is a favorite nesting place for birds.
10. On the bed was a quilt that had been in the family for generations.

□EXERCISE 5

1. My paper was on the whole greatly improved by my revision.
2. It's much better I think than my previous draft.
3. Focused free writing I find helps me write more easily.
4. The position that you told me about has been filled.
5. This is the suit that I bought before Easter.
6. This suit which I bought before Easter is really too small for me.
7. More than a hundred years ago Hanson Gregory captain of a schooner and dabbler in the culinary art is said to have first put the hole in the doughnut.
8. My dad who has never cared for football really enjoyed that game.
9. The man who had been assigned to the job didn't report for work.
10. That novel by Charles Dickens a nineteenth-century author has been made into a movie.

□EXERCISE 6

1. The motion that we adjourn was greeted with applause.
2. Greenland the largest island in the world is partly buried under an ice cap.
3. There's more room in this car Kent.
4. Come here Debra and help me hold this ladder.
5. The people who are in charge of the project seem to be making progress.
6. He had in spite of his inexperience won the confidence of his peers.
7. And we said furthermore that we would support him in anything he chose to do.
8. I'm sure the man who lost his wallet will soon come back for it.
9. Those who want their term papers returned should sign this list.
10. The examination which should not worry anyone will be given on Tuesday.

□EXERCISE 7

1. The photography contest which is open to all students will be judged by a three-member panel.
2. Do you think Curt that you'll enter any photographs?

3. Conductor what time do we get to Galesburg?
4. The city of Nassau is located on the island of New Providence which is 21 miles long.
5. The place where Cabot landed is marked by a bronze plaque.
6. Williamsburg which was at one time the capital of Virginia has been restored to its original eighteenth-century appearance.
7. The area which covers 170 acres contains over 500 colonial buildings.
8. It's a place certainly that's well worth visiting.
9. The book that was at the top of the best-seller list last week is in the library now.
10. I've decided however that I don't have time to read it.

☐EXERCISE 8

1. A man's character and his garden it has been said both reflect the amount of weeding done during the growing season.
2. I tell you Jon you are making a mistake.
3. All those who had worked in the political campaign felt rewarded by the outcome of the election.
4. Getting everyone to vote we have found is a difficult job.
5. The watercolor that he had painted in high school hung in the living room.
6. The coldest permanently inhabited place in the world is a small town in Siberia where the temperature reached −96° F. in 1964.
7. My stamp collection which I've been working on for almost ten years is now quite valuable.
8. The largest and heaviest animal in the world and probably the biggest creature that has ever existed is the blue whale.
9. Hippocrates who is known as the father of medicine set forth the Hippocratic oath which is still respected by modern doctors.
10. George Bernard Shaw who became one of England's most famous writers made only $30 during his first nine years of writing.

☐EXERCISE 9

1. Ski resorts in the East which used to worry about the weather now give the weather little thought.
2. New snowmaking systems which are more efficient than the old ones provide 12 different kinds of snow, such as base, corn, frozen, granular, and machine.
3. The only kind of snow they don't provide obviously is real snow.
4. The new systems make more snow for every gallon of water and every cubic foot of air pumped, and they are able furthermore to make snow in warmer and more humid weather.

5. Killington resort in Vermont which has 90 trails and 16 lifts can now operate from mid-October to late May or even mid-June.
6. And Stowe in Vermont which advertises that it has more than 20 feet of natural snowfall per year supplements the natural snow with one of New England's most extensive snowmaking systems.
7. The snowmaking systems however are expensive.
8. Costs at Hunter Mountain in New York for one season were estimated at $1 million.
9. It's not surprising therefore that the price of ski-lift tickets has increased.
10. The extra money beyond a doubt goes to the making of snow.

JOURNAL WRITING

Write six sentences using the six comma rules given in the following box.

Review of the Comma

THE SIX COMMA RULES

1. Put a comma before *and, but, for, or, nor, yet, so* when they connect two independent clauses.
2. Put a comma between items in a series.
3. Put a comma after an introductory expression or afterthought that doesn't flow smoothly into the sentence.
4. Put commas around the name of a person spoken to.
5. Put commas around an interrupter, like *however, moreover*, etc.
6. Put commas around nonessential material.

Add the necessary commas to these sentences.

1. Many Americans do not know about Highway 1 which is an overseas highway.
2. It is 109 miles long and with its 42 bridges links the string of keys or islands that run from Miami to Key West.
3. The keys which go southwestward from the mainland of Florida form a dividing line between the Gulf of Mexico and the Atlantic Ocean.
4. The keys are great places for shell collecting bird watching and fishing.
5. Shell collectors who say the keys beaches are the best places in the United States for shells have the best luck just after high tide.
6. Bird watchers are interested in the herons pelicans and egrets that stop in the keys on their migratory routes.
7. Various kinds of coral abound but their sharp edges must be handled with gloves.
8. Many Spanish galleons were shipwrecked on these razor-sharp reefs and sank with their treasures.
9. On Grassy Key is the Flipper Sea School which trains dolphins for show business or for experiments.
10. On some of the smaller keys are found key deer which weigh less than 100 pounds.
11. Almost extinct 20 years ago they are now however making a comeback.
12. Key West which is the end of the Overseas Highway is nearer to Havana Cuba than it is to Miami.
13. With its freewheeling lifestyle and its marvelous weather it has become a popular vacation spot.
14. Walking is a good way to see Key West but bicycling is even better.
15. Among the famous artists and writers who have found inspiration at Key West over the years are James Audubon Hart Crane and Ernest Hemingway.

QUOTATION MARKS

Put quotation marks around the exact words of a speaker (but not around an indirect quotation).

He said, "I'll go." (his exact words)
He said that he would go. (not his exact words)

Whenever *that* precedes the words of a speaker (as in the last example), it indicates that the words are not a direct quotation and should not have quotation marks around them.

If the speaker says more than one sentence, quotation marks are used only before and after the entire speech.

He said, "I'll go. It's no trouble. I'll be there at six."

The words telling who is speaking are set off with a comma unless, of course, a question mark or exclamation mark is needed.

"I'll go," he said.
He said, "I'll go."
"Do you want me to go?" he asked.
"Come here!" he shouted.

Every quotation begins with a capital letter. But when a quotation is broken, the second part doesn't begin with a capital letter unless it's a new sentence.

"Ninety percent of the friction of daily life," said Arnold Bennett, "is caused by tone of voice."

"A friend is a person with whom I may be sincere," said Emerson. "Before him, I may think aloud."

Begin a new paragraph with each change of speaker.

"Will you come with me?" I asked Barbara as I got up and walked toward the door.

"What for?" she said.

"Just because I want you to," I replied.

Put quotation marks around the name of a story, poem, essay, or other short work. For longer works such as books, newspapers, plays, or movies, use underlining, which means they would be italicized in print.

I like Robert Frost's short poem "Dust of Snow."

Have you seen the movie *Never Cry Wolf*?

James Thurber's short story "The Secret Life of Walter Mitty" is found in his book *My World—and Welcome to It.*

I read about it in *Newsweek.*

EXERCISES

Punctuate the quotations, and underline or put quotation marks around each title.

□EXERCISE 1

1. Let's get something to eat she said.
2. Do you want to go now or after the movie he asked.
3. Why not both times she said.
4. Snow and adolescence are the only problems that disappear if you ignore them long enough my father says.
5. Some people stay longer in an hour than others can in a week said William Dean Howells.
6. After her weekend visitors left, she remarked that guests always bring pleasure—if not in the coming, then in the going.
7. Doing work I like is more important to me than making a lot of money my sister said.
8. With all its sham, drudgery, and broken dreams said Adlai Stevenson it is still a beautiful world.
9. We went to see The Wild Duck, a play by Henrik Ibsen.
10. Our future as a nation is going to depend not so much on what happens in outer space as on what happens in inner space—the space between our ears said the lecturer.

□EXERCISE 2

1. The actions of some children said Will Rogers suggest that their parents embarked on the sea of matrimony without a paddle.
2. The best time to tackle a small problem said my father is before he grows up.
3. When Mom goes shopping says Kip she leaves no store unturned.
4. I agree with the Spanish proverb how beautiful it is to do nothing and then rest afterward.
5. He found her munching chocolates and reading a book entitled Eat, Drink, and Be Buried.
6. Mark Twain said when I was a boy of 14, my father was so ignorant I could hardly stand to have the old man around. But when I got to be 21, I was astonished at how much the old man had learned in seven years.
7. Mark Twain said the parts of the Bible which give me the most trouble are those I understand the best.
8. Work consists of whatever a body is obliged to do, and play consists of whatever a body is not obliged to do said Mark Twain.

9. On observing the great number of civic statues, Cato, a famous Roman, remarked I would rather people would ask why there is not a statue of Cato than why there is.
10. One does not complain about water because it is wet said Abraham Maslow nor about rocks because they are hard.

☐EXERCISE 3

1. I've just read Barn Burning, a short story by William Faulkner.
2. The construction of an airplane wrote Charles Lindbergh is simple compared to the evolutionary achievement of a bird.
3. If I had the choice Lindbergh continued I would rather have birds than airplanes.
4. Of war, George Bernard Shaw said that the men should all shoot their officers and go home.
5. An art critic once said that there are three kinds of people in the world: those who can't stand Picasso, those who can't stand Raphael, and those who've never heard of either of them.
6. Pablo Casals, the great cellist, spent hours on a single phrase. He said people say I play as easily as a bird sings. If they only knew how much effort their bird has put into his song.
7. As it is the mark of great minds to say many things in a few words wrote La Rochefoucauld so it is the mark of little minds to use many words to say nothing.
8. William James said that the essence of genius is to know what to overlook.
9. Whatever you have you must either use or lose said Henry Ford.
10. A span of time either leaves you better off or worse off wrote John Gardner there is no neutral time.

☐EXERCISE 4

1. Finish every day and be done with it said Ralph Waldo Emerson tomorrow is a new day.
2. Life can only be understood backward said Kierkegaard but it must be lived forward.
3. The most valuable of all talents is that of never using two words when one will do said Thomas Jefferson.
4. The only conquests that are permanent and leave no regrets Napoleon said are our conquests over ourselves.
5. Nearly all men can stand adversity, but if you want to test a man's character, give him power said Lincoln.
6. Freud said that to have mental health a person has to be able to love and to work.

7. In the novel Fathers and Sons by Turgenev the main character says that the chief thing is to be able to devote yourself.
8. Nobody can carry three watermelons under one arm says a Spanish proverb.
9. The taller the bamboo grows the lower it bends says a Japanese proverb.
10. The man who does not do more work than he's paid for said Abraham Lincoln isn't worth what he gets.

☐EXERCISE 5

1. The cost of a thing is the amount of what I call life which is required to be exchanged for it, immediately or in the long run said Henry David Thoreau.
2. A man is rich said Thoreau in proportion to the number of things he can afford to let alone.
3. Viewing the multitude of articles exposed for sale in the marketplace, Socrates remarked how many things there are that I do not want.
4. I have been reading Comfortable Words, a book about word origins by Bergan Evans.
5. Perhaps the most valuable result of all education said Thomas Huxley is the ability to make yourself do the thing you have to do, when it ought to be done, whether you like it or not.
6. James B. Conant, former president of Harvard, said that a liberal education is what remains after all you have learned has been forgotten.
7. Education does not mean teaching people to know what they do not know said John Ruskin it means teaching them to behave as they do not behave.
8. Sometimes when fate kicks us and we finally land and look around, we find we have been kicked upstairs said Carl Sandburg.
9. At the end said Richard E. Byrd only two things really matter to a man, regardless of who he is; and they are the affection and understanding of his family.
10. There are at least as many stars wrote Sir James Jeans as there are grains of sand upon all the seashores of the earth.

☐EXERCISE 6

Are we nearly there Alice managed to pant out at last.

Nearly there! the Queen repeated why, we passed it ten minutes ago! Faster! And they ran on for a time in silence, with the wind whistling in Alice's ears, and almost blowing her hair off her head, she fancied.

Now! Now! cried the Queen Faster! Faster! And they went so fast that at last they seemed to skim through the air, hardly touching the ground with their feet, till suddenly, just as Alice was getting quite exhausted, they stopped, and she found herself sitting on the ground, breathless and giddy.

The Queen propped her up against a tree, and said kindly you may rest a little now.

Alice looked round her in great surprise why, I do believe we've been under this tree the whole time! Everything's just as it was!

Of course it is said the Queen what would you have it?

Well, in *our* country said Alice, still panting a little, you'd generally get to somewhere else—if you ran very fast for a long time as we've been doing.

A slow sort of country! said the Queen now, *here*, you see, it takes all the running you can do to keep in the same place. If you want to get somewhere else, you must run at least twice as fast as that.

—Lewis Carroll, *Through the Looking-Glass*

JOURNAL WRITING

To practice using quotation marks, write a conversation that has taken place in your home recently. Start a new paragraph with each change of speaker.

CAPITAL LETTERS

Capitalize

1. The first word of every sentence.

2. The first word of every direct quotation.

He said, "We've jogged two miles."
"We've jogged two miles," he said, "and I feel great." (The *and* is not capitalized because it doesn't begin a new sentence.)
"We've jogged two miles," he said. "It makes me feel great." (*It* is capitalized because it begins a new sentence.)

3. The first, last, and every important word in a title. Don't capitalize prepositions, short connecting words, the *to* in front of a verb, or *a, an, the.*

I've been reading Bulfinch's *The Age of Fable.*
We read Swift's "A Modest Proposal" last year.

4. Names of people, places, languages, races, and nationalities.

Grandfather Brown	Japan	Chicano
Uganda	English	Indian

5. Names of months, days of the week, and special days, but not the seasons.

February	Fourth of July	spring
Wednesday	Thanksgiving	summer

6. A title of relationship if it takes the place of the person's name, but not otherwise. If *my* (or a similar word) is in front of the word, a capital is not used.

I think Mother wrote to her.	*but* I think my mother wrote to her.
I'm sorry, Grandfather.	*but* Our grandfather is an artist.
She visited Aunt Rhonda.	*but* She visited her aunt.
He phoned Dad last night.	*but* He phoned his dad.

7. Names of particular people or things, but not general ones.

I spoke to Professor Warnock.	*but* I spoke to the professor.
We sailed on the Wabash River.	*but* We sailed on the river.
Are you from the Midwest?	*but* We turned west.
I take Art 300 and French 101.	*but* I take art and French.
I went to St. Joseph's High School.	*but* I was in high school last year.
He goes to Chaffey College.	*but* He's going to college now.

EXERCISES

Add the necessary capital letters.

☐EXERCISE 1

1. I discussed the matter with my professor.
2. We were studying Robert Frost's poem "The death of the hired man."
3. All freshmen take history and english.
4. Usually college classes begin the day after labor day.
5. You know, dad, I haven't had the car all week.
6. The detour took us south, then west, then north.
7. The doctor sent her to the hospital last wednesday.
8. After graduating from high school, he went to Sawyer college.
9. My aunt is president of her club this fall.
10. My cousin plays hockey for Colorado state university.

☐EXERCISE 2

1. My father wants me to go to a state university, but I want to go to Indiana vocational technical college at Columbus.
2. She spent the summer with her aunt in the east.
3. In high school I seldom studied, but college has changed that.
4. The headline read, "tougher meat laws needed in ontario."
5. I hope to go to the west coast this summer and then on to the yukon.
6. We visited yosemite national park and a lot of state parks.
7. Last spring she enrolled in San Bernardino valley community college.
8. My uncle came to our house on summer evenings and told us stories.
9. Usually aunt Angela came with him.
10. My aunt and my uncle had no children of their own.

☐EXERCISE 3

1. The fastest growing region in the world today is latin america.
2. Including mexico and central and south america, that area grew from 86 million people in 1925 to an estimated 350 million in 1982.
3. Next year I plan to take french, history, english, and physics.
4. I gave a report on *the autobiography of Benjamin Franklin* last week.
5. After high school my dad went to community college of Philadelphia.
6. The entertainer had performed before kings and presidents.
7. The John G. Shedd aquarium in grant park in Chicago is the largest aquarium in the world.
8. Have you read Eudora Welty's short story "A worn path"?

9. He shouted, "what's happening?"
10. "Nothing's happening," she called back, "except that I've fallen off the ladder and broken my back."

☐EXERCISE 4

1. My brother and I both went to Bishop Ward high school but now go to different colleges.
2. He is going to Alvin community college in Texas, and I'm going to the university of Missouri at Saint Louis.
3. May I have the car, dad, or is mother going to use it?
4. My mother usually wants the car on thursday afternoons, when she goes to the Muncie women's club.
5. We traveled east to Boston, where the pronunciation of certain words left no doubt that we were in the east.
6. We went swimming in the river every sunday when I was a boy.
7. Everyone would congregate in front of the stores on main street on saturday nights.
8. My grandmother grew up in the south, but grandfather was born in the east.
9. An Erie canal has no way of knowing how many ways a Mississippi river has of going wrong.
10. "The tragedy of life," Thomas Carlyle said, "is not so much what men suffer but rather what they miss."

☐EXERCISE 5

1. The sugar maple and the hemlock are both native to canada.
2. She graduated from Spokane Falls community college and now is attending Weber state college in Utah.
3. My mother likes plane travel, but dad would rather drive.
4. Last spring we took a trip through the black hills of South Dakota.
5. Then we drove south into Nebraska and west to Estes park in Colorado.
6. We're studying about world war II in history now.
7. I've always liked literature and have decided to make it my major.
8. Next semester I'm going to take psychology 101, history 210, and English 300; then the following semester I'll take math and physics.
9. The band from Pierce college was on our campus last weekend.
10. "I'd rather be a big duck in a little pond," she said, "than a little duck in a big pond."

☐EXERCISE 6

1. My granddad used to take us boating on the river on weekends.
2. The Missouri river has some exceptionally swift currents.

3. But granddad was always able to maneuver the boat safely.
4. When I went away to college, I of course had no time for boating.
5. At the state technical institute at Knoxville, I really worked.
6. But then in the summer I got a job as a counselor at a camp near Barren river lake, and again I had time for boating.
7. I'll always be grateful for the training granddad gave me.
8. Now I'm finishing my second year of college.
9. My professors all demand good english on written work.
10. I hope to get good grades and then go to McNeese state university next year.

☐EXERCISE 7

1. Sixty years ago the united kingdom ruled over one-fourth of the human race.
2. Now the colonial empires of britain and france are gone.
3. We read Poe's short story "The fall of the house of Usher."
4. Are you going to take spanish or psychology as an elective?
5. I hear she's decided to go to Tacoma community college.
6. He enjoyed the fourth of July but paid up for it on the fifth.
7. She belongs to the business and professional women's club.
8. Hey, dad, let's quit the yard work for today.
9. Have you read Huxley's *Brave new world?*
10. The university with the largest enrollment in the world is the university of Calcutta in India.

Review of Punctuation and Capital Letters

Punctuate these sentences. They include all the rules for punctuation and capitalization you have learned. Correct your answers carefully by those at the back of the book. Most sentences have several errors.

□EXERCISE 1

1. The Taj Mahal which is in Agra is often called the most beautiful building in the world.
2. Do you read Time or Newsweek.
3. I'm glad it's snowing now we can go skiing tomorrow.
4. Skiing skating and tobogganing were their chief winter sports.
5. Figure skating which I'm just learning takes hours of practice.
6. His knapsack contained the following items food matches and a canteen.
7. The sign in the dentist's office read support your dentist eat candy.
8. There is much inferior paint on the market but most consumer dissatisfaction arises from bad application.
9. A little old lady from Boston refused to travel saying Why should I travel I'm already here.
10. My sister is on the swim team at Polk community college.

□EXERCISE 2

1. No he didn't come we'll miss him.
2. You'll find them where you left them son.
3. The boy fought bit kicked and screamed but his mother remained calm.
4. When I was in high school I memorized Robert Frost's poem the road not taken.
5. An arabian proverb says I had no shoes and complained until I met a man who had no feet.
6. You can get the document by writing to the Superintendent of Documents Government Printing Office Washington DC.
7. My mother who is not a writer herself is still a good critic of my writing.
8. He tried to improve his vocabulary by looking up new words by keeping word lists and by using the words in conversation.
9. Have you read Yeats' poem The lake isle of Innisfree.
10. Reading improves your understanding of human nature writing improves your understanding of yourself.

☐EXERCISE 3

1. I've been reading about insects which are the most numerous of land animals.
2. Adult insects have six legs and the majority also have wings.
3. Although they are often destructive they can also be beneficial.
4. Some destroy crops but others kill more harmful insects.
5. We followed the trail into the clearing then we turned south.
6. In 1973 in Transvaal South Africa humans made their deepest penetration into the earth, a shaft of 11,391 feet.
7. Although I've not read Ghosts I've read other plays by Ibsen.
8. We wanted to see that movie but couldn't get tickets.
9. The trouble with the average family said Bill Vaughan is it has too much month left at the end of the money.
10. Coming out of the capitol the senator said you save a billion here and a billion there and it soon mounts up.

☐EXERCISE 4

1. I've been trying to teach my small son to ride a bike but it's difficult.
2. He rides a few feet then he falls off.
3. He's just not coordinated however I don't want him to get discouraged.
4. He keeps trying and I keep encouraging.
5. It's harder on me than on him but I must keep helping him.
6. I finished high school two years ago and am now attending the university of southern Colorado.
7. The official land speed record of 622 mph was set on the Bonneville Salt Flats Utah on October 23 1970.
8. Can the story be true then that we read in the paper.
9. The Christian Science Monitor and the Wall Street Journal are excellent papers.
10. Life said Samuel Butler is like playing a violin solo in public and learning the instrument as one goes on.

Proofreading Exercise 1

Try to find all eight errors in this student paper before you check with the answers at the back of the book. You may have to go through the paper several times to find them all. Challenge your instructor to find all eight on the first try!

THOSE FAULTY PARTS

I was only ten years old, but I had all the confidence of a great scientist. I had already built a little electric motor and fixed the electric parts in all the toys anyone would bring me. And now I had a magazine article that told how to build a simple battery-powered radio. The directions looked straightforward all I needed was the parts.

My world extended only as far as my bicycle could take me, so the only place I knew of that sold radio parts was the TV repair shop five blocks away. I don't know what the men there first thought of a ten-year-old kid trying to build a radio but I persisted until one of them gathered up the parts and sold them to me. It cost a few weeks' allowance money, but I new it was going to be worth it.

Well, after a few days of work, I had it finish. Admittedly, my wiring didnt look as neat as that in the picture. As a matter of fact, those people had used a few more wires than I had, but I didn't feel that all of them were really necessary.

But my radio didn't work! And my ten-year-old mind concluded that it must be that the TV repair shop had sold me faulty parts. I bicycled back with my new radio under my arm and demanded an explanation I was upset. After a long discussion, one of the men finally took my radio and started working on it. I think he was afraid I might cry or something.

In about half an hour, and after many changes, he got it working.

"No charge kid," he said.

"Thank you," I said in my most polite voice, thrilled at the sound of music coming from my radio.

What a feeling of accomplishment! It was as if Id invented something great. I guess the TV repairman must have had a bit of feeling of accomplishment too as a beaming ten-year-old rode away with a little radio that worked under his arm.

Proofreading Exercise 2

This student paper is marred by one fragment and three run-together sentences. Make the necessary corrections. You're on your own now. No answers are provided at the back of the book for this exercise.

I DON'T WANT TO

I must have tried to give up smoking a dozen times. Sometimes I'd last a month. And sometimes only a day or two. Always I'd start again. Then it hit me. The trouble was I didn't really want to stop I was one of those who say they want to stop but really don't. If people truly wanted to stop, I reasoned, they would. What I really needed, then, was simply to not want to smoke.

One day I added up all the negative aspects of smoking—the cost, the yellow stains on my fingers, the nervousness, the bad breath, the rotten taste in my mouth every morning, the smoker's cough, the danger to my health. Then, too, I told myself that smoking was a sign of weakness. I was unable to control myself I was caught in a habit that big tobacco companies were continuously promoting. That bothered me. I was, against my will, doing exactly what some big companies wanted me to do it was then I decided that I really didn't want to smoke.

The day I decided I didn't want to smoke, I simply stopped. Oh, it took a couple of weeks of effort to break the habit, but it's been three years now, and I haven't had another cigarette. All it took was just not to want to.

Proofreading Exercise 3

Here is another student paper to proofread. This one has six errors. No answers are provided at the back of the book for this exercise.

CURB THAT ENTHUSIASM

There we were, the two of us, in an eight-foot rubber raft, approaching Three Forks Rapids. Neither of us had ever tried river rafting before and it was scary. We had our life jackets strapped on tight and were bracing ourselves for what might come.

As we were swept along in the incredibly swift current, I held the two oars and tried to direct the raft. Nick, in the front, was suppose to watch for rocks and yell out which direction to head but already the thunder of the water hurtling through the rapids had drowned out his voice. Anyway I was really rowing as hard as I could just to keep the raft pointing downstream, let alone directing it more specifically.

Then came the first big drop! Its an amazing feeling riding over a sudden four-foot drop in a river. But somehow we stayed upright and landed below in the white foaming water. We cheered and congratulated each other for a moment but then braced ourselves for the next big drop coming right up.

Amazingly we did it. We managed to keep the raft afloat again with both of us still in it.

"Great!" I yelled. "We made 'em both."

"We're good!" Nick shouted.

Giving a whoop, he turned around but then as we yelled and laughed, we both happen to lean the same way, and sure enough, after running the rapids unscathed, we now found the raft tiping sideways, and over we went into the calm water . . . .

The *next* time, we told each other as we righted the raft and climbed back on board, we're going to curb our enthusiasm.

Comprehensive Test

In these sentences you will find all the errors that have been discussed. Correct them by adding apostrophes, punctuation, and capital letters and by crossing out incorrect expressions and writing the corrections above. Most sentences have several errors. A perfect—or almost perfect—score will mean that you've mastered the text.

1. Its useless to wait hes probably not coming.
2. If one wants a larger vocabulary you should study word roots.
3. Spending entirely too much time on that one coarse last semester.
4. Dad ask my sister and me to water the lawn we was glad to do it.
5. While they were waiting for there daughter, they're motor stalled.
6. I cant decide whether to finish my math, study my history, or whether I should take it easy for a change.
7. If you're going to be hear Dawn you can answer the phone for me.
8. Your going with me, aren't you.
9. We freshmen helped a upperclass student with registration he really appreciated it.
10. I was quiet sure that Rons car was in the driveway.
11. When we were on our trip we visited some cities in the south.
12. Which had many beautiful old homes and lovely gardens.
13. Its Mr. Petersons car but hes not driving it.
14. Each of the students are planning a individual report.
15. Looking under the car, the missing baseball was found.
16. Christines grades are always higher than Jackies.
17. Ill be ready in a minute Jeanne said.
18. This semester I'm taking french, history, and english.
19. The united nations receives more brickbats than bravos yet it remains the only real hope for peace.
20. She told her sister she needed a new purse.
21. They didnt think however that they would have time to come back.

22. She was suppose to read the short story The Elephant's Child from Rudyard Kipling's book Just So Stories.
23. Whether you agree with me or whether you follow your own ideas.
24. We waited as long as we could than we went on without her.
25. Whats done to children, they will do to society wrote Karl Menninger.

4

Writing

4 Writing

You learn to write by writing—not by reading long discussions *about* writing. Therefore the instructions in this section are brief. In fact, they are boiled down to just eight steps that you need to take to write good papers. Take these eight steps, one at a time, and you'll write more effectively and also more easily. Here are the steps:

EIGHT STEPS TO BETTER WRITING

I. Do some free writing.
II. Limit your topic.
III. Write a thesis statement.
IV. Support your thesis with reasons or points.
V. Organize your paper from your thesis.
VI. Organize each paragraph.
VII. Write and rewrite.
VIII. Proofread ALOUD.

I. DO SOME FREE WRITING

"Writing is good for us," Oliver Wendell Holmes said, "because it brings our thoughts out into the open, as a boy turns his pockets inside out to see what is in them." Try "turning your pockets inside out" by writing as fast as you can for five minutes. Write anything that comes into your mind. Put your thoughts down as fast as they come. What you write may not make sense, but that doesn't matter. Write fast. Don't stop a moment. Don't even take your pen off the page. If you can't think of anything to write, just write, "I can't think of anything to write," over and over until something occurs to you. Look at your watch and begin.

This free writing should limber up your mind and your pen so that you'll write more freely.

Now try another kind of free writing—focused free writing. Write for five minutes as fast as you can, but this time stick to one subject—travel. Look at your watch and begin.

Did you focus on travel that long? Did you think of family trips, of backpacking, of the most beautiful place you've ever seen, of trips to your grandmother's when you were small, of places you'd like to see?

You didn't have time to include all those things of course. Once more write for ten minutes and add more to your discussion of travel. Begin.

Focused free writing is a good way to begin any writing. When you are assigned a paper, write for ten minutes putting down all your thoughts on the subject. It will let you see what material you have and will help you figure out what aspect of the subject (what topic) to write about.

II. LIMIT YOUR TOPIC

Finding the right topic is sometimes the hardest part of writing. For one thing, you need to limit your topic so that you can handle it in a paper of 300 to 500 words. The subject travel, which you used for free writing, was obviously too big. You could limit it by saying

A Canoe Trip
Our Best Family Vacation
Backpacking

but even those topics are too big. Keep making your topic smaller

Backpacking in the Wilderness

and smaller

Backpacking in Algonquin Park

and smaller

One Day of Backpacking in Algonquin Park

Now you have a topic limited enough to write about in a short paper.

Usually the more you limit your topic, the better your paper will be, for then you'll have room to add plenty of specific details. And it's specific details that will interest your reader.

EXERCISE 1 Make each of these topics more and more limited until it would be a possible topic for a short paper. After you have finished, compare your topics with those suggested at the back of the book.

1. Cooking for Two

   Cooking Breakfast for Two

   Two Cook Breakfast for Two

2. Photography as a Hobby

3. Buying a Bike

4. The State Park near my Home

5. Training a Pup

6. A High School Swim Meet

7. Playing in the College Band

8. Being a Lifeguard

9. Finding a Summer Job

The following two assignments emphasize the first two Steps to Better Writing.

Assignment 1 A Significant Incident

Think of some incident in your life that had a profound effect upon you. It might be from your childhood or from later years, but it should be an incident that had so much significance for you that you will long remember it.

First do some free writing telling about the experience. Put down all the details you can think of. For example, if you are going to tell about the time you won a trophy, you'll want to say more than that it was a great moment. You'll want to tell what you saw at that moment, what you heard, how you felt. If you are groping for details, remember your five senses—sight, hearing, smell, taste, and touch. Each of them may call forth some details you hadn't thought of before.

When you've done all the free writing you can, then make sure your topic is limited. If you're writing about winning a trophy, you won't tell about the entire season but only about actually receiving the award.

Before you start to write, you might like to read two student papers on this assignment. Both students were having difficulties with spelling and sentence structure. At first their papers were so full of errors that they were almost impossible to read, but after a number of rewritings, they are now clear and understandable. These students had something interesting to say, and it was worth their while to get rid of the errors so that their writing can be read easily.

THE DAY I STOOD AND BECAME A MAN

I reached the door of my home, sweating not from exhaustion but from fear. I opened the door. A calm feeling came over me as I sat down. One more day I had escaped. But no more would I run or hide. I would stand and be a man and fight. The next day as I walked to school, out from behind a tree the bully came. We stood toe to toe and eye to eye. Fear ran through my body. Then he swung and I swung. As blood ran from his nose, my fear turned to courage. But then something happened. The fight stopped. We stood toe to toe for a minute. No words were said, and then he smiled and I smiled.

JASON

Two years ago at the District wrestling tournament, where I was wrestling with the team, halfway through the meet I noticed an apparently retarded boy talking to and annoying everyone. Some of the crowd moved to other seats. Everybody was watching and laughing, including the guys on the bench where my team was seated. I leaned over to the guy next to me, whom I've known for several years, and I said, "Ron, look at that weirdo up there." Ron then replied proudly, "He's my older brother Jason. He's a mongoloid." I felt like a real jackass!

Later when there was a break in the tournament, Ron's brother came down on the mat and attempted to wrestle like Ron does. Of course everyone was watching Jason in hysterical laughter. Ron then lovingly and proudly walked onto the mat and embraced Jason, and they walked off together. The whole gymnasium hushed, and a tear came into my eye.

Now write your paper for this assignment. Imagine that you are telling someone about your significant experience, and write what you would say.

Finally, spend some time thinking of a good title. Just as you are more likely to read a magazine article with a catchy title, so your reader will be more eager to read your paper if you give it a good title. (And remember that every important word in a title is capitalized.) Which of these titles from student papers would make you want to read further?

An Interesting Experience
Knees Shaking
Toss It Away
Jail outside a Jail
Inchworms Get There
My Favorite Class
Say Cheese

Assignment 2 A Place I'll Never Forget

What place means more to you than any other place in the world? It might be a place you know now or one you knew in childhood—a playroom, your workshop, a backyard, a playing field . . . .

Do some free writing to bring to your mind specific details that will help your reader see your place. Telling some things that happened there will also help your reader participate in your memory of it.

After you have done all the free writing about it that you can, ask yourself whether your topic is limited enough. Take it through several steps of limiting to see whether you can turn it into a more manageable topic before you begin to write.

Here is a student paper, a third draft. With each draft the writer added specific details about what he saw, what he did, and how he felt. The reader can now visualize the place and understand how the writer feels about it.

THE SCHOOL YARD

It's the school yard that I remember. Oh sure, things went on inside the school—lessons, reports, projects—but it's the school yard that I'll never forget.

All the other paper boys and I would hang around the school yard after finishing our routes. We'd have toy car races in the dirt or play with waterguns or trade baseball cards. The older boys wouldn't let us play baseball with them, and of course the girls were sissies who none of us liked, but we never tired of our own entertainment.

We even had our own version of baseball. We'd make a big square "Strike Zone" on the school wall with chalk, and then a batter would stand in front of it and try to hit the baseball (actually a tennis ball) that someone would pitch. When the batter had had three strikes, a player from the other team would come up to bat. I've never played a baseball game since then that could come up to those games in excitement.

In the winter we'd throw snowballs at each other or at the girls—but never at the bigger boys. When it was really cold, we'd play hockey on the school yard rink. I remember putting on my skates in the warmth of our kitchen and then walking the two blocks to school with my skates on.

And there were big events too, like Athletics Day when the whole school turned out for races. Once our fifth grade lined up on one side of the school yard and then at the starting gun raced as fast as we could to the other side. That was a great day for me because at the finish a teacher grabbed me and took me over to the finalists' table, where I was given a little pin for second place. I still have the pin.

That school yard is a part of me.

III. WRITE A THESIS STATEMENT

For any kind of writing, and particularly for writing that explains something or defends an idea, you need to be sure you know what point you want to get across to your reader.

The limited topic we wrote on page 197, "One Day of Backpacking in Algonquin Park," doesn't say anything. It doesn't make any point. What about that day? What did it do for you? What point about that day would you like to get across to your reader? You might write

> One day of backpacking in Algonquin Park taught me the importance of getting in shape beforehand.

or

> One day of backpacking in Algonquin Park showed me that I have more resourcefulness than I was aware of.

or

> One day of backpacking in Algonquin Park made me a confirmed backpacker.

Now you have said something. **When you write in one sentence the point you want to get across to your reader, you have written a thesis statement.**

All good writers have a thesis in mind when they begin to write. Whether they are writing articles, novels, short stories, poems, or plays, they have in mind an idea they want to present to the reader. They may develop it in various ways, but back of whatever they write is their ruling thought, their reason for writing, their thesis.

For any writing assignment, after you have done some free writing and limited your topic, your next step is to write a thesis statement. As you write it, keep two things in mind.

1. A thesis statement must be a sentence (not a title or topic).

TITLE	THESIS
One Day of Backpacking in Algonquin Park	One day of backpacking in Algonquin Park made me a confirmed backpacker.
Quitting Smoking	My decision to quit smoking was the best decision I ever made.
Poachers in Yosemite	New laws are needed to protect Yosemite from poachers.

2. A thesis statement must be a statement that you can explain or defend (not simply a fact that no one would deny).

FACT	THESIS
Many accidents involve drunken drivers.	Tougher laws should be passed concerning drinking and driving.
Jobs are scarce	A good interview can land a job.
My doctor told me to lose weight.	I'm following three rules to take off weight.

EXERCISE 2 Which of the following are merely titles or facts, and which are thesis statements that you could explain or defend? In front of each, write TITLE, FACT, or THESIS. Check your answers with those at the back of the book.

__________ 1. Cross-country skiing

__________ 2. I felt grown up the day I got my first bike

__________ 3. Alaska has great mineral resources

__________ 4. The state fair in our city

__________ 5. A day I'll never forget

__________ 6. Teaching a pup to heel takes patience

__________ 7. Developers shouldn't be allowed in Tonto National Forest

__________ 8. My job gives me an ego boost

__________ 9. The weather bureau predicts a hot summer

__________ 10. Painting a room

__________ 11. Group therapy taught me a lot about myself

__________ 12. In painting a room, four steps are necessary

__________ 13. For some students, standard English is a second language

__________ 14. Our trip to Mesa was the best our family ever had

EXERCISE 3 Now make thesis statements from all the preceding that are only titles or facts. Compare your thesis statements with those suggested at the back of the book.

IV. SUPPORT YOUR THESIS WITH REASONS OR POINTS

Now you are ready to support your thesis with reasons or points. That is, you will think of ways to convince your reader that your thesis is true. How could you convince your reader that a day of backpacking made you a confirmed backpacker? You might write

A day of backpacking in Algonquin Park made me a confirmed backpacker. (because)*

1. I liked traveling without suitcases.
2. I liked getting out into the wilds.
3. I met interesting people.

The points supporting a thesis are not always reasons. They may be examples (to make your thesis clear) or steps (in a how-to paper). Whatever they are, they should convince your reader that your thesis is true.

EXERCISE 4 Add supporting points (sentences) to these thesis statements.

I've decided not to quit college.

(reasons)
1.
2.
3.

Learning to write is like learning to swim.

(examples)
1.
2.

Our house is a madhouse when we're leaving on a trip.

(examples)
1.
2.
3.
4.

To increase your vocabulary, you need to take three steps.

(steps)
1.
2.
3.

* (Sometimes if you imagine a "because" at the end of your thesis statement, it will help you write your reasons clearly.)

Learning to write a good thesis statement with supporting points is perhaps the most important thing you can learn in this course. Most writing problems are not really writing problems but thinking problems. Whether you are writing a term paper or merely an answer to a test question, working out a thesis statement is always the best way to organize your thoughts. If you take enough time to think, you will be able to write a clear thesis statement with supporting points. And if you have a clear thesis statement with supporting points, organizing your paper won't be difficult.

Of course not all writing follows this "thesis and support" form. Experienced writers vary their writing. Using this form, however, is an excellent way to begin learning to write because it will help you think logically, and logical thinking is important for all writing.

Assignment 3 Two Thesis Statements with Supporting Points

Think of some decision you are trying to make. Are you wondering what major to choose, whether to drop out of college for a time, whether to give up smoking, whether to try out for the next dramatic production? Think of a decision that really matters to you. Only then will you be able to write something others will care to read. When you have decided on a topic, write a thesis statement for *each side*. For example, if you are wondering whether to major in physical education or in business, you would write

> I've decided to major in physical education.
> I've decided to major in business.

Then you would support each of those thesis statements with reasons. You might write

I've decided to major in physical education.

1. My real interest is in sports.
2. I'd like to influence kids.
3. I'll be able to get a job either as a teacher or as a coach.

I've decided to major in business.

1. Age won't disqualify me later.
2. I'll have more job opportunities.
3. I'll make my living in business and keep sports for a hobby.

Three reasons usually work well, but you could have two or four. Be sure your reasons are all sentences.

V. ORGANIZE YOUR PAPER FROM YOUR THESIS

Once you have worked out a good thesis with supporting points, organizing your paper will be easy.

First, you need an introductory paragraph. It should catch your reader's interest and should either include or suggest your thesis statement. It may also list the supporting points, but usually it's more effective to let them unfold paragraph by paragraph rather than to give them all away in your introduction. (Your instructor may ask you to write your complete thesis statement with supporting points at the top of your paper so that it may be referred to easily.) Even if your supporting points don't appear in your introduction, your reader will easily spot them later in the paper if your paper is clearly organized.

Your second paragraph will present your first supporting point—everything about it and nothing more.

Your next paragraph will be about your second supporting point—all about it and nothing more.

Your next paragraph will be about your third supporting point. Thus each of your points will have its own paragraph.

Finally you will need a brief concluding paragraph. In a short paper it isn't necessary to restate all your points. Even a single clincher sentence to round out the paper may be sufficient.

Your paper will, therefore, have five paragraphs. (If you have two or four supporting points rather than three, that of course will change the number of your paragraphs.)

Paragraph 1.	Introduction arousing your reader's interest and indicating your thesis
Paragraph 2.	First supporting point
Paragraph 3.	Second supporting point
Paragraph 4.	Third supporting point
Paragraph 5.	Clincher paragraph

Learning to write this kind of paper will teach you to write logically. Then when you are ready to write a longer paper, you'll be able to organize it easily. A longer paper may divide each of the supporting points into several paragraphs, and it may not present the thesis statement until later in the paper. But no matter how the material is presented, it will still have some kind of logical pattern.

Here are the introductory and concluding paragraphs from a student paper. Note that the introductory paragraph arouses the reader's interest and suggests the thesis statement. And the brief concluding paragraph simply ties the whole paper together.

Introductory paragraph	When we finally decided to snap off the TV for good on school days, we had a revolution. Our two youngsters—seven and nine—staged a protest so violent that it would have been worthy of any war-torn country. For two weeks our house was in a state of siege. Then three things happened.
	(The writer tells in three paragraphs the changes in attitude that took place.)
Concluding paragraph	The finale to our drama came yesterday. I had turned the TV on for the weather but had been called to the phone and had forgotten about it. When our youngsters rushed in after school, they stopped still at the door. . . . Then Kristin walked into the living room and calmly snapped off the TV.

Transition expressions are a great help to a reader in moving from one point to the next. It's a good idea to start your supporting paragraphs with a transition expression such as

My first reason	Another example
Second	Furthermore
Also	Finally
Even more important	

Transition expressions are also valuable within a paragraph to indicate the movement from one detail or example to the next.

VI. ORGANIZE EACH PARAGRAPH

Organizing a paragraph is easy because it's organized just the way an entire paper is. Here's the way you learned to organize a paper:

Thesis statement in introductory paragraph
  First supporting point
  Second supporting point
  Third supporting point
Clincher paragraph

And here's the way to organize a paragraph:

Topic sentence
  First supporting detail or example
  Second supporting detail or example
  Further supporting details or examples
Concluding sentence if needed

You should have at least two or three points to support your topic sentence. If you find that you have little to say after writing your topic sentence, ask yourself what details or examples will make your reader see that your topic sentence is true.

The topic sentence doesn't have to be the first sentence in the paragraph. It may come at the end or even in the middle, but having it first is the most common way and the way we'll use in the materials that follow.

Each paragraph should contain only one main idea, and no detail or example should be allowed to creep into the paragraph if it doesn't support the topic sentence. Note how the following paragraph is organized.

> On Sunday afternoon I drove on some of my favorite country roads and was glad to see that most of the roadsides had not been mowed and thus remained a haven for birds and small animals as well as an encouraging place for wild flowers. The black-eyed Susans were plentiful among the white-flowered fleabanes and Queen Anne's lace. I even saw a few plants from the endangered species list. As I approached Troublesome Creek, several quail were in the road and were reluctant to make way for my car. It was plain that it was their territory and that I was an intruder. Then a squirrel raced across the road, and some baby rabbits hopped about among the low bushes. After a while I returned to the highway and to the monotonous border of miles and miles of mowed grass.

The rather long topic sentence states that unmowed roadsides are a haven for birds, small animals, and plants. Then abundant details follow, and the final clincher sentence adds emphasis to the topic sentence.

EXERCISE 5 Here is the topic sentence for a paragraph:

Hawaii is now burning bagasse as one alternative to foreign oil.

Which of the following statements support that topic sentence and therefore should be included in the paragraph? Mark them *S* (support). Check your answers with those at the back of the book.

_____ 1. Bagasse is the fibrous residue from sugar cane.
_____ 2. Hawaii was formerly dependent on foreign oil.
_____ 3. Hawaii has one of the most equable climates in the world.
_____ 4. The Environmental Protection Agency halted dumping bagasse in the Pacific.
_____ 5. The Pacific beaches are one of the world's great playgrounds.
_____ 6. Tourism is one of Hawaii's main industries.
_____ 7. Burning bagasse provides electricity and also gets rid of waste.
_____ 8. A ton of bagasse produces as much electricity as a barrel of oil.
_____ 9. Hawaii is also developing solar, wind, and geothermal power sources.
_____ 10. Bagasse now provides seven percent of Hawaii's electrical needs.

Assignment 4 Writing a Paragraph

For practice in writing paragraphs, choose one (or more) of the following topic sentences and add support sentences. You may alter each topic sentence slightly if you wish.

1. A single experience got me over my fear of computers.
2. I'm improving my vocabulary by making myself use new words.
3. In a disagreement, I've learned to ask the question, "What's important here?"
4. A simple change in my eating habits helped me lose weight.
5. I've learned to travel light.
6. Finally I acted on the motto, "If you don't love your job, get out."
7. The first step in preparing for an interview is to learn all you can about the job.
8. It's important to have the right shoes for jogging.

The easiest and most natural way to practice writing paragraphs is to write them as part of a paper. You'll have an excellent opportunity to practice writing paragraphs in the assignments that follow.

Assignment 5 A Decision I Have Made

Return to the two thesis statements with supporting points about a decision you are trying to make (Assignment 3, p. 205). Choose one of those thesis statements to write about. Even if your mind is not really made up, you must choose one side for this assignment. You may mention in your introduction the arguments on the other side, but you must focus on one side if your paper is to be effective.

Write a rough draft of your paper, giving enough specific details in each of your supporting paragraphs to convince your reader that you have made the right decision.

Then take Step VII, which follows.

VII. WRITE AND REWRITE

If possible, write your paper several days before it's due. Let it sit for a day. When you reread it, you'll see ways to improve it. After rewriting it, put it away for another day, and again try to improve it.

Great writers don't just sit down and write their books in a first draft. They write and rewrite. Hemingway said, "I wrote the ending to *Farewell to Arms*, the last page of it, 39 times before I was satisfied." And Leo Tolstoy wrote, "I can't understand how anyone can write without rewriting everything over and over again."

Here's a checklist of questions to ask yourself as you begin to rewrite:

1. Will my introductory paragraph make my reader want to read further?
2. Does each paragraph support my thesis statement?
3. Does each paragraph contain only one main idea?
4. Do I have enough specific details in each paragraph to support the topic sentence, and are all the details relevant?
5. Have I used transition expressions to tie my paragraphs together?
6. Does my concluding paragraph sum up my paper in a persuasive way?
7. Are my sentences properly constructed and clear?
8. Have I checked all questionable spellings?
9. Is my punctuation correct?
10. Is my title interesting?

Don't call any paper finished until you have worked through it two or three times. **REWRITING IS THE BEST WAY TO LEARN TO WRITE.**

Your final rewriting should be typed, double-spaced, or written legibly in ink on 8½-by-11-inch paper on one side only. An inch-and-a-half margin should be left on each side of the page for your instructor's comments. Paragraphs should be indented about five spaces.

Part of the success of a paper depends on how it looks. The same paper written sloppily or neatly might well receive different grades. If, however, when you do your final proofreading, you find a word repeated or a word left out, don't hesitate to make neat corrections in pen. So long as your paper gives a neat appearance, no one will mind a few minor corrections.

VIII. PROOFREAD ALOUD

Finally, read your finished paper ALOUD. If you read it silently, you're sure to miss some errors. Read it aloud slowly, word by word, to catch omitted words, errors in spelling and punctuation, and so on. Make it a rule to read each of your papers aloud before handing it in.

As you do the following assignments, be sure to take each of the EIGHT STEPS TO BETTER WRITING.

Assignment 6 Children and My Hometown

Do you consider your hometown or your neighborhood a good place to bring up children? If so, why? If not, why not? After doing some free writing and limiting your topic, spend plenty of time working out a good thesis statement with two or three supporting reasons, and remember that specific details are essential to make a paper effective.

Assignment 7 A Letter to a Parent

Most of us think our parents failed in some way, large or small, in bringing us up. First do some free writing. Then work out a good thesis statement telling what you think your parents (or one parent) did wrong. Then write another thesis statement telling what you think one or both of them did right. Choose one of these thesis statements and write a paper in the form of a letter to one or both of your parents.

Even though you are writing a letter, it will still be in the form of an essay—introduction, a paragraph for each supporting reason, and a conclusion. Your introduction might well be a brief statement of the other side of the question. That is, if you are writing about the things your parents did wrong, you might in your first paragraph mention a number of things they did right. But the bulk of your paper must be on one side or the other. And remember . . . specific details make any paper come alive.

Assignment 8 Getting Along with Someone

Write down the name of someone you have trouble getting along with. You may make up a name, but have a real person in mind. Write a thesis statement listing ways in which you wish that person would change so that the two of you could get along better.

As we all know, however, it's difficult to get someone else to change. Therefore now write a thesis statement listing ways in which *you* could change to make the relationship better. Perhaps you are saying, "Impossible." Think. There are always ways. Think until you have a realistic, possible thesis statement for your paper. This paper will be harder to write than if you wrote about how the other person should change, but it will teach you more about writing. Remember that learning to write is learning to think.

Assignment 9 How to Do Something

Nothing will get rid of the clutter in your writing like writing a "how to" paper. Every sentence will have to be clear and to the point.

Write a short paper telling someone how to do something—how to paint a table, how to choose a stereo, how to put a three-year-old to bed, how to make a piece of costume jewelry, how to change the oil in one's car . . . .

First you'll need an introductory paragraph—a sentence will do—to interest your reader, then a step-by-step explanation, and finally a concluding paragraph, which again may be just one sentence. You may want to add some humor to your introduction or conclusion to make your paper more interesting.

Assignment 10 Choosing a Career

What career are you considering? Be specific. Rather than saying Teaching, say Elementary School Teaching. Give the reasons that make you think you'd like that career. If you have no idea what you want to be, simply choose any likely possibility.

Assignment 11 A Quotation

Turn to pages 179–81 and read the quotations. Then choose one as a topic for a paper. Either show how the quotation applies to your life, giving two or three examples, or else show how you might benefit by following the idea of the quotation, again giving two or three examples.

Assignment 12 A Surprise

What has surprised you most since coming to college? It might be a surprise about social life, about the attitude of professors, about the attitude of students . . . . Just how is college different from what you thought it would be? After you have done some free writing and limited your topic, work out a good thesis statement, giving two or three examples to support your opinion.

Assignment 13 My Opinion on a Current Problem

Choose one of the problems below and present your arguments for one side. Write a carefully thought-out thesis statement, supported by reasons, before you begin your paper. In your introduction or conclusion you may want to mention briefly the reasons you can see for the opposite side.

A. As an admissions officer of your college, you have only one space left in the freshman class for the coming fall, and you are trying to decide between two applicants. One is a straight *A* student who has won honors in high school speech and debate and has participated in dramatics. The other is a minority student who lettered in two high school sports but has only a *B* average. The college, however, is trying to increase its percentage of minority students. Which student will you admit and why?

B. A boatload of people from a war-torn country has landed illegally on a U.S. shore. The people claim they are afraid for their lives and ask for asylum. The United States, however, has too many illegal aliens already and is plagued with unemployment. If you were on the congressional committee to make the decision, what would your response be and why?

C. The college bookstore, where you work part-time, is losing a lot of money to shoplifters and has asked all employees to be on the watch and to report any suspect. This morning you happen to notice a friend of yours trying on a T-shirt on the opposite side of the store. Then, as you are watching, he slips his jacket over the T-shirt and goes out the door. What should you do? The problem is complicated by the fact that he has twice befriended you—once by standing up for you when you were falsely accused in an athletic tangle and once by taking time to talk you out of quitting college. You feel indebted to him, and yet you feel an obligation to your employer and a desire to take a stand for honesty. What are you going to do? As you are thinking all this, the manager steps up to you and says, "I saw you watching that student. Did he swipe that T-shirt?" What will you say?

WRITING A SUMMARY

A good way to learn to write concisely is to write 100-word summaries. Writing 100 words sounds easy, but actually it isn't. Writing 200- or 300- or 500-word summaries isn't too difficult, but condensing all the main ideas of an essay or article into 100 words is a time-consuming task—not to be undertaken the last hour before class. If you work at writing summaries conscientiously, you will improve both your reading and your writing. You will improve your reading by learning to spot main ideas and your writing by learning to construct a concise, clear, smooth paragraph. Furthermore, your skill will carry over into your reading and writing for other courses.

Assignment 14 A 100-Word Summary

Your aim in writing your summary should be to give someone who has not read the article a clear idea of it. First read the article, and then follow the instructions given after it.

Can It!

Speeding along the highway, she tosses a paper cup out the car window. Walking across the campus, he drops a candy wrapper on the grass. Finishing their picnic lunch, they leave their paper plates beside a stream.

Why do people litter? Although they like a clean sandy beach, a well-kept park, an uncluttered avenue, yet they litter. They do to public places what they would never think of doing to their own yards. Why do they do it? A research project found that people litter when they feel no personal responsibility for the property, when they know someone else will clean up after them, and when litter has already accumulated. They say, "Everybody does it, and there's nothing I can do about it."

Well, now something is being done about it. An antilitter campaign called the Clean Community System is spreading across the country and producing some startling changes. Sponsored by Keep America Beautiful, Inc., it's not merely a cleanup campaign but rather a plan to change people's attitudes. Its slogan is "Put Litter in Its Place—Can It."

Of prime importance in the campaign is a system of community education that starts in kindergarten with the "Waste in Place" program and continues throughout the schools and on into public forums. An example of how well the community education program is working is the Earth

Sources: Roger W. Powers, "Litterbugs—Beware!" *New Jersey Municipalities,* March 1980; "A Clean Sweep," *Time,* May 19, 1980.

Group in a Plainfield, New Jersey, high school that is assisting the city by identifying trash-filled alleyways and vacant lots, locating the owners, and sometimes even helping with the cleanup. Another example of effective community education and action is in Atlanta, Georgia, where schoolchildren are collecting aluminum cans for recycling, and where the Rapid Transit Authority has installed closed-circuit TV at each new subway station. Anyone who drops a gum wrapper or a cigarette package will hear a voice from a loudspeaker saying, "Pick it up, please."

The campaign makes use of an objective litter-measuring technique that enables each community, with the aid of a camera and a yardstick, to keep an accurate record of its progress in getting rid of loose trash in streets and lots. And as the residents see the litter level decreasing, they want to become involved in the program. People begin to believe they *can* make a difference when they learn that they *have* made a difference.

The program even makes financial sense. In Cincinnati, for example, sanitation crews used to spend half a day cleaning up after outdoor events. Now a few Clean Community System workers with trash bags mingle with the crowds and encourage them to "think tidy," with the result that the cleanup time of the sanitation crews the next day is cut in half.

Since its introduction in 1976, the plan has helped reduce the litter level in cities as large as Houston (population 1.7 million) and towns as small as Holly Ridge, North Carolina (population 415). In Sioux Falls, in Chattanooga, in Indianapolis, in Kansas City, in San Bernardino . . . the plan is working. Depending more on popular support than on money, the Clean Community System is succeeding in 331 communities in 40 states.

A good way to begin a summary of an article is to figure out the thesis statement. In this article the first two paragraphs merely try to catch the reader's interest. Not until the third paragraph do we find the thesis statement, the main idea the author wants to get across to the reader. Write that idea down BEFORE READING FURTHER.

You probably wrote something like this: *An antilitter campaign is spreading across the country and reducing litter levels in many communities.* Using your thesis statement as your first sentence, summarize the article by choosing the most important points. Since examples are not necessary in a summary, you will not need to mention specific cities. Your first draft may be 150 words or more. Now cut it down by including only essential points and by getting rid of wordiness. Keep within the 100-word limit. You may have a few words less but not one word more. (And every word counts—even *a*, *and*, and *the*.) By forcing yourself to keep within the 100 words, you will get to the kernel of the author's thought and understand the article better.

When you have written the best summary you can, then, *and only then,* compare it with the summary on page 299. If you look at the model sooner, you will cheat yourself of the opportunity to learn to write summaries because once you read the model, it will be almost impossible not to make yours similar. So do your own thinking and writing, and *then* compare.

Even though your summary is different from the model, it may be just as good. If you are not sure how yours compares, ask yourself these questions:

Did I include as many important ideas?
Did I omit all unnecessary words?
Does my summary read smoothly?
Would someone who had not read the article get a clear idea of it from my summary?

Assignment 15 A 100-Word Summary

Here is another article to summarize. You're on your own now. No summary is given at the back of the book for this article. After you finish writing, simply ask yourself whether someone who had not read the article would get a clear idea of it from your summary.

Let 'em Eat Leftovers

Mike McGrady

Last year my wife and I traded roles. Every morning she went off to an office and earned the money that paid the bills. I cooked and cleaned, picked up after three kids, went head-to-head with bargain-hunting shoppers, pleaded for a raise in allowance and lived the generally hellish life that half the human race accepts as its lot.

The year is over now but the memories won't go away. . . .

At the heart of my difficulty was this simple fact: for the past two decades I had been paid for my work. I had come to feel my time was valuable. Suddenly my sole payment was a weekly allowance given to me with considerable fanfare by my bread-winning wife. I began to see that as a trap, a many-strings-attached offering that barely survived a single session in the supermarket and never got me through a neighborhood poker game. . . .

Some people seem to feel that the housewife's lot would be bettered if she were given a new title, one that takes into account the full range and complexity of her role, something along the lines of "household engineer" or, perhaps, "domestic scientist." Wonderful. You come and take care of my house and my kids and you can be the Empress of the Domestic Arts, the Maharanee of the Vacuum Cleaner.

A more intriguing suggestion is that husbands pay their wives salaries for housework. I suggested this to my wife and she said I don't make enough money to pay her to do that job again. Neither, according to her, does J. Paul Getty. I am coming to the feeling that this is a job that should not be done by any one person for love or for money.

This is not to put down the whole experience. By the end of the year, I had succeeded in organizing my time so that there were a few hours for the occasional book, the random round of golf. Then, too, it was a pleasure to be more than a weekend visitor in my kids' lives. While my wife and I are now willing to de-emphasize housekeeping, neither of us would cut back on what some people call parenting and what I look at as the one solid reward in this belated and male motherhood of mine.

Of course, I had it easy—relatively easy anyway. This was my little experiment, not my destiny. There is a considerable difference between a year in prison and a life sentence.

It will be argued: well, *someone* has to do these things. Not necessarily. In the first place, some two can do most of these things. Secondly, I can think of no area in modern life that could more easily sustain a policy of benign neglect than the home. I'm arguing here in favor of letting the dust gather where it may; in favor of making greater use of slow cookers and nearby fish-and-chips stands; of abolishing, as far as possible, the position of unpaid servant in the family.

Many men surely will find this line of thought threatening. That's just as it should be. Few plantation owners were enthusiastic about the Emancipation Proclamation. What is more surprising is that these thoughts will prove equally threatening to many women. OK. Those females who demand the right to remain in service should not necessarily be discouraged—we all know how hard it is to find decent household help these days.

I suspect the real reason for many women's reluctance to break bonds is fear of the world that exists outside the home. They sense the enormous complexity of their husbands' lives, the tremendous skills required to head up a team of salesmen or to write cigarette commercials or to manufacture lawn fertilizer. The mind that feels these fears may be beyond the reach of change.

It is another sort of mind, the mind that finds itself in constant rebellion against the limitations of housewifery, that concerns me more here. To this mind, this person, we should say: go ahead. There is a world out here, a whole planet of possibilities. The real danger is that you won't do it. If Gutenberg had been a housewife, I might be writing these words with a quill pen. And if Edison had been a housewife, you might be reading them by candlelight.

No escape is simple and a certain amount of toughness will be required. How do you do it? You might start by learning how to sweep things under the rug. You might have to stop pampering the rest of the family—let 'em eat leftovers. And be prepared for the opposition that will surely develop. Even the most loving family hates to lose that trusted servant, that faithful family retainer, that little old homemaker, you. No one enjoys it when the most marvelous appliance of them all breaks down. But if it will be any comfort to you, the life you save will surely be your own.

Assignment 16 A 100-Word Summary

Once more you're on your own. No summary is given at the back of the book for this article nor for the two that follow.

Biking's New Breed

Michael Hofferber

From the early part of the century through the mid-1950s, America's youngsters grew up on the balloon tires and upright handlebars of the two-wheeler—that tried-and-true workhorse of a bicycle turned out by such famous names as Schwinn, Rollfast, Roadmaster and Columbia.

But the two-wheeler had all but faded into oblivion by the early 1960s, eclipsed by sleek, lightweight European three-speed and 10-speed models. The splendidly skeletal foreign bikes outran and outshone the traditional but clunky-looking two-wheeler. Even newspaper boys dropped the American-builts for the skinny-tired racers that bespoke the modern age of bicycling.

Well, hold on to your curved handlebars—the two-wheeler is staging a comeback. It's back in a new form called a "mountain bike," or "klunker." Boasting the multiple gears and hand brakes of a European lightweight plus superlight alloy frames and precision components borrowed from 10-speed technology, this revamped two-wheeler is a new breed of bicycle. The mountain bike goes places where 10-speeds fear to tread—up mountains, down rutted sideroads and trails, and through both mud and snow.

From high mountain paths to rocky canyon floors, mountain bikes are as at home in the outdoors as a mule. Proponents say they can climb like a mountain goat and glide like a hawk. Their wide, knobby tires and sturdy frames carry riders over terrain never before explored by bicyclists.

Not just kids are riding these mountain bikes. Adults have discovered them, too, and for many it has been a nostalgic reunion with the bicycle of their childhood. As one middle-aged mountain-biker exclaimed after his first ride, "It's been a long time since I felt like I was 14 again!"

Fittingly, mountain bikes were born in the mountains of Colorado and California. About seven years ago bicyclists there began looking for something to ride on the logging roads and hiking trails that wind across many Western states. The popular 10-speeds were too delicate and easily damaged to take off-pavement. The heavy two-wheelers, on the other hand, had some definite advantages. They were solid and rugged and could take the beating off-road riding would give them.

Reprinted courtesy of *Ford Times,* June 1983.

Bicycle builders who enjoyed off-road bicycling began to tinker with old two-wheelers they found at garage sales or the dusty back rooms of hardware stores. They wanted to make them faster, lighter and better climbers. One of the first and most important additions to the conventional two-wheeler was the "derailleur," or multiple-speed gear changer. With 5, 10 and even 15 speeds to choose from, bicyclists found they could cruise up hillsides that were unapproachable with one speed.

In the late 1970s, a small group of bicycle framebuilders began constructing two-wheelers out of the same lightweight chrome-molybdenum alloy tubing as the European 10-speeds. These superlight metals were as hard as steel but not nearly as heavy. A frame sturdy enough to withstand the rigors of off-road riding only had to weigh a pound or two more than a 10-speed. The new two-wheelers could actually be carried up terrain that couldn't be ridden over, like portaging a canoe.

Next came the wide, knobby tires that could grip gravel, loose dirt or wet leaves as surely as pavement. . . . The new tires seemed to flow over rocks, logs and ditches with scarcely a bump. Their awesome traction and cornering ability made them perfect for high-speed descents down heart-stopping slopes.

The revolution in two-wheelers was complete. No longer were they resigned to being heavy, clumsy beasts. As the new "mountain bikes," they could corner sharper, climb higher and take more of a beating than any 10-speed—and many bicyclists began taking notice.

. . . . .

Whether it becomes the most popular bike or not, the mountain bike appears to have found a place in the hearts of a wide variety of bicyclists —racers looking for adventure, tourists expanding their horizons, commuters who want an indestructible bike, and beginners who just like its ease of riding.

From mountains to city, the two-wheeler has returned.

Assignment 17 A 100-Word Summary

Here is an excerpt from an article by a University of Michigan Law School professor whose specialty is environmental and public land law. Note that difficult words are defined in the margin.

Will the National Parks Survive?

Joseph L. Sax

If you look carefully, you will see in every national park an unobtrusive bronze tablet dedicated to Steve Mather, the Chicago mining magnate who was the first director of the Park Service. Its brief inscription ends with the words "There will never come an end to the good that he has done." Mather was the sort of public servant who seems wholly to have vanished from our national life. He rode around the parks in a big Packard touring car, with the license number USNPS-1, greeting park visitors; when a facility was needed at Yosemite, and Congress refused to appropriate funds, Mather reached into his own pocket and financed the purchase; and when a concessioner refused to remove an illegal sawmill in Glacier Park, Mather personally appeared on the scene, invited guests from the nearby hotel to come outside for a demonstration, and, as if he were laying a cornerstone, lighted a fuse and blew up the sawmill with thirteen charges of TNT. With each detonation, he became more cheerful. "Just celebrating my daughter's nineteenth birthday," he said.

unobtrusive—not readily noticeable
magnate—influential person
detonation—explosion

The serious business of the parks, then as now, was to control the itch of commercial and industrial interests to get their hands on the spectacular untapped resources the national parks represented, and it was in resisting these pressures that Mather was at his best. There is hardly a scheme that has not at some time been put forward for what a Senate Committee once called "the vandalism of improvement" of the great western parks. For years entrepreneurs sought to build a steam-powered elevator to take visitors down into the Grand Canyon of the Yellowstone, and in the 1920s a San Fran-

entrepreneur—one who organizes and assumes the risks of an enterprise

University of Chicago Magazine, Spring 1983.

cisco engineer named Davol put forward a scheme to string a cableway across the Grand Canyon, all the way from the El Tovar Hotel on the south to the North Rim. Perhaps the gravest threat was a plan to dam up Yellowstone National Park for water power and irrigation. Recognizing that the Yellowstone project would set a shaping precedent for the entire park system, Mather fought it relentlessly, and ultimately successfully, in the years following World War I.

relentlessly—persistently
ultimately—finally

Since then, the national parks have been conceded to be off limits to water and energy development, commercial lumbering and mining. There have, of course, been some exceptions, and there were still a few great battles to be fought: Proposed dams that would have backed water up into Grand Canyon brought the Sierra Club to national prominence in the 1960s; and during World War II, Interior Secretary Harold Ickes fought and won a bitter battle to save Olympic Park's massive sitka spruces from military procurement and eager Washington State lumber interests. Grazing is still an issue in Utah's Capitol Reef National Park, and there has been a uranium mine on the south rim of Grand Canyon. All in all, however, the national park borders were secured, and Mather's foresight vindicated.

conceded—acknowledged

procurement—taking possession of

vindicated—shown to be right

The parks were reasonably safe until the oil shock of the mid-1970s renewed the old threats with a savage new twist. While respecting parklands themselves, energy developers moved up to their borders, lines on maps that neither wildlife nor water systems are able to respect. Coal mining now stands poised just at the edge of Glacier and Bryce Canyon Parks; oil and gas exploration is threatened on one side of Yellowstone Park and geothermal development on the other. The Department of Energy would like to install the national nuclear waste dump just outside Canyonlands National Park on a site that would be reached by trainloads of radioactive waste following the path of the Colorado River. The threats literally number in the hundreds, and they range from mining at the remotest areas, such as the Indian ruins at Chaco Canyon in northern New Mexico, to a nuclear power plant that was scheduled for construction just beyond the

geothermal—pertaining to the internal heat of the earth

boundary of the Indiana Dunes National Lakeshore.

. . . . .

The external threat problem has been well known for years to those who keep an eye on national park matters. Congress has spent tens of millions of dollars trying to repair the damage done to Redwoods National Park by commercial logging on private lands adjacent to the park. The Park Service fought (for a while) and lost (ultimately) in an effort to keep developers from desecrating the site of Gettysburg National Battlefield. It took a Supreme Court decision, years of politicking and an Act of Congress to prevent the Forest Service and Walt Disney Enterprises from building a high speed road through Sequoia National Park in order to turn California's Mineral King Valley into a winter ski resort. . . .

desecrating—taking away the sacredness of

There is no other word to describe the present situation than the much overused term crisis. Without dramatic action to buffer them, the national parks simply will not survive the next few decades as the nearly-pristine natural landscapes that have made them the envy and model of the world for 110 years.

pristine—unspoiled

Assignment 18 A 100-Word Summary

Now that you have had some practice in writing summaries, make use of your skill in reading your textbooks. When you finish reading a chapter, summarize it immediately, and you'll not only understand it better but will remember it longer and have the summary ready for review.

Here is part of a chapter from an astronomy textbook. Because it contains so much important information, you'll have to choose for your 100-word summary only the most striking facts, ones that you will want to remember.

The Nature of the Universe

Thomas L. Swihart

The Universe is the sum of all things that can be scientifically measured, at least in principle, so it is not possible to make a complete list of its contents. It is possible to describe a few of the major ingredients, however, and the background this gives will help to show how the details to be studied later fit into the whole.

GALAXIES

Matter is not spread evenly throughout the Universe, but is concentrated into large bunches called *galaxies*. A galaxy is an extremely large collection of stars that is held together by the force of gravity. A galaxy may contain tens or hundreds of billions of stars, each star being about as large and bright and hot as the Sun. Billions of galaxies are known to exist. There may also be large amounts of matter in space between the galaxies, although the evidence to date indicates that this isn't the case.

The size of galaxies and the distances between them are so large as to be almost beyond comprehension. Distances in astronomy tend to be so big that the speed of light is often used to measure them. Light travels at a speed of about 186,000 miles or 300,000 kilometers each second—that's nearly *eight* times around the Earth in 1 second. At this speed, light reaches us from the Moon in a little more than 1 second, while it takes 8 minutes to arrive here from the Sun. According to scientific ideas held today, it is not possible to move faster than light: It is the ultimate in speed. Yet some galaxies are so big that it takes 100,000 years or more for light just to cross from one side to the other.

In one year light can travel a distance of about 6 trillion miles. (A trillion is written 1,000,000,000,000.) This distance is called a *light-year* (not a length of time), and it is convenient to measure large distances in light-years. We live in a large galaxy called the *Milky Way*, and it has a diameter of about 100,000 light-years. The Milky Way is one of the larger galaxies, although it is by no means the largest.

A certain area of the sky is known as the constellation of Andromeda (an-DROM-e-da). On a very dark, clear night a person with good eyes might barely be able to see a faint hazy spot in Andromeda, although it is easily seen with binoculars. The object is called the *Andromeda galaxy*, and it is over 2 million light-years away. This means that when you look at the Andromeda galaxy, you are seeing it as it appeared over 2 million years ago; what you are seeing is the light that was emitted by the stars in that galaxy before modern man appeared on the Earth. Thus looking out at great distances is also looking back at times far in the past. In spite of its great distance, the Andromeda galaxy is one of the closest ones to us.

. . . . .

Is there a limit to how many galaxies exist and how far away they extend? Is there a limit to how far into the past they have existed and how long they will last? Or does the Universe have an infinite size and age? So far, astronomers have been able to give only very incomplete answers to these intriguing questions, and I do not believe that we will ever be able to answer them with much confidence. Past experience also reveals that when answers are found to "ultimate" questions, other ultimate questions, unimaginable earlier, arise to take their place. This continuous search for answers does give astronomers a very exciting profession.

WRITING AN APPLICATION

Assignment 19 A Letter of Application

You may not need to do much writing in the career you have chosen, but almost certainly you will at some time need to write a letter of application. Write a letter of application now, either for a job this coming summer or for a job you might want to apply for after you finish college. Then write a separate personal data sheet. Follow the forms given here.

240 West 37th Avenue
San Mateo, CA 94403
January 9, 1985

Ms. Dorothy Ames
Camp Fire Service Center
270 Washington Street
Santa Clara, CA 95050

Dear Ms. Ames:

My friend Kathy Church, who is going to be a counselor at your Camp Wastahi in August, has told me that you still have a few openings for counselors. I'd certainly like to be considered for a position.

I'm now in my second year at the College of San Mateo, where I'm majoring in biology and minoring in physical education. I was a member of the Varsity Swim Team in 1984 and won All Conference Honors in the Individual Medley. I also placed third in the State Meet in the same event. I have completed my Senior Life Saving Certification and at present am enrolled in the Water Safety Instructors Course.

Because going to Camp Fire Camp was one of the highlights of my own high school days, I'd like to help other girls have a good camp experience. I'd enjoy taking them on bird hikes and nature walks, and I'd value the opportunity to gain teaching experience by helping with swimming instruction and other sports.

I'm enclosing a data sheet and will be glad to come for an interview at your convenience.

Sincerely,

Jane Doe

Jane Doe

PERSONAL DATA SHEET

Jane Doe
240 West 37th Avenue
San Mateo, CA 94403
Telephone: 000-000-0000

PERSONAL
Age 20
Height 5 feet, 4 inches
Weight 130 pounds
Unmarried

EDUCATION
1983–85 College of San Mateo. Major in biology; minor in physical education
1979–83 Palo Alto High School, Palo Alto, CA

ACTIVITIES
1983–85 Varsity Swim Team, College of San Mateo. In 1984 won All Conference Honors in Individual Medley. Won third place in State Meet in same event.

WORK EXPERIENCE
1984 summer Worked at College of San Mateo Cafeteria
1983 summer Worked as a volunteer assistant in the East Palo Alto Montessori Day Care Center

REFERENCES
Mr. George Blitz
Biology Department
College of San Mateo
San Mateo, CA 94402

Ms. Joeann Ingraham
Department of Physical Education/Athletics
College of San Mateo
San Mateo, CA 94402

Mr. Russell Whiteford
Mid Peninsula Youth & Community Services, Inc.
2400 Ralmar Court
East Palo Alto, CA 94303

WRITING AN EVALUATION

Assignment 20 An Evaluation of My Performance

Do five minutes of free writing in preparation for writing a short paper on your performance in this course. Don't evaluate the course—it may have been bad or good—but simply evaluate how you performed. Although you may need to mention some weakness or strength of the course, the emphasis should be on how you reacted to that weakness or strength.

Don't be afraid to be honest. This isn't an occasion for apple-polishing. If you've gained little, you'll write a better paper by saying so than by trying to concoct phony gains. Someone who has gained little may write a better paper than someone who has gained much. How well the paper is organized and whether there are plenty of specific examples will determine the effectiveness of the paper.

Before starting your paper, write your thesis statement, listing your supporting points. If you've made gains, list the kinds—gain in writing skill, gain in confidence, gain in study habits . . . . Or, if you've gained little, list the reasons why—lack of time, lack of interest, getting off to a bad start . . . .

Since no one will have all gains or all losses in any course, you may want to include in your introduction or conclusion a sentence about the other side.

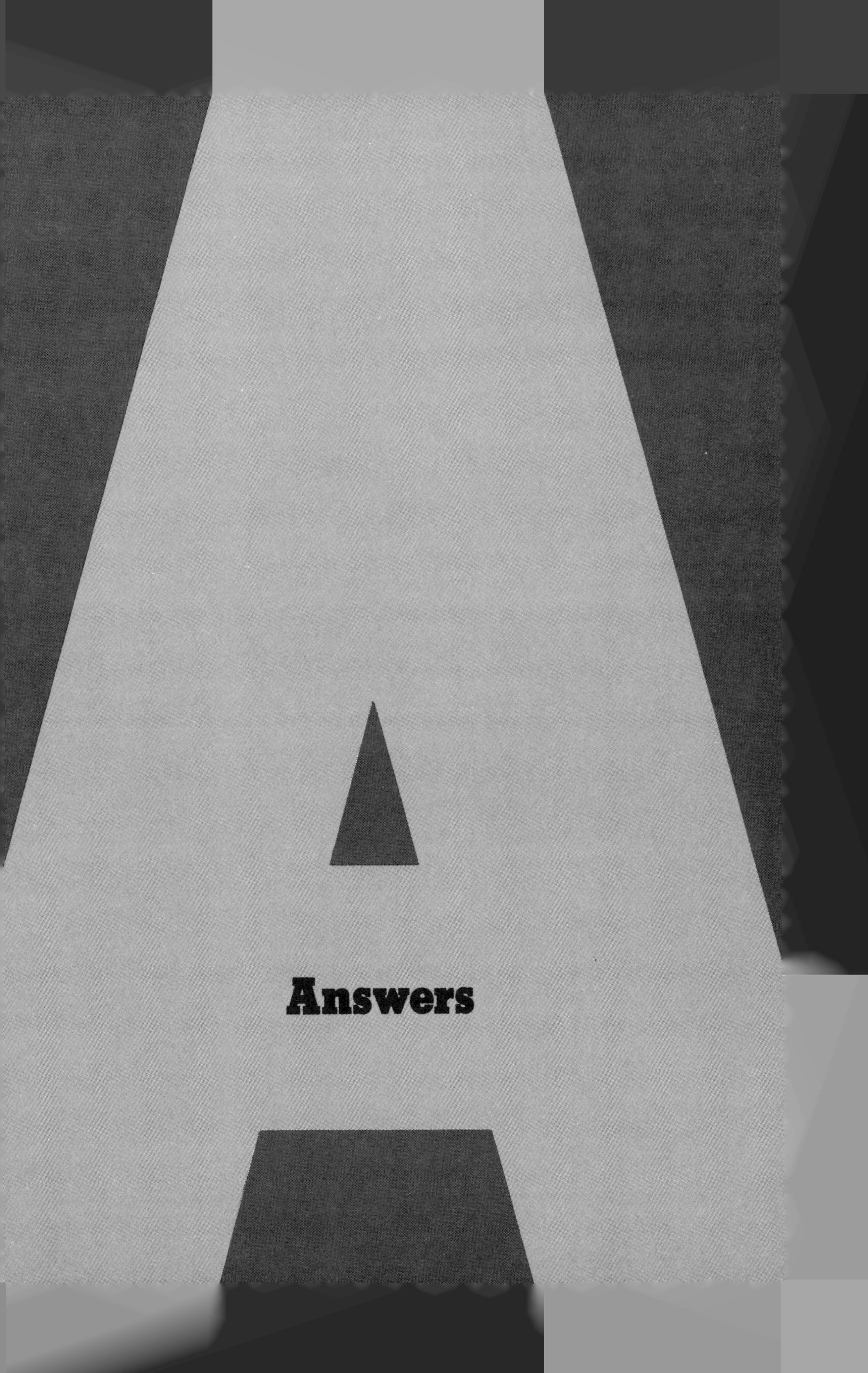

Answers

Answers

Words Often Confused (p. 10)

EXERCISE 1

1. course, have
2. already, know, do
3. an, effect
4. accept, advice
5. It's, knew, course
6. conscious, no
7. choose, new
8. no, do
9. hear
10. all ready, a, new

EXERCISE 2

1. cloths, coarse
2. except, knew, have
3. conscience, a
4. already, due, do
5. all ready, except, cloths
6. our, brakes
7. breaking
8. dose
9. new
10. conscious, course, its

EXERCISE 3

1. new, already
2. doesn't, it's
3. know, affect, its
4. advice, compliment
5. except, here
6. choose, are
7. course, know
8. conscious, our
9. affect, an
10. have, or

EXERCISE 4

1. an, due
2. chose, know
3. It's, effect
4. know, have
5. it's, all ready
6. course, an
7. does, accept
8. it's, effect
9. Our, are
10. hear, doesn't

EXERCISE 5

1. an
2. knew, know, it's, our
3. Its, its
4. effect
5. conscious
6. or, an
7. chose, an
8. its, its
9. an
10. feel, does

EXERCISE 6

1. Here, are, our
2. new, desert
3. know, it's
4. no, do
5. already, our
6. accept, advice
7. an, break
8. chose, fourth
9. course, effect, its
10. know, it's, an

EXERCISE 7

1. our, course
2. clothes, new
3. chose, know
4. new, fill
5. course, conscious, here
6. our
7. choose, feel
8. accept
9. all ready, desert
10. no, an

EXERCISE 8

1. choose, clothes
2. It's, already
3. new, a
4. doesn't, except
5. chose, complement
6. feel, choose, clothes
7. does, advise
8. do, accept, advice
9. course, break
10. conscience, forth

EXERCISE 9

1. an, our
2. course, already, knew, it's
3. conscious, its
4. have, do, it's, an
5. knew
6. know, it's
7. an
8. no
9. know, does
10. course, already

EXERCISE 10

1. chose, except
2. new, already
3. break, here
4. do, it's
5. doesn't, does
6. advice
7. It's
8. are
9. course, dessert
10. conscious, do, have

Words Often Confused (continued) (p. 19)

EXERCISE 1

1. piece, quite
2. have, than
3. You're, dessert
4. Here, choose
5. know, advice
6. course, doesn't
7. It's, too
8. break, your
9. Who's, woman
10. knew, past

EXERCISE 2

1. Where, threw
2. loose, lose
3. It's, already
4. knew, quite
5. know, write
6. fourth, it's
7. It's, does
8. principal, too
9. have, past
10. course, effect

EXERCISE 3

1. an
2. It's, new
3. there
4. are, courses
5. It's
6. course, there, their
7. than
8. loose, weather, whether
9. their
10. through

EXERCISE 4

1. piece, loose
2. brakes, then, there, no
3. right
4. It's, quite
5. where
6. than, too
7. led, its
8. lead, their
9. morale, than, it's
10. they're

EXERCISE 5

1. advice
2. its, than
3. passed
4. It's
5. hear
6. passed, there
7. quite
8. women's
9. course, women, passed
10. It's, too, whether, their

EXERCISE 6

1. break
2. do
3. do, an
4. there
5. threw, write
6. where, know, whether, or
7. course, an
8. write, then, right
9. led, quite
10. too, principal

EXERCISE 7

1. morale, personnel, where
2. personal, their
3. They're, their
4. whose
5. Our, quite, woman, through
6. principles, moral
7. personnel, their
8. quite, lose, our, principal
9. know, where
10. There, right

EXERCISE 8

1. quiet, except
2. peace
3. whether, dessert
4. do, there
5. weather, dessert
6. two, are
7. through, then
8. two, whether
9. you're
10. Then, where

EXERCISE 9

1. know, whether
2. principal, course, does
3. it's, our, write
4. our
5. quite
6. or
7. course, than
8. know
9. know, where
10. quite, through

EXERCISE 10

1. whether, weather, affect
2. all ready
3. Where, piece
4. quite, there
5. coarse
6. You're, right, it's
7. past, then, Fourth
8. doesn't, whether
9. our
10. know, woman, who's

Proofreading Exercise (p. 24)

. . . an old wind-up . . . . I knew . . . . There sure . . . . back where they logically . . . . all through . . . . And of course

Contractions (p. 26)

EXERCISE 1

1. I'm, didn't
2. I'd, I'd
3. I'm, didn't
4. I'd, didn't
5. didn't, I've
6. It's, it's
7. It's, I'll
8. can't, isn't
9. can't, they've
10. I'm, I'll, I've

EXERCISE 2

1. I'm, I've
2. isn't, it's
3. I've, there's
4. hasn't, we've
5. who's, can't
6. It's, who's
7. I'm, who's, I'll
8. I'm, they're
9. I've, there's
10. I've, wouldn't

EXERCISE 3

1. I've
2. They're, can't
3. They've
4.
5. it's
6. they're
7. can't, aren't
8. it's
9. aren't
10. They're

EXERCISE 4

1. I've, it's
2. I'd, I'd
3. I'd
4. you've, it's
5. it's
6. you'll
7. you're, you'll
8. you're
9. It's, you're, don't
10. you'll

EXERCISE 5

1. I've
2. didn't, they've
3. they'd, they've
4. They'd
5. Isn't, didn't
6. We've
7. It's, isn't
8. What's
9. haven't, that's
10. It'll, they've

EXERCISE 6

1. Haven't
2. I've
3. aren't, they're
4. aren't, they're
5. There's
6. you've, you'll
7. they're
8. It's
9. It's
10. it's, they're

EXERCISE 7

1. I've, can't, that's
2. There's, didn't
3. I'll
4. It's
5. I'd
6. It's
7. there's
8. You'll, you'll
9. It's, I'm
10. I'm

EXERCISE 8

1. I'm, it's
2. I'd, it's
3. I've, they're
4. I've
5. I'm, don't
6. It's, I've
7. I've
8. I'm, I'm
9. it's, what's
10. I've, can't

EXERCISE 9

1. I've, didn't
2. It's
3. didn't
4. hadn't
5. didn't
6. didn't
7. wasn't, didn't
8. It's
9. aren't
10. I'll

EXERCISE 10

1. I've, they're
2. can't
3. aren't, it's
4. won't
5. It's
6. that's, can't
7. doesn't
8. don't
9. doesn't
10. she's

Possessives (p. 33)

EXERCISE 1

1. man's
2.
3. Kimberley's, Sarah's
4. Alfredo's
5.
6. Everyone's
7. college's
8. Saturday's
9. yesterday's
10. governor's

EXERCISE 2

1. everybody's
2. professor's
3. Someone's
4. person's
5. students'
6. students'
7. Jim's
8. Michael's
9. Mike's
10. team's

EXERCISE 3

1. day's
2. Tony's, Sue's
3. Sue's
4. Scouts', orthodontist's
5. day's
6. mother's
7. today's
8. Chicago's, Miami's
9. tomorrow's
10. children's

EXERCISE 4

1. Women's
2. senator's
3. president's
4. chairperson's
5. senator's
6. audience's
7. anybody's
8. library's
9. Jennifer's
10. women's

EXERCISE 5

1. visitor's
2.
3. museum's
4. Children's
5. museum's, visitors'
6. Indians'
7. loom's
8. museum's
9. theater's
10.

EXERCISE 6

1. Sally's
2. butterfly's
3. butterfly's, moth's
4. moth's
5. insects'
6. butterfly's
7. insects'
8. butterfly's
9. Sally's
10. flowers'

EXERCISE 7

1. Lincoln's
2. settlers'
3. Beethoven's
4. people's
5. Children's
6. Girls'
7. Pablo's, Leroy's
8. Cheryl's
9. Heather's
10. day's

EXERCISE 8

1. Dad's
2. father's
3. mother's
4. Jones'
5. Jones'
6.
7.
8. Johnsons'
9. Eric's, Dennis'
10. Charles'

EXERCISE 9

1. Saturday's
2. everybody's
3. men's, women's
4. boys', men's
5. children's
6. niece's
7. sister's
8. parents'
9. morning's
10. people's

EXERCISE 10

1. Matthew's
2. Victor's
3. Jeffrey's
4. else's
5. Haley's
6. judge's
7. anyone's
8. brother-in-law's
9. Rebecca's
10. wife's

Review of Contractions and Possessives (p. 37)

EXERCISE 1

1. I've
2. I'd, don't
3. doesn't
4. it's
5. plant's
6.
7. plant's
8. That's, I'd, don't
9. they're, they're
10. they're

EXERCISE 2

1. I'd, we'd
2. Doug's
3.
4. we'd, we've
5. We'd, it's, country's
6. world's
7. It's, they've
8. visitors'
9. we'd
10. Earth's

EXERCISE 3

1. can't
2. she's, family's
3. She's
4. She's
5. it's
6. everything's
7. I've
8.
9. They've
10. snake's

EXERCISE 4

It's going to be a summer of traveling for my brothers. They're going to the West Coast in Mark's car. They had thought of taking Miles' van, but it's a gas guzzler. Mark's VW won't be so expensive to run. They haven't planned their route yet, but they'll no doubt hit Idaho because Mark's best friend lives there, and a few nights' lodging and a few free meals won't be unwelcome. The boys will be gone a month or maybe longer if they're lucky enough to find jobs. Their aim is to see whether they'd like to settle in the West and also just to see a part of the country they haven't seen before.

Proofreading Exercise (p. 39)

. . . but it's hard . . . . where there were about 20 . . . . people's homes. We could choose . . . . I must have cleaned . . . . didn't make a cent

Doubling the Final Consonant (p. 42)

EXERCISE 1

1. putting
2. controlling
3. admitting
4. mopping
5. planning
6. hopping
7. jumping
8. knitting
9. marking
10. creeping

EXERCISE 2

1. returning
2. swimming
3. singing
4. benefiting
5. loafing
6. nailing
7. omitting
8. occurring
9. shopping
10. interrupting

EXERCISE 3

1. beginning
2. spelling
3. preferring
4. fishing
5. hunting
6. excelling
7. wrapping
8. stopping
9. wedding
10. screaming

EXERCISE 4

1. feeling
2. murmuring
3. turning
4. adding
5. subtracting
6. streaming
7. expelling
8. missing
9. getting
10. stressing

EXERCISE 5

1. forgetting
2. misspelling
3. fitting
4. planting
5. pinning
6. trusting
7. sipping
8. flopping
9. reaping
10. carting

Progress Test (p. 43)

1. B
2. B
3. B
4. A
5. B
6. A
7. B
8. B
9. A
10. A
11. B
12. B
13. B
14. A
15. B

Subjects and Verbs (p. 56)

EXERCISE 1

1. trees are
2. They grow
3. They are
4. Redwoods grow
5. They resist
6. bark resists
7. trees live
8. Many were
9. many are
10. wood varies

EXERCISE 2

1. we saw
2. fire swept
3. smoke was
4. flames were
5. flames rose
6. motorist saw
7. he alerted
8. fighters spread
9. They had
10. cabin burned

EXERCISE 3

1. instructor stresses
2. attitude is
3. I keep
4. I worked
5. paper has
6. I typed
7. papers make
8. paper satisfies
9. I worked
10. (You) give

EXERCISE 4

1. koala is
2. It is
3. koala looks
4. animal has
5. food consists
6. it eats
7. Leaves are
8. koala is
9. It crawls
10. koala rides

EXERCISE 5

1. cloud was
2. lizard darted
3. Locusts swarmed
4. sound grew
5. we saw
6. wind shifted
7. mountains rose
8. sun sank
9. prairie became
10. We were

EXERCISE 6

1. Persians built
2. windmills meet
3. windpower provides
4. future looks
5. government supports
6. It encourages
7. It gives
8. windmills are
9. they provide
10. windpower has

EXERCISE 7

1. state has
2. cardinal is
3. states chose
4. states are
5. bird is
6. It belongs
7. nene is
8. bird is
9. wren was
10. bird is

EXERCISE 8

1. Oceans cover
2. oceans are
3. waters join
4. they make
5. sea is
6. fluids are
7. This is
8. oceans give
9. They send
10. clouds supply

EXERCISE 9

1. sea gives
2. one-fifth comes
3. sea provides
4. People play
5. people like
6. 30 percent live
7. People like
8. pleasures include
9. pleasures include
10. Divers explore

EXERCISE 10

1. I took
2. I visited
3. It contains
4. I learned
5. Seurat used
6. Picasso burned
7. Van Gogh applied
8. paintings interested
9. I bought
10. (You) try

Subjects Not in Prepositional Phrases (p. 61)

EXERCISE 1

1. Some of my friends went to the game with me.
2. Most of the bleachers were full.
3. But all of us found good seats in the middle of the bleachers.
4. During the game the atmosphere was tense.
5. Three of the players were on probation.
6. Neither of the teams scored during the first half.
7. Some of the spectators left at the end of the first half.
8. The most exciting part of the entire game was the last quarter.
9. In the last two minutes our team made a touchdown.
10. But the outcome of the game was a tie between the two teams.

EXERCISE 2

1. All of my classes are on the top floor of Carwood Hall.
2. Most of my courses require a lot of homework.
3. Most of my professors give true-false tests.
4. But one of my professors gives essay tests.
5. All of us find the true-false tests easier.
6. One of the requirements of my economics course is a term paper.
7. Much of my time goes into that term paper.
8. In most classes an ability in writing helps.
9. A term paper with good organization gets a higher grade.
10. And writing without errors is also a plus.

EXERCISE 3

1. Two of my friends went with me on a vacation.
2. All of us wanted to see more of California.
3. Above all, we wanted to see Muir Woods.
4. The road to the woods is long and winding.
5. But all of us were enchanted with the cathedral-like woods.
6. The quietness of the scene among the big trees was breathtaking.

7. All ~~of us~~ learned a great deal that day ~~about redwoods~~.
8. The next place ~~on our list~~ was Golden Gate Park.
9. ~~With its aquarium, arboretum, and museums~~, it kept us busy ~~for an entire day~~.
10. Finally the three ~~of us~~ had tea ~~in the Oriental Tea Garden~~.

EXERCISE 4

1. Hibernation differs
2. animals relax
3. life stops
4. breathing becomes
5. beating becomes
6. body is
7. kinds freeze
8. Mammals prepare
9. They store
10. Groundhogs become

EXERCISE 5

1. bird is
2. it is
3. eagles are
4. Cedar Glen is
5. they gather
6. they stay
7. area is
8. eagles perch
9. eagles spend
10. Havens ensure

EXERCISE 6

1. One is
2. I pursue
3. rung was
4. I made
5. rung was
6. coat finished
7. One was
8. metal was
9. I cleaned
10. coat made

EXERCISE 7

1. Great Pyramid exists
2. Egyptians used
3. Hanging Gardens were
4. gardens were
5. pump watered
6. one was
7. meaning is
8. It stood
9. it toppled
10. someone sold

EXERCISE 8

1. wonders are
2. one is
3. arch spans
4. bridge is
5. tributary carved
6. it arches
7. It is
8. width is
9. it is
10. It is

EXERCISE 9

1. Making is
2. sap rises
3. Indians taught
4. farmer bores
5. He inserts
6. sap drips
7. Sap ferments
8. farmer sends
9. tree yields
10. it takes

EXERCISE 10

1. we visited
2. island stands
3. peaks rise
4. natives call
5. It is
6. havens are
7. Admiralty Island is
8. firm wants
9. government passed
10. it takes

More about Verbs and Subjects (p. 66)

EXERCISE 1

1. fires have been
2. fires were started
3. Conditions must be
4. Vegetation contains, will burn
5. fires start, spread
6. Fire can race
7. land can change
8. rain will extinguish
9. number has increased
10. vigilance is

EXERCISE 2

1. she had been collecting
2. She would identify
3. she would place
4. Limpets had been
5. shells could be found
6. Others could be found
7. she awoke, scanned
8. She went, wandered
9. She gathered, took
10. she, friends went, had

EXERCISE 3

1. Harvesting is
2. It sells
3. rice is, is
4. Indians used
5. Minnesota produces, has
6. harvesting leaves, is
7. Indians harvest
8. ricers must obtain, may harvest
9. They row, tap
10. ricers must cope, must beware

EXERCISE 4

1. Library is
2. items are included
3. items are added
4. forms are included
5. It was established
6. it has become
7. Libraries can borrow
8. people can go, use
9. manuscripts, photographs, recordings, reels are
10. It houses

EXERCISE 5

1. papers are stored
2. pieces may be found
3. collection is included
4. Two-thirds are
5. book is
6. volume is
7. collections are housed
8. building is
9. sculptures, paintings, murals were produced
10. Visitors are given

EXERCISE 6

1. I have been reading
2. explosion was
3. It buried, killed
4. blast was, occurred
5. It was
6. blast blew, caused
7. miles were buried
8. eruption occurred
9. blast had, caused
10. volcanoes are

EXERCISE 7

1. Galileo made
2. Improvements have been made
3. astronomers have been
4. atmosphere has interfered
5. telescope was put
6. telescope was operated
7. it orbited
8. It made
9. It could detect
10. That would be

EXERCISE 8

1. He opened, looked
2. days were
3. Night came, lasted
4. tracks could be seen
5. tracks could be seen
6. mountains, cliffs looked
7. cabin was
8. lights appeared
9. cause is
10. belts are

EXERCISE 9

1. Yellow has been
2. Pencils have sold
3. pencils are sold
4. pencil can draw
5. America could conserve
6. cans can be separated, can be put
7. cities are recovering
8. cans are being recycled
9. America is realizing
10. environmentalists are

EXERCISE 10

1. I have been learning
2. roots mean
3. flowers do turn
4. roots mean
5. odor gave
6. daisy is
7. tulip comes, means
8. Dandelion has come
9. points do look
10. I am enjoying, want

Correcting Run-together Sentences (p. 72)

EXERCISE 1

1. Pronunciations change, words are being added
2. (You) read, you will learn
3. (You) note, they will help
4. Keeping is, you can review
5. (You) use. It's
6. (You) use, you will forget
7. handguns circulate, million are sold
8. Half are committed
9. people believe, resent
10. others enumerate, they are working

EXERCISE 2

1. I am writing, he is
2. He has designed, he won
3. He has designed, achievement has restored
4. complex consists, it has
5. building, courthouse are included
6. courthouse is, roof is
7. Robson Square is, it is
8. Robson Square has
9. tank is heated, cooled; buildings are heated, cooled
10. I've learned, I hope

EXERCISE 3

1. clear. Not
2. lake. It
3. lake. Then
4. afternoon,
5. fish. We
6.
7.
8. country,
9. them. We
10. explorations,

EXERCISE 4

1. problems,
2. West. Now
3. Park,
4. natural,
5. bears,
6. well,
7. campgrounds,
8. homes,
9. dumps,
10. habits;

EXERCISE 5

1. blowing. Our
2. torrents;
3. shore. We
4.
5. quiet. Only
6.
7. cold;
8. cracks,
9.
10. downstream. It

EXERCISE 6

1. farm;
2. TV. He
3. books;
4. succeed. He
5. way;
6.
7. work,
8.
9. years,
10. them,

EXERCISE 7

1. violent. They
2. hour. Some . . . higher,
3.
4. long;
5. small, and . . . short,
6. knowing. They
7. walls. Shield
8. floor. Closets
9. shelter,
10. season,

EXERCISE 8

1.
2. fence,
3. tunneling;
4. West,
5. West. More
6. fence,
7. night,
8. country. Only
9. side,
10. barrier,

EXERCISE 9

1. Museum. It
2. *Louis.* Here
3. spacecraft. They
4.
5. *Workshop.* Here
6. ceiling,
7.
8. sensational;
9.
10. Institution. It

EXERCISE 10

1. Last spring we were driving through Arizona and decided to see the Petrified Forest. Therefore we took the 27-mile drive through that strange landscape. Trees have turned to stone, and thousands of great stone logs lie on the ground. We learned a great deal about petrified wood and were glad for the experience. We had seen a new part of our country. The National Park Service is preserving the area for future generations.
2. The most striking feature of the oceans is their vast size. The next most striking feature is the constant motion of their surfaces. One cause of the motion is the wind. It may make waves from an inch to over 60 feet in height. Another cause of waves is geologic disturbances such as earthquakes and volcanic eruptions below the surface of the oceans. Waves from geologic disturbances are sometimes incorrectly called tidal waves, but they have no relation to the tides.

Correcting Fragments (p. 80)

EXERCISE 1

1. I refused to go because I had homework to do.
2. I could make good grades if I studied.
3. After I finish college, I'll get a job.
4. They were out playing Frisbee while he was studying.
5. Her essay would have been better if she had rewritten it.
6. Unless you return your library book today, you'll have to pay a fine.
7. A large vocabulary is the characteristic that most often accompanies outstanding success.
8. He was searching for the money that he had dropped in the snow.
9. Although he looked a long time, he couldn't find it.
10. Until you understand subjects and verbs, you cannot understand clauses.

EXERCISE 2

1. If you are too busy for a vacation
2. Although I studied
3. If you want to learn to write
4. After I rewrite
5. When the sun went down
6. As it became dark
7. that may be the largest object in the universe
8. Whereas the Earth's diameter is about 8,000 miles
9. If you stood on the moon and looked back toward Earth
10. which was built in the third century B.C.

EXERCISE 3

1. As he ran to catch the ball, he missed it.
2.
3.
4. Because no one had told me about the new ruling, I was late with my report.
5. When I finally decide to really work, I can accomplish a lot.
6.
7. If I can just spend a couple of hours on my math, I can pass that test.
8.

9. When I'm finished with both of them, I can relax.
10.

EXERCISE 4

1.
2. As the ambulance came racing down the street, a crowd gathered.
3. When a book is really interesting, I read it rapidly.
4.
5. As we learned more about the problem, we sympathized with him.
6. Because I had so much homework for that evening, I stayed at home.
7. Unless something goes wrong, we're going to win.
8. While everyone else was studying, he was watching TV.
9.
10.

EXERCISE 5

1. Since the afternoon was hot,
2. Although there was no breeze in the woods,
3. As we sat under a large oak,
4. Although we could not see any birds,
5. And two yellowthroats were calling to each other as they . . . .
6. Because some bees were buzzing around a flower,
7. Since we didn't want to get stung,
8. While we sat there quietly, a downy . . . .
9. We watched in delight as it . . . .
10. When I made a light movement, it . . . .

EXERCISE 6

1. Although we think of apples as food for people,
2. Since bears are led by their sense of smell,
3. Apple leaves are eaten by deer while apple seeds . . . .
4. Because birds also eat young apple buds, apple growers have been . . . .
5. Now most apple growers accept the debudding because it actually . . . .
6. Although some trees hold their fruit all winter,
7. When the apples on the ground rot,
8. Since worms flourish in the enriched soil,
9. John Chapman, who was a nineteenth-century missionary from Massachusetts, traveled . . . .
10. As news of his work spread,

EXERCISE 7

1. Although this course is difficult,
2. Since I've been working on spelling,
3. My dad has commented that even . . . .
4. I like writing papers because . . . .

5. Although I like to hear other students' papers read,
6. Although they sometimes sound terrible,
7. When I do all the exercises,
8. When occasionally I don't do all the exercises,
9. Although I'm really not sure of myself,
10. Even though learning all this has been a struggle,

More about Fragments (p. 86)

EXERCISE 1

1. After answering the telephone and taking the message, she left.
2.
3. After falling on the ice and breaking his leg, he could no longer compete.
4. The announcement that there would be no classes on Friday was welcome.
5.
6. I don't know whether . . . .
7. My parents want . . . .
8. Not wanting to disappoint them, I made the effort to go.
9. My father is . . . .
10. Having always done his best in school, he graduated with honors.

EXERCISE 2

1. We had walked . . . .
2. We walked where . . . .
3. Trying to keep the fire burning, we gathered more wood.
4.
5. Having traveled almost 200 miles, we were weary.
6. It was a boring . . . .
7. I had nothing to do . . . .
8. Her family enjoyed the gracious . . . .
9. She needed a place . . . .
10. She finished the day . . . .

EXERCISE 3

1. They were facts . . . .
2. My hobby is not expensive.
3. She came at a time . . . .
4. Although neither of us was eager to undertake the job, we did it.
5. Each of us hoped . . . .
6. He was a fellow . . . .
7. Even though we were told that the game might be postponed, we went anyway.
8. I was sure . . . .
9.
10. The audience applauded wildly and called . . . .

EXERCISE 4

Individuals can help save our forests. Americans waste vast amounts of paper because they don't think of paper as forests. They think nothing of wasting an envelope because an envelope is only a tiny piece of paper, but it takes two million trees to make the yearly supply of 112 billion envelopes.

Even small savings can encourage others to save until finally the concerted efforts of enough individuals can make a difference.

EXERCISE 5

Future historians will probably call our age the time when humans began the exploration of space. Some historians say that space exploration marks a turning point in the history of the world. Some people criticize space exploration saying that the money should have been spent on the poor here on earth. Others say, however, that we wouldn't have spent the money on anything of greater human value. The annual space budget is less than one percent of federal spending whereas the bulk of federal spending goes to defense and to health, education, and welfare. There have been practical payoffs from space exploration. One is the transoceanic television broadcasts that can be relayed by communications satellites. Another payoff is the daily weather picture that appears on television screens. Still another payoff is the earth-resources satellites that circle the earth and help map remote regions, search for water and minerals, and monitor crops and timber. And the final payoff is military reconnaissance that helps make possible arms limitation agreements among nations.

EXERCISE 6

Welcome to Stouffer's Lasagna and more than 40 delicious entrees. It's food that good cooks appreciate. And they appreciate it even more because we've done the work.

Set yourself free with Stouffer's.

EXERCISE 7

Hartmann has an interesting angle on luggage—the right angle.

When we make Hartmann luggage, we never cut corners. We keep them nice and square for good reason. . . .

And you can pack more neatly too because your clothes fit snugly right against the corner. . . .

Our master craftsmen tailor each exquisite detail of our luggage stitch by stitch from the handle to the inside lining. . . .

You'll never find a production shortcut—or a cut corner in a Hartmann. And that is why Hartmann isn't the cheapest luggage you can buy. . . .

Review of Run-together Sentences and Fragments (p. 90)

1. In the 1960s Lake Erie was so polluted that experts feared there wouldn't be a single living organism in it within 20 years. Strict antipollution laws in the United States and Canada, however, have eliminated much of the industrial pollution. Also better sewage-treatment methods have reduced the flow of phosphorus into the lake. Now the waters are teeming with fish again, and the beaches are crowded with swimmers.
2. How to dispose of hazardous chemical wastes is one of the greatest environmental problems. Society has benefited from the chemicals that control pain and disease and those that create new industrial products, but almost 35,000 chemicals used in the United States are classified as possibly hazardous to human health. The Environmental Protection Agency estimates that the United States is generating more than 77 billion pounds of hazardous chemical wastes a year and that only 10 percent are being handled safely. At least half of the wastes are being dumped indiscriminately, poisoning the earth and the underground water supplies. Toxic chemicals are adding to disease according to the Surgeon General, and virtually the entire population is carrying some body burden of these chemicals.
3. The science of medicine has had a long history. It began with superstitions, and illness was attributed to evil spirits. The ancient Egyptians were among the first to practice surgery. Anesthesia was, of course, unknown. Therefore the patient was made unconscious by a blow on the head with a mallet. Surgery was also practiced in early Babylonia, and the Code of Hammurabi lists the penalties that an unsuccessful surgeon had to pay. For example, if a patient lost an eye through poor surgery, the surgeon's eye was put out.
4. In 1598 the famous Globe Theater was built across the Thames from London. Shakespeare became a shareholder, and his plays were produced there. The theater was octagonal and held about 1,200 people. The "groundlings" stood on the floor and watched the play, but the wealthier patrons sat in the two galleries. Those paying the highest fees could sit upon the stage. The stage jutted out into the audience; thus the players and the audience had a close relationship.
5. The pronghorn has one of the shortest "childhoods" of any mammal. Within three or four days after birth it can outrun a man. In a year it becomes the fastest long-distance runner on this continent.

Proofreading Exercise (p. 91)

. . . the driver's attention, the . . . .

. . . five centuries, it's . . . .

Using Standard English Verbs (p. 95)

EXERCISE 1

1. walk, walked
2. am, was
3. has, had
4. do, did
5. needs, needed
6. helps, helped
7. want, wanted
8. attends, attended
9. talks, talked
10. suppose, supposed

EXERCISE 2

1. am, was
2. do, did
3. has, had
4. ask, asked
5. enjoy, enjoyed
6. finishes, finished
7. learns, learned
8. works, worked
9. listen, listened
10. play, played

EXERCISE 3

1. doesn't, do
2. expect, changed
3. suggest, watch
4. bothers, missed
5. did, wanted
6. were, are
7. did, did
8. asked, wasn't
9. were, weren't
10. were, returned

EXERCISE 4

1. joined, like
2. played, play
3. needs, hopes
4. doesn't, are
5. work, learn
6. expects, insists
7. practice, have
8. enjoys, benefits
9. watch, do
10. were, praised

EXERCISE 5

1. liked, work
2. learned, discussed
3. explained, did
4. do, hope
5. liked, dropped
6. checked, decided
7. picked, did
8. encouraged, listened
9. is, is
10. advises, treats

EXERCISE 6

1. started, was
2. collect, have
3. asked, were
4. wanted, decided
5. want
6. disposed, received
7. are, have
8. are, measure
9. help, impress
10. intend

EXERCISE 7

1. finished, returned
2. asked, had
3. occurred, was
4. happened, reported
5. expected, appeared
6. did, happened
7. were, weren't
8. was, wasn't
9. arrived, rested
10. enjoy, am

EXERCISE 8

1. impressed, changed
2. bores, do
3. needs, intend
4. asked, did, could
5. sealed, dropped
6. discovered, are
7. happened, was
8. asked, walked
9. seemed, asked
10. expect

EXERCISE 9

1. pleased, came
2. ordered, finished
3. handed, finished
4. loaned, want
5. complained, disliked
6. dropped, had
7. occurs, need
8. observed, started
9. wants, refuses
10. is

Standard English Verbs (compound forms) (p. 104)

EXERCISE 1

1. finish, finished
2. finish
3. finished, finish
4. finishing
5. finished
6. finished
7. finish
8. finished
9. finish
10. finished

EXERCISE 2

1. speak, begun
2. seems, want
3. know, become
4. imitating, use
5. teach, beginning
6. like
7. spoken, learned
8. intend, began
9. were, realized
10. helped, were, beginning

EXERCISE 3

1. were, saw
2. seen, begun
3. driven, eaten
4. offered, did
5. ate, asked
6. written, asked, received
7. come, begun
8. saw, suggested
9. gone, washed, prepared
10. saw, were, drove

EXERCISE 4

1. decided, seen
2. frozen, reached
3. was, come
4. observed, saw
5. announced, won
6. smiled, received
7. were, done
8. Were, accepted
9. discussed, impressed
10. analyzed, quoted

EXERCISE 5

1. said, visit
2. hoping, come
3. were, drove
4. seen, grown
5. taken, taking
6. was, stay
7. occupied, took
8. seen, were
9. asked, like
10. were, collected

Avoiding Dialect Expressions (p. 108)

EXERCISE 1

1. brother did well
2. I was never . . . anyway I don't have
3. He'd rather fix his car himself
4. looked and looked, couldn't . . . anywhere
5. This book is
6. did, any
7. wanted . . . didn't have any
8. haven't read any of those
9. Where did you find all those
10. well

Proofreading Exercise (p. 110)

. . . that led . . . .

. . . easy, but . . . wasn't going well. . . . were growing, and . . . while there was any hair . . . .

Progress Test (p. 111)

1. B
2. A
3. B
4. A
5. B
6. B
7. A
8. A
9. A
10. B
11. B
12. B
13. A
14. B
15. B

Making Subjects, Verbs, and Pronouns Agree (p. 114)

EXERCISE 1

1. is
2. is
3. is
4. doesn't
5. is, his
6. were
7. doesn't
8. has
9. think
10. intend

EXERCISE 2

1. is
2. has
3. has
4. hopes
5. likes
6. were
7. live
8. were
9. was
10. was

EXERCISE 3

1. is
2. helps
3. are
4. has
5. were, were
6. depends
7. doesn't
8. work
9. requires
10. is

EXERCISE 4

1. has her
2. like
3. lives
4. doesn't
5. has
6. has her
7. doesn't
8. were
9. were
10. spend

EXERCISE 5

1. are
2. take
3. are
4. are
5. were
6. spend
7. are
8. takes
9. have
10. were

EXERCISE 6

1. are
2. exhibits
3. was
4. is
5. come
6. like
7. were, weren't
8. were, were
9. were
10. feels

EXERCISE 7

1. are
2. has, her
3. have, their
4. doesn't
5. expect
6. hope, intend
7. enjoy
8. spend
9. go
10. takes

EXERCISE 8

1. is, his
2. are, their
3. intend
4. presents
5. expects
6. admires
7. promises
8. send
9. is
10. play

EXERCISE 9

1. is
2. was
3. doesn't
4. Weren't
5. are
6. were
7. were
8. remain
9. doesn't
10. were

EXERCISE 10

1. thinks, he is
2. doesn't
3. is
4. Doesn't
5. have
6. were
7. has
8. have
9. sleep
10. were

Choosing the Right Pronoun (p. 119)

EXERCISE 1

1. me
2. I
3. he
4. he and I
5. we
6. he and I
7. her
8. her
9. I
10. I

EXERCISE 2

1. My sister and I
2. me
3. I
4. I
5. him
6. him
7. he
8. he
9. him
10. he

EXERCISE 3

1. us
2. We
3. us
4. me
5. him, me
6. he
7. us
8. me
9. Lou and I
10. I

EXERCISE 4

1. He and I
2. he and I
3. us
4. him
5. him and me
6. me
7. me
8. Dad and I
9. I
10. us

EXERCISE 5

1. me
2. her
3. me
4. me
5. me
6. me
7. My wife and I
8. David and I
9. me
10. I

Making the Pronoun Refer to the Right Word (p. 122)

EXERCISE 1

1. I put the omelet on the table, took off my apron, and began to eat.
2. I was pleased that they offered me a job.
3. Trying to decide what trip to take isn't easy.
4. She said to her sister, "My room is a mess."
5. I have a pair of glasses, but my eyes are so good that I don't use the glasses except for reading.
6. The president said to the dean, "You have been too lenient."
7. The child was pleased when I praised the finger painting.
8. I thought he would phone, and I waited all evening for the phone to ring.
9. The teachers arranged for a play center where the children can play on swings, slides, and jungle gyms.
10. Felipe said to the professor, "Your watch is wrong."

EXERCISE 2

1. When I picked up the dog's dish, the dog began to whine.
2. Because I have always been interested in coaching football ever since I was in high school, I have decided to become a coach.
3. My family was annoyed because I decided not to accept the summer job.
4. She asked her sister, "Why wasn't I invited to the party?"
5. His father said to Jay, "You can take my new tennis racket to school."
6. I have always liked French Provincial furniture and have finally decided to buy a French Provincial dresser.
7. She said to her instructor, "You don't understand what I'm saying."
8. She likes to swim; in fact she spends most of her summer swimming.
9. She was chosen student body president because she is good in her studies even though she is not very good in sports.
10. The boss was really despondent when he talked with Ed.

EXERCISE 3

1. His motorcycle swerved into the side of a house, but the house was not damaged.
2. As I approached the playpen, the baby began to cry.
3. As soon as the fender was repaired, I drove the car home.
4.
5. The instructor said, "Your typewriter needs a new ribbon."
6. He said to his father, "I ought to wash the car."
7. I walked into the room, climbed on the ladder, and began to paint the ceiling.
8.

9. She said to her mother, "You need to be positive before making such a big decision."
10. We couldn't find a single bottle and blamed Rudy for drinking all the Cokes.

EXERCISE 4

1. Andy said to his brother, "Your car has a flat tire."
2. It would be cold in New England at this time of year, and I don't like the cold.
3. He asked the mechanic, "Why am I having trouble?"
4. Her sister came in crying at 4 A.M.
5. As I tried to attach the leash, the dog ran away.
6.
7. The cars whizzed past, but no one even looked my way.
8. As soon as I approached the robin's nest, the robin flew away.
9. I've decided to save all my money for a trip although saving that much won't be easy.
10. She said to her daughter, "I missed my appointment."

EXERCISE 5

1. He said, "Dad, I need a new suit."
2. Since we couldn't find the cake plate, we realized the children must have eaten the cake.
3.
4. The child screamed when I moved the tricycle.
5. I have adjusted the steering wheel, and you can take your car home.
6. After I read about Lindbergh's life, I decided I want to be an airline pilot.
7. He said to the man, "Won't you come back when I have time to talk?"
8. Jerome was very angry when he talked to his father.
9. Ben said, "Dad, you ought to get a refund for the faulty tire."
10. When I opened the door of the kennel, the puppy ran away.

Correcting Misplaced or Dangling Modifiers (p. 126)

EXERCISE 1

1. While I talked on the phone, the cake . . . .
2. I came across my grandfather sound . . . .
3. I saw a furry little caterpillar crawling . . . .
4. As he took her in his arms, the moon . . . .
5. Years later you will . . . .
6.
7. Lincoln Park is the most interesting park I have seen in the city.
8. She was engaged to a man named Smith, who had a . . . .
9. When I was 14, my . . . .
10. We gave all the food we didn't want to . . . .

EXERCISE 2

1. After I had cleaned my room, my dog . . . .
2. A son weighing eight pounds was . . . .
3. I don't enjoy his company because he's . . . .
4. I don't care for cucumbers unless they are pickled.
5. I tried to quiet the screaming and kicking child.
6. The car I bought from a used car dealer had a . . . .
7. I saw the broken ladder leaning . . . .
8. After watching TV all evening, I found the dirty dishes . . . .
9. When I was six, my . . . .
10.

EXERCISE 3

1. I brought the dog, badly in need of a bath, into . . . .
2. I watched the horses in the pasture quietly . . . .
3. Having been born and raised in the country, I naturally find the old cookstove appealing.
4. Excited and eager to go, we saw the bus waiting. . . .
5. The house where I was born is . . . .
6. I stopped and talked to the child who was . . . .
7. As we unwrapped gift after gift, the puppy . . . .
8. I decided to give the clothes I had no use for to . . . .
9. Although his car was almost eight years old, he refused to turn it . . . .
10. She put the sandwiches that she had not eaten back . . . .

EXERCISE 4

1. When I was ten, my . . . .
2. We could see little white pieces of paper falling . . . .
3. While she was on a two-week vacation, the office . . . .
4. I saw in the evening paper that . . . .

5. Because I played Frisbee all evening, I did not get my English paper finished.
6. Consulting the Lost and Found section of the paper, we soon had the dog safe . . . .
7. Just as we arrived, the youngster went careening down the driveway on . . . .
8. After eating lunch hurriedly, we started in two taxis . . . .
9. We saw the parade moving . . . .
10. We bought a duck decoy that had been refinished.

EXERCISE 5

1. While tobogganing down the hill, we saw a huge bear come into view.
2. The class made me aware of some little speech habits, which I got rid of very soon.
3.
4. The monkey watched us as it peeled . . . .
5. On the way to school I saw . . . .
6. Dressed in a long blue evening gown, she seemed to him prettier than ever.
7. Living in a small town, one . . . .
8. Everyday you can read . . . .
9. Because I had gone to too many parties, my . . . .
10. The series of lectures we are having on religions of the world will . . . .

Using Parallel Construction (p. 131)

EXERCISE 1

1. and sleeping late . . . .
2. and by taking him . . . .
3. or making an oral report.
4. and with modern . . . .
5. and studied for . . . .
6. and packed the car . . . .
7. the pleasant boss . . . .
8. and camping out.
9. and to get along . . . .
10. and bubble gum.

EXERCISE 2

1. waited for Sue . . . .
2.
3. and by cooking economy . . . .
4.
5. and an old popcorn . . . .
6. than to have a great . . . .
7. and entertaining.
8. and to read better books.
9. and concluded . . . .
10. and rewriting all . . . .

EXERCISE 3

1. and understanding . . . .
2.
3. and security.
4. and all kinds . . . .
5. sometimes even sat and . . . .
6. and to come when called.
7. then went to bed.
8. inches wide.
9. and can't even smell.
10. and then getting myself

EXERCISE 4

1. and judo lessons.
2.
3. and unhappy.
4. and friendly children . . . .
5. and his fear.
6. and interested in . . . .
7. and then placed it . . . .
8. and unselfish.
9. and finally how to add the fertilizer.
10.

EXERCISE 5

1.
2. and a bank teller.
3. and making . . . .
4. keep the display counters neat and of course wait . . . .
5. demanding, satisfying, and challenging.
6. meets people, can help people, and has . . . .
7. and gets along . . . .
8. and to have a vacation.
9. and an Indian blanket.
10. and by train.

EXERCISE 6

1. and cold weather . . . .
2.
3. and the sounds of insects.
4. and entertaining.
5. and the anemone blossoms waving in the wind.
6. and a redheaded woodpecker tapping . . . .
7. and watching for birds . . . .
8. or swim without . . . .
9.
10. and educational.

EXERCISE 7

1. and to be able to . . . .
2. and the increase in crime.
3. and by air.
4. charm and tact.
5. and how to change . . . .
6. and get some gas.
7.
8. and probably a dessert.
9.
10.

EXERCISE 8

1. Every college student should know how to type.
   1. Some instructors require typed papers.
   2. Typing, if one is good at it, saves time.
   3. A typed paper often gets a higher grade.

2. Going home every weekend is unwise.
   1. I spend too much time on the bus.
   2. I get behind in my college work.
   3. It is too expensive.
   4. I miss out on weekend activities at college.

3. Commercial billboards along highways should be prohibited.
   1. They often cause accidents.
   2. They mar the scenery.

4. Learning to sew is valuable.
   1. Sewing your own clothes saves money.
   2. Sewing teaches you to be creative.

Correcting Shift in Time (p. 138)

EXERCISE 1

1. saw, looked
2. came
3. came
4. becomes
5. thinks, becomes
6. came
7. remembered
8. turned
9. writes
10. tells

EXERCISE 2

1. went
2. surprised
3. escapes
4. gets
5. gave, had
6. crawled
7. have
8. went
9. ran
10. didn't

EXERCISE 3

As I traveled down the highway, I signaled to turn left. I started the turn . . . . I pulled off the road. . . . I stopped the truck and got out . . . .

EXERCISE 4

My mother stood . . . because she was afraid I was going to fall off the roof. In spite of her I finally got it up . . . . I was listening . . . . Eventually I decided I wanted . . . . Mostly I just listened and worked . . . .

EXERCISE 5

He says . . . . He says . . . .

EXERCISE 6

. . . trees provided . . . . and they lived . . . . Several families lived . . .

EXERCISE 7

. . . he decided that the routine of study was . . . . he tramped, taught school, made shoes, and edited . . . . he was writing poetry . . . . he found himself famous.

Correcting Shift in Person (p. 143)

EXERCISE 1

1. you should
2. when I
3. as we grew up we became
4. I really have
5. Students should have study schedules. Otherwise they won't get all their
6. my brain
7. I couldn't take it easy the way I
8. they have to set
9. you should read,
10. get their equipment

EXERCISE 2

1. I made a piece . . . . I did this on my own
2. give us two work sheets . . . if we didn't do them . . . keep after us until we did . . . . we could tell our problems to.
3. made us feel we were getting . . . prepared us . . . .

EXERCISE 3

1. She received a mountain of presents.
2. Jogging is good for one's health.
3. To stay healthy one should get some exercise every day.
4. I was upset when I heard about the accident.
5. As the plane took off, we could see the entire city below.
6. I was delighted to receive his letter.
7. My desk was in a mess.
8. When we had gone a hundred miles, we could hear a thumping in the engine.
9. We've improved our garden.
10. To lose weight one must cut out sugar and stick to a rigid diet.

EXERCISE 4

It was my sign of independence. It was my ticket to freedom. I didn't have to ask to borrow the family car, and I didn't have to explain where I was going or when I'd be back . . . . every accessory imaginable . . . . Funny how it costs freedom to support freedom.

EXERCISE 5

we could see the people below . . . . as close to floating on a cloud as it's possible to get. We couldn't feel the wind, of course, because we were drifting with it, but we could see the ground moving along beneath us . . . . when we went high, we could see for miles . . . . Few experiences can compare with floating on a cloud.

Correcting Wordiness (p. 149)

EXERCISE 1

1. I woke up at four this morning.
2. We were considering whether to charge admission.
3. Many people never read a book.
4. After our eight-hour hike, we were hungry.
5. He had tried football, basketball, and hockey.
6. He can be depended upon to do what he says he will.
7. I was surprised yesterday when my college roommate stopped to see me.
8. I think she's planning to go.
9. I had no money by the end of the year.
10. The three kinds of stones we found were unique.

EXERCISE 2

1. No doubt our team will win.
2. They carried him home drunk.
3. There is more permissiveness today than formerly.
4. Justice is too slow in our country.
5. Justice should be swift and sure.
6. He has worked hard all his life.
7. His height makes him a good basketball player.
8. The melons were large and sweet.
9. Most students don't leave campus on weekends.
10. Finally one should learn more at college than what is learned in courses.

EXERCISE 3

1. Many people were there.
2. At present thousands of acres along the river are under water.
3. Something should be done to prevent flooding.
4. No one seems to be working on the problem.
5. Finally the doctor arrived but could do nothing for her.
6. The plane circled the airport for half an hour and then disappeared.
7. I was unaware that she had arrived.
8. He left college because he wanted some business experience.
9. The wealthier countries should aid the developing countries.
10. In 1981 my brother accepted a job with Bell and Howell of Chicago.

EXERCISE 4

1. Most people spend too much time watching TV.
2. I forgot about last night's meeting.
3. Most writers use too many words.
4. A new car should not be driven too fast for the first 500 miles.

5. I'm happy to accept your invitation.
6. I intend to finish my year here and then look for a job.
7. Most people want a clear, concise business form.
8. The president should bring the motion to a vote.
9. I thought she was just pretending to be ill.
10. I'm trying to get rid of wordiness in my papers.

EXERCISE 5

To help new students find their way around the Library, the staff offers orientation programs. Many faculty members also bring their classes to particular subject areas for orientation. And printed handouts, such as special subject bibliographies and instructions for using periodical indexes and psychological abstracts, are available.

Avoiding Clichés (p. 153)

EXERCISE 1

1. Since I hadn't opened a book all weekend, I decided to do a little studying before I went to bed.
2. But then I changed my mind.
3. I decided I'd rather do some cooking.
4. Therefore I went to the kitchen and got out my equipment.
5. But there were no eggs in the fridge and no cake mix in the cupboard.
6. I couldn't figure out what to bake.
7. Since I couldn't find any ingredients, I decided to clean the kitchen.
8. I worked hard and soon had everything clean.
9. But finally I decided to do some studying.
10. I studied late that night, but the next morning I was up early and ready for my exam.

Review of Sentence Structure and Agreement (p. 154)

1. B	6. B	11. B	16. B	21. A
2. A	7. A	12. A	17. B	22. A
3. A	8. B	13. A	18. A	23. B
4. B	9. B	14. B	19. A	24. A
5. B	10. B	15. A	20. B	25. B

Punctuation (p. 159)

EXERCISE 1

1. Hurry!
2.
3. late;
4. Lake Placid. We'd
5. crusty. It
6. week.
7. best:
8. trips. It
9. parks:
10.

EXERCISE 2

1. following materials:
2. out. He
3. shed.
4. appeared. By
5. 1924. That
6. States. That
7. competition. Then
8. compacts.
9. advantages:
10. Japanese;

EXERCISE 3

1. years. He
2. places:
3. countryside. A
4. rock. He's
5. animals. They
6. rocks;
7. fern;
8. leaf;
9.
10. park. It

EXERCISE 4

1. clocks. They
2.
3. hourglass. It
4. 1354. It
5. pendulum. His
6. popular. Not
7. parts. Each
8. too. The
9. short;
10. parts. The

EXERCISE 5

1. president. Taft
2. college. Three
3. following:
4.
5. president; John
6. 42. He
7. assassinated:
8. resign. He
9. television;
10. terms. He

EXERCISE 6

1. farms?
2. energy. Now
3. jobs:
4. soil;
5. morning. Tractors
6. years. The
7. itself. Other
8. food;
9. can. However
10. farms. They

EXERCISE 7

1. Michigan?
2. village. It's
3. past. Then
4. Dearborn. Then
5. carriage. Next
6. great;
7.
8. buildings. He
9. museum. One
10. life. Ford

EXERCISE 8

1. metric?
2. metric. Gas
3.
4. metric:
5. change. A
6. cut;
7. signs. Industry
8. switched. Furthermore
9. schools. Thus
10. management. Then

EXERCISE 9

1. player. Then
2. up. He
3. 1980. His
4. leg. Some
5. weather:
6. perseverance. They
7. him. He
8. up. The
9. miles. Furthermore
10. point.

EXERCISE 10

1. moved. They
2. theirs. It's
3. garden. All
4. tame. It
5. small. It's
6. distance. They
7. advantage. It
8. gallon. Now
9. errand. Now
10. difference.

Commas (p. 166)

EXERCISE 1

1. trip,
2. brochures,
3. time,
4. newspapers, encyclopedias,
5. Yes,
6. away,
7. planning,
8. college,
9. Hawaii, Tahiti,
10. far,

EXERCISE 2

1. lately,
2. years,
3. dull,
4. lecture,
5. me,
6. daydreaming,
7. off,
8.
9. marks,
10. all,

EXERCISE 3

1.
2. sentences,
3. answer,
4. exercises,
5. statement,
6.
7. finish,
8. finished,
9. writing,
10. writing,

EXERCISE 4

1. animal,
2. 1800s,
3. West,
4. settlers, by sportsmen,
5. supply,
6. States,
7. management, the . . . comeback,
8. Yellowstone National Park, National Bison Range in Montana,
9. free,
10. heritage,

EXERCISE 5

1. States,
2. Maine, Shenandoah in Virginia, Mammoth Cave in Kentucky, Everglades in Florida,
3.
4. summer,
5. stalagmites,
6. cave,
7. water,
8. purple, brown,
9. cave,
10. levels,

EXERCISE 6

1. River, Frozen Niagara,
2. left,
3. parks,
4. acres,
5. created,
6. geysers, hot springs, lakes, rivers,
7. Yellowstone,
8. 1870,
9. nature,
10. prohibited,

EXERCISE 7

1. hour,
2. "swift creature,"
3. delicate,
4. today,
5. measured,
6. head,
7. leaves, twigs,
8. branch, draws . . . lips,
9. acacia,
10.

EXERCISE 8

1. harm,
2. anyone,
3. eat,
4. animals,
5. world,
6. ignored, and . . . chips, bread, cheese,
7. animals,
8.
9. laws,
10. thoughtlessness,

EXERCISE 9

1. skiing,
2. it,
3. skiing,
4. slalom, giant slalom, and downhill
5. States,
6. two,
7.
8.
9. with,
10. ambitious,

Commas (continued) (p. 172)

EXERCISE 1

1. Bill, who . . . asleep,
2.
3.
4. hoping, Elizabeth,
5. car, it seems,
6. have, of course,
7.
8. wife, who . . . kindergarten,
9. odd, Rosa,
10. tried, nevertheless,

EXERCISE 2

1. Yes, Oswaldo,
2. imagined, moreover,
3.
4.
5.
6. was, beyond a doubt,
7. should, I think,
8.
9. Minnesota,
10. Kilauea, which . . . Hawaii,

EXERCISE 3

1.
2. Amazon, flowing . . . Atlantic, and the Nile,
3.
4.
5. country, of course,
6. need, many think,
7. punishment, they say,
8.
9.
10. Atchison, where . . . born,

EXERCISE 4

1.
2.
3.
4. Mel,
5. positive, however,
6.
7. gardening, it seems,
8. spot,
9. Place, 30 acres . . . timber,
10.

EXERCISE 5

1. was, on the whole,
2. better, I think,
3. writing, I find,
4.
5.
6. suit, which . . . Easter,
7. ago, Hanson Gregory, captain . . . art,
8. dad, who . . . football,
9.
10. Dickens, a nineteenth-century author,

EXERCISE 6

1.
2. Greenland, the . . . world,
3. car,
4. here, Debra,
5.
6. had, in spite of his inexperience,
7. said, furthermore,
8.
9.
10. examination, which . . . anyone,

EXERCISE 7

1. contest, which . . . students,
2. think, Curt,
3. Conductor,
4. Providence,
5.
6. Williamsburg, which . . . Virginia,
7. area, which . . . acres,
8. place, certainly,
9.
10. decided, however,

EXERCISE 8

1. garden, it has been said,
2. you, Jon,
3.
4. vote, we have found,
5.
6.
7. collection, which . . . years,
8. world, and . . . existed,
9. Hippocrates, who . . . medicine, set . . . oath,
10. Shaw, who . . . writers,

EXERCISE 9

1. East, which . . . weather,
2. systems, which . . . ones,
3. provide, obviously,
4. able, furthermore,
5. Vermont, which . . . lifts,
6. Vermont, which . . . year,
7. systems, however,
8.
9. surprising, therefore,
10. money, beyond a doubt,

Review of the Comma (p. 177)

1. Many Americans do not know about Highway 1,
2.
3. The keys, which go southwestward from the mainland of Florida,
4. The keys are great places for shell collecting, bird watching,
5. Shell collectors, who say the keys beaches are the best places in the United States for shells,
6. Bird watchers are interested in the herons, pelicans,
7. Various kinds of coral abound,
8.
9. On Grassy Key is the Flipper Sea School,
10. On some of the smaller keys are found key deer,
11. Almost extinct 20 years ago, they are now, however,
12. Key West, which is the end of the Overseas Highway, is nearer to Havana, Cuba,
13. With its freewheeling lifestyle and its marvelous weather,
14. Walking is a good way to see Key West,
15. Among the famous artists and writers who have found inspiration at Key West over the years are James Audubon, Hart Crane,

Quotation Marks (p. 179)

EXERCISE 1

1. "Let's get something to eat,"
2. "Do you want to go now or after the movie?"
3. "Why not both times?"
4. "Snow and adolescence are the only problems that disappear if you ignore them long enough,"
5. "Some people stay longer in an hour than others can in a week,"
6.
7. "Doing work I like is more important to me than making a lot of money,"
8. "With all its sham, drudgery, and broken dreams," said Adlai Stevenson, "it is still a beautiful world."
9. We went to see *The Wild Duck,*
10. "Our future as a nation is going to depend not so much on what happens in outer space as on what happens in inner space—the space between our ears,"

EXERCISE 2

1. "The actions of some children," said Will Rogers, "suggest that their parents embarked on the sea of matrimony without a paddle."
2. "The best time to tackle a small problem," said my father, "is before he grows up."
3. "When Mom goes shopping," says Kip, "she leaves no store unturned."
4. I agree with the Spanish proverb "How beautiful it is to do nothing and then rest afterward."
5. He found her munching chocolates and reading a book entitled *Eat, Drink, and Be Buried.*
6. Mark Twain said, "When I was a boy of 14, my father was so ignorant I could hardly stand to have the old man around. But when I got to be 21, I was astonished at how much the old man had learned in seven years."
7. Mark Twain said, "The parts of the Bible which give me the most trouble are those I understand the best."
8. "Work consists of whatever a body is obliged to do, and play consists of whatever a body is not obliged to do,"
9. On observing the great number of civic statues, Cato, a famous Roman, remarked, "I would rather people would ask why there is not a statue of Cato than why there is."
10. "One does not complain about water because it is wet," said Abraham Maslow, "nor about rocks because they are hard."

EXERCISE 3

1. I've just read "Barn Burning,"
2. "The construction of an airplane," wrote Charles Lindbergh, "is simple compared to the evolutionary achievement of a bird."
3. "If I had the choice," Lindbergh continued, "I would rather have birds than airplanes."
4.
5.
6. Pablo Casals, the great cellist, spent hours on a single phrase. He said, "People say I play as easily as a bird sings. If they only knew how much effort their bird has put into his song."
7. "As it is the mark of great minds to say many things in a few words," wrote La Rochefoucauld, "so it is the mark of little minds to use many words to say nothing."
8.
9. "Whatever you have you must either use or lose,"
10. "A span of time either leaves you better off or worse off," wrote John Gardner. "There is no neutral time."

EXERCISE 4

1. "Finish every day and be done with it," said Ralph Waldo Emerson. "Tomorrow is a new day."
2. "Life can only be understood backward," said Kierkegaard, "but it must be lived forward."
3. "The most valuable of all talents is that of never using two words when one will do,"
4. "The only conquests that are permanent and leave no regrets," Napoleon said, "are our conquests over ourselves."
5. "Nearly all men can stand adversity, but if you want to test a man's character, give him power,"
6.
7. In the novel *Fathers and Sons*
8. "Nobody can carry three watermelons under one arm,"
9. "The taller the bamboo grows the lower it bends,"
10. "The man who does not do more work than he's paid for," said Abraham Lincoln, "isn't worth what he gets."

EXERCISE 5

1. "The cost of a thing is the amount of what I call life which is required to be exchanged for it, immediately or in the long run,"
2. "A man is rich," said Thoreau, "in proportion to the number of things he can afford to let alone."
3. Viewing the multitude of articles exposed for sale in the marketplace, Socrates remarked, "How many things there are that I do not want."
4. I have been reading *Comfortable Words,*

5. "Perhaps the most valuable result of all education," said Thomas Huxley, "is the ability to make yourself do the thing you have to do, when it ought to be done, whether you like it or not."
6.
7. "Education does not mean teaching people to know what they do not know," said John Ruskin. "It means teaching them to behave as they do not behave."
8. "Sometimes when fate kicks us and we finally land and look around, we find we have been kicked upstairs,"
9. "At the end," said Richard E. Byrd, "only two things really matter to a man, regardless of who he is; and they are the affection and understanding of his family."
10. "There are at least as many stars," wrote Sir James Jeans, "as there are grains of sand upon all the seashores of the earth."

EXERCISE 6

"Are we nearly there?" Alice managed to pant out at last.

"Nearly there!" the Queen repeated. "Why, we passed it ten minutes ago! Faster!" And they ran on for a time in silence, with the wind whistling in Alice's ears, and almost blowing her hair off her head, she fancied.

"Now! Now!" cried the Queen. "Faster! Faster!" And they went so fast that at last they seemed to skim through the air, hardly touching the ground with their feet, till suddenly, just as Alice was getting quite exhausted, they stopped, and she found herself sitting on the ground, breathless and giddy.

The Queen propped her up against a tree, and said kindly, "You may rest a little now."

Alice looked round her in great surprise. "Why, I do believe we've been under this tree the whole time! Everything's just as it was!"

"Of course it is," said the Queen. "What would you have it?"

"Well, in *our* country," said Alice, still panting a little, "you'd generally get to somewhere else—if you ran very fast for a long time as we've been doing."

"A slow sort of country!" said the Queen. "Now, *here*, you see, it takes all the running you can do to keep in the same place. If you want to get somewhere else, you must run at least twice as fast as that."

—Lewis Carroll, *Through the Looking-Glass*

Capital Letters (p. 184)

EXERCISE 1

1.
2. "The Death of the Hired Man"
3. English
4. Labor Day
5. Dad
6.
7. Wednesday
8. College
9.
10. State University

EXERCISE 2

1. Vocational Technical College
2. East
3.
4. "Tougher Meat Laws Needed in Ontario"
5. West Coast, Yukon
6. Yosemite National Park
7. Valley Community College
8.
9. Aunt
10.

EXERCISE 3

1. Latin America
2. Mexico, Central and South America
3. French, English
4. *The Autobiography*
5. Community College
6.
7. Aquarium, Grant Park
8. "A Worn Path"
9. "What's
10.

EXERCISE 4

1. High School
2. Community College, University
3. Dad, Mother
4. Thursday, Women's Club
5. the East
6. Sunday
7. Main Street, Saturday
8. South, Grandfather, East
9. Canal, River
10.

EXERCISE 5

1. Canada
2. Community College, State College
3. Dad
4. Black Hills
5. Park
6. World War
7.
8. Psychology, History
9. College
10.

EXERCISE 6

1.
2. River
3. Granddad
4.
5. State Technical Institute
6. River Lake
7. Granddad
8.
9. English
10. State University

EXERCISE 7

1. United Kingdom
2. Britain, France
3. Fall of the House of Usher
4. Spanish
5. Community College
6. Fourth
7. Business and Professional Women's Club
8. Dad
9. *New World*
10. University of Calcutta

Review of Punctuation and Capital Letters (p. 187)

EXERCISE 1

1. The Taj Mahal, which is in Agra,
2. Do you read *Time* or *Newsweek*?
3. I'm glad it's snowing;
4. Skiing, skating,
5. Figure skating, which I'm just learning,
6. His knapsack contained the following items: food, matches,
7. The sign in the dentist's office read, "Support your dentist. Eat candy."
8. There is much inferior paint on the market,
9. A little old lady from Boston refused to travel saying, "Why should I travel? I'm already here."
10. My sister is on the swim team at Polk Community College.

EXERCISE 2

1. No, he didn't come. We'll
2. You'll find them where you left them, Son.
3. The boy fought, bit, kicked, and screamed,
4. When I was in high school, I memorized Robert Frost's poem "The Road Not Taken."
5. An Arabian proverb says, "I had no shoes and complained until I met a man who had no feet."
6. You can get the document by writing to the Superintendent of Documents, Government Printing Office, Washington,
7. My mother, who is not a writer herself,
8. He tried to improve his vocabulary by looking up new words, by keepin word lists,
9. Have you read Yeats' poem "The Lake Isle of Innisfree"?
10. Reading improves your understanding of human nature;

EXERCISE 3

1. I've been reading about insects,
2. Adult insects have six legs,
3. Although they are often destructive,
4. Some destroy crops,
5. We followed the trail into the clearing;
6. In 1973 in Transvaal, South Africa,
7. Although I've not read *Ghosts*,
8.
9. "The trouble with the average family," said Bill Vaughn, "is that it has too much month left at the end of the money."
10. Coming out of the Capitol, the senator said, "You save a billion here and a billion there, and it soon mounts up."

EXERCISE 4

1. I've been trying to teach my small son to ride a bike,
2. He rides a few feet;
3. He's just not coordinated;
4. He keeps trying,
5. It's harder on me than on him,
6. I finished high school two years ago and am now attending the University of Southern
7. The official land speed record of 622 mph was set on the Bonneville Salt Flats, Utah, on October 23, 1970.
8. Can the story be true, then, that we read in the paper?
9. The *Christian Science Monitor* and the *Wall Street Journal*
10. "Life," said Samuel Butler, "is like playing a violin solo in public and learning the instrument as one goes on."

Proofreading Exercise 1 (p. 189)

THOSE FAULTY PARTS

I was only ten years old, but I had all the confidence of a great scientist. I had already built a little electric motor and fixed the electric parts in all the toys anyone would bring me. And now I had a magazine article that told how to build a simple battery-powered radio. The directions looked straightforward. ~~all~~ *All* I needed was the parts.

My world extended only as far as my bicycle could take me, so the only place I knew of that sold radio parts was the TV repair shop five blocks away. I don't know what the men there first thought of a ten-year-old kid trying to build a radio, but I persisted until one of them gathered up the parts and sold them to me. It cost a few weeks' allowance money, but I ~~new~~ *knew* it was going to be worth it.

Well, after a few days of work, I had it ~~finish~~ *finished*. Admittedly, my wiring ~~didnt~~ *didn't* look as neat as that in the picture. As a matter of fact, those people had used a few more wires than I had, but I didn't feel that all of them were really necessary.

But my radio didn't work! And my ten-year-old mind concluded that it must be that the TV repair shop had sold me faulty parts. I bicycled back with my new radio under my arm and demanded an explanation. I was upset. After a long discussion, one of the men finally took my radio and started working on it. I think he was afraid I might cry or something.

In about half an hour, and after many changes, he got it working.

"No charge, kid," he said.

"Thank you," I said in my most polite voice, thrilled at the sound of music coming from my radio.

What a feeling of accomplishment! It was as if Id invented something great. I guess the TV repairman must have had a bit of feeling of accomplishment too as a beaming ten-year-old rode away with a little radio that worked under his arm.

Comprehensive Test (p. 192)

1. It's useless to wait. He's probably not coming.
2. If one wants a larger vocabulary, one should study word roots.
3. I spent entirely too much time on that one course last semester.
4. Dad asked my sister and me to water the lawn. We were glad to do it.
5. While they were waiting for their daughter, their motor stalled.
6. I can't decide whether to finish my math, study my history, or take it easy for a change.
7. If you're going to be here, Dawn, you can answer the phone for me.
8. You're going with me, aren't you?
9. We freshmen helped an upperclass student with registration. He really appreciated it.
10. I was quite sure that Ron's car was in the driveway.
11. When we were on our trip, we visited some cities in the South.
12. They had many beautiful old homes and lovely gardens.
13. It's Mr. Peterson's car, but he's not driving it.
14. Each of the students is planning an individual report.
15. Looking under the car, I found the missing baseball.
16. Christine's grades are always higher than Jackie's.
17. "I'll be ready in a minute," Jeanne said.
18. This semester I'm taking French, history, and English.
19. The United Nations receives more brickbats than bravos, yet it remains the only real hope for peace.
20. She said to her sister, "I need a new purse."
21. They didn't think, however, that they would have time to come back.
22. She was supposed to read the short story "The Elephant's Child" from Rudyard Kipling's book *Just So Stories*.
23. I don't care whether you agree with me or whether you follow your own ideas.
24. We waited as long as we could. Then we went on without her.
25. "What's done to children, they will do to society," wrote Karl Menninger.

Writing

EXERCISE 1 (p. 198)

1. Cooking for Two
   Cooking Breakfast for Two
   Two Cook Breakfast for Two
2. Photography as a Hobby
   Learning to Compose Photographs
   Composing a Winning Photograph
3. Buying a Bike
   Buying a Used Ten-Speed
   Questions to Ask before Buying a Used Ten-Speed
4. The State Park near My Home
   Working at a State Park
   Hashing at a State Park Inn
5. Training a Pup
   Teaching My Pup to Obey
   Teaching My Pup to Sit
6. A High School Swim Meet
   The High Dive Contest
   Getting Ready to Make the High Dive
7. Playing in the College Band
   Playing the Drums in a College Band
   Playing the Drums in a Band Contest
8. Being a Lifeguard
   A Lifeguard's Day
   Two Minutes in a Lifeguard's Day
9. Finding a Summer Job
   Working at a Supermarket
   Learning to Bag at Kroger's

EXERCISE 2 (p. 203)

title 1. Cross-country skiing
thesis 2. I felt grown up the day I got my first bike.
fact 3. Alaska has great mineral resources.
title 4. The state fair in our city
title 5. A day I'll never forget
thesis 6. Teaching a pup to heel takes patience.
thesis 7. Developers shouldn't be allowed in Tonto National Forest.
thesis 8. My job gives me an ego boost.
fact 9. The weather bureau predicts a hot summer.
title 10. Painting a room
thesis 11. Group therapy taught me a lot about myself.

thesis 12. In painting a room, four steps are necessary.
fact 13. For some students, standard English is a second language.
thesis 14. Our trip to Mesa was the best our family ever had.

EXERCISE 3 (p. 203)

1. Cross-country has four advantages over downhill.
3. The Sierra Club is trying to save Misty Fjords in Alaska from developers.
4. Winning a blue ribbon at the State Fair encouraged me to continue baking.
5. The day I won a speech contest was the happiest of my childhood.
9. We're doing two things to get our house ready for a hot summer.
10. I painted my room for less than $20.
13. I'm learning a lot from helping a student for whom English is a second language.

EXERCISE 4 (p. 204)

I've decided not to quit college.

1. I'd have difficulty finding a job.
2. I'll get a better job later if I have a college degree.
3. I really like some of my courses.

Learning to write is like learning to swim.

1. First one has to learn the strokes in swimming or the rules in writing.
2. Then one has to practice until the skill becomes automatic.

Our house is a madhouse when we're leaving on a trip.

1. Everyone is shouting orders.
2. No one wants to do the breakfast dishes.
3. Our luggage won't all fit into the car.
4. No one can find the road map.

To increase your vocabulary, you need to take three steps.

1. Read a lot and look up words that interest you.
2. Look for word roots to give you clues to meaning.
3. Use your new words in speaking and writing.

EXERCISE 5 (p. 209)

Statements that should be marked S: 1, 2, 4, 7, 8, 10.

Summary of "Can It!" (p. 215)

An antilitter campaign is spreading across the country and reducing litter levels in many communities. Its slogan is "Put Litter in Its Place—Can It!" Not merely a cleanup campaign, it sponsors an education program starting in kindergarten and continuing throughout the schools and in public forums. People's attitudes are changing as a litter-measuring technique shows them that they *can* make a difference. The program is even proving financially successful by cutting down on time spent by cleanup crews after public events. Depending more on popular support than on money, the campaign is succeeding in 331 communities in 40 states.

Index